Crossing the Ethnic Divide

AMERICAN ACADEMY OF RELIGION
ACADEMY SERIES

SERIES EDITOR
Kimberly Rae Connor, University of San Francisco

A Publication Series of The American Academy of Religion
and Oxford University Press

AMERICAN ACADEMY OF RELIGION

Crossing the Ethnic Divide

The Multiethnic Church on a Mission

KATHLEEN GARCES-FOLEY

OXFORD

UNIVERSITY PRESS

2007

OXFORD
UNIVERSITY PRESS

Oxford University Press, Inc., publishes works that further
Oxford University's objective of excellence
in research, scholarship, and education.

Oxford   New York
Auckland   Cape Town   Dar es Salaam   Hong Kong   Karachi
Kuala Lumpur   Madrid   Melbourne   Mexico City   Nairobi
New Delhi   Shanghai   Taipei   Toronto

With offices in
Argentina   Austria   Brazil   Chile   Czech Republic   France   Greece
Guatemala   Hungary   Italy   Japan   Poland   Portugal   Singapore
South Korea   Switzerland   Thailand   Turkey   Ukraine   Vietnam

Copyright © 2007 by The American Academy of Religion

Published by Oxford University Press, Inc.
198 Madison Avenue, New York, New York 10016

www.oup.com

Library of Congress Cataloging-in-Publication Data
Garces-Foley, Kathleen, 1972–
Crossing the ethnic divide: the multiethnic church on a mission /
Kathleen Garces-Foley.
    p. cm.—(American Academy of Religion academy series)
Includes bibliographical references and index.
ISBN-13 978-0-19-531108-2
ISBN 0-19-531108-6
1. Church and minorities.   2. Church work with minorities.
3. Ethnicity—Religious aspects—Christianity.   4. Reconciliation—
Religious aspects—Christianity.   5. Christianity and culture.
6. Multiculturalism—Religious aspects—Christianity.   I. Title.
II. Series.
BV639.M56G37   2007
277.3'083089—dc22   2006014122

9 8 7 6 5 4 3 2 1

Printed in the United States of America
on acid-free paper

To Anthony,
with all my love

Acknowledgments

This book could not have been completed without the help of many individuals and organizations. My thanks go first to the members of Evergreen Baptist Church of Los Angeles and the staff of the Los Angeles Division of the InterVarsity Christian Fellowship, who shared their experiences, hopes, and frustrations with me. In particular, I want to thank Pastor Ken Fong and Church Administrator Jetty Fong, from Evergreen, and Doug Schaupp, director of the Los Angeles Division of InterVarsity, for allowing me access to their organizations and fielding my many questions. In the research phase, this project was financially supported by a Graduate Student Researcher position with the Religious Pluralism in Southern California Project, funded by the Ford Foundation, and in the writing stage by grants from the Louisville Institute and the Interdisciplinary Humanities Center at the University of California at Santa Barbara. Much gratitude is due to my mentors at UCSB, Wade Clark Roof, Catherine Albanese, Paul Spickard, Rudy Busto, and Richard Hecht, and to my colleagues Gerardo Marti and Russell Jeung, for thought-provoking conversations on the subject of multiethnic churches, as well as helpful advice. I also want to thank my parents, Professors Marie and John Foley, for their careful reading of the manuscript. Lastly, my children, Jonah and Eva Marie, deserve my unending gratitude for their patience, and my partner, Anthony, for his loving and practical support, without which this project would not have been possible.

Contents

Crossing the Ethnic Divide

Introduction

Looking for the Promised Land

The year 2004 marked the fiftieth anniversary of the *Brown v. Board of Education* decision that ended legal segregation in the public schools. While some celebrated this achievement, many wondered what had become of the Promised Land that Martin Luther King, Jr., believed was not far off. What happened to his dream of a country in which all Americans would have equal rights and equal opportunities? Five decades after the civil rights movement, the dream remains alive for many Americans, and it is experiencing a resurgence in Christian churches. Churches remain overwhelmingly homogeneous, but the desire to change this historic pattern is strong and growing.

Like many churches, Greenwood Acres Full Gospel Baptist Church wants to be a multiethnic church.[1] This five-thousand member African American church in Shreveport, Louisiana, wants to be a gathering of all the tribes and all the nations, as described in the New Testament Book of Revelation. After joint ministry projects and pulpit-sharing with White churches failed to bring any non-Blacks through his doors, Bishop Fred Caldwell decided to take more drastic measures. He announced one Sunday morning in 2003 that he would pay White people to come to services. He was willing to give two thousand dollars from his own pocket to pay them to come to his church during the month of August: five dollars an hour on Sundays and ten dollars an hour on Thursdays. When word got out, many people, especially neighboring pastors, accused him of trying to buy souls, but he explained his actions in this way: "Our churches are too segregated, and the Lord never intended for that to happen. It's time for something radical." That month Greenwood Acres had 125 White and six Native American visitors, many of whom refused to take the money. I imagine this was a very exciting time at Greenwood Acres, culminating in the decision by one White couple to sign the membership book. The euphoria could not have lasted long, however, because this couple quickly faded out of sight, as did the rest of the visitors. One month and over one thousand dollars later, Greenwood Acres was still a Black church.

There is much more to this story than failure. After his bold announcement, Bishop Caldwell was inundated with requests for interviews. He spoke on fifty talk shows, including an interview on CNN that was broadcast globally to more than a billion people. He received letters of support from people all over the world, which have prompted him to write a book on creating multiethnic churches. When I spoke with Bishop Caldwell six months after the experiment, he shared with me how exciting it has been to receive so much encouragement. This attention does not surprise him, since, in his words, "It was God's idea, and God knows what He is doing." The outpouring of support from all over the world is, in Bishop Caldwell's assessment, a sign that the world is ready for multiethnic churches.

Fifty years after the civil rights movement began, are American Christians ready for multiethnic churches? Despite the energy and resources that churches like Greenwood Acres, as well as denominational bodies and church-related organizations, are putting toward the creation of multiethnic churches, success stories are hard to find. According to the most comprehensive study on the subject, the Multiracial Congregations Project, only 5.5 percent of Christian churches are multiracial.[2] Nonetheless, I encountered the desire for this new kind of church everywhere I looked. There is clear evidence, from books to sermon series to conferences on the subject, that many Christians have a strong interest in bridging the historic ethnic divisions between Whites and Blacks, as well as the more recent divisions among Christians of Latin, Asian, and African heritage. In fact, it has become increasingly difficult for any Christian organization to find legitimate grounds on which to oppose ethnic diversity. As I researched the subject, I was told repeatedly that my topic is quite timely; everyone wants to know how to create a multiethnic church. But the more I encountered this desire, the more I wanted to understand it: Who wants to know, and why? Why now?

Obviously people find the *idea* of multiethnic churches attractive, but they seem to be more attracted to an imagined ideal rather than to joining the real multiethnic churches that already exist. Those few churches that do succeed in crossing the ethnic divide are doing something quite exceptional in the history of American religious life.[3] While Christian theologians and ministers from across denominations have written extensively in recent years on the subject of the multiethnic church, it has not received much attention from a sociological perspective.[4] We know very little about this emerging social institution and its inner workings. What does it mean to describe a church as multiethnic? How does ethnic diversity affect congregational life? What kind of people are attracted to multiethnic churches, and why?

While it seems quite plausible that an ethnically diverse group of people can form a community around shared beliefs, in practice shared beliefs have not been enough to overcome historic ethnic divisions within Christianity. For the multiethnic church to exist, individuals must literally cross these dividing lines by walking into the religious space of the ethnically "other." However the ideal multiethnic church is imagined, it most certainly means more than occupying the same physical space, which can so easily replicate the divisions of the surrounding society. Internal divisions must also be crossed by literally walking from one side of the room to another. To understand the multiethnic church as a new social institution, then, we must look concretely at how real people live out their values in congregational life.

Through an ethnographic study of one congregation, Evergreen Baptist Church, this book takes an in-depth look at why and how a community of people in search of an ideal Christian community transformed their relatively homogeneous church into a multiethnic one. This book tells their story—the pitfalls they have encountered and the measures of their success—but their story, like Bishop Caldwell's, is only a starting point for understanding a much larger narrative of the changing ethnic dynamics in America and how religious institutions are responding to and shaping these changes. By looking closely at the efforts of one community, while also examining the broad social context in which these efforts are embedded, we can come to understand not only what is unique about the multiethnic church, but also what the desire for this kind of community reveals about who we are as an ethnically diverse country and who we desire to become.

Evergreen Baptist Church and the Evangelical Racial Reconciliation Movement

In 2001, the *Los Angeles Times* ran a full-page article, titled "Building on the Gospel of Inclusion," describing Evergreen Baptist Church of Los Angeles.[5] Like many other evangelical churches in Southern California, Evergreen offers worship services with dynamic music, technological aids, and great preaching, as well as a smorgasbord of programs on topics ranging from financial advice to parenting skills. Situated in one of the most diverse cities in the world, Evergreen has allowed itself to be shaped by the surrounding cosmopolitan milieu. Founded in 1945 as a mission church for Japanese immigrants, Evergreen became a mixed Japanese/Chinese church in the 1980s, growing to over a thousand members. In 1997, Evergreen split in two, and the Evergreen Los Angeles branch took on a new identity as a multi-Asian/multiethnic community. Since then, its Asian American membership has shifted from 98 percent to 75 percent of the total, and has broadened to include people of seventeen distinct Asian and Pacific Rim ethnicities. By 2001, 25 percent of Evergreen's members identify themselves as Black, Latino, White, or multiracial.

There are dozens of other multiethnic churches in Los Angeles that could have easily served as the focal point of this study, so why Evergreen? The region is predominantly Roman Catholic, with an Archdiocese actively promoting multiculturalism in parish ministry, so focusing on a multiethnic parish might have seemed an obvious choice.[6] Instead I chose to study a Protestant church for the simple reason that while Catholics are expected to attend their local parish church, Protestants are not restricted by parochial boundaries and thus have much greater freedom in choosing a church. In practice, some Roman Catholics do church-shop, and diversity of membership is certainly a factor in their decision, but the process of church-shopping is much more transparent for Protestant Christians, and I wanted to know if diversity is a significant factor in choosing a church.

Beyond this criterion, Evergreen Baptist Church made an appealing case study for two reasons. First, this congregation is intentionally and publicly addressing diversity issues, while many multiethnic churches do not. By addressing diversity issues through theological reflection in sermons, the church newsletter and Web site, and programs and discussion groups, Evergreen makes public, and thus accessible to the researcher, the inner workings of its multiethnic efforts. These arenas of ongoing internal dialogue were an invaluable source of insight into the institutional culture of Evergreen, which served to supplement the formal interviews I conducted with forty members of the church, including six of the paid ministry staff. Second, as a predominantly Asian American church Evergreen stands outside the White/Black divide that has dominated the study of race relations in the United States. Important as this framework is for understanding how race functions in America, it is inadequate for understanding the development of multiethnic churches in areas of the country, such as Los Angeles, where the dynamics of diversity are far more complicated. Too often books on multiethnic churches have focused on the dynamics between Whites and people of color, forgetting that relations among people of color are also negotiated and fraught with tension.[7] Rather than focusing on a White church that has opened its doors to people of color, I chose to base this study on a non-White multiethnic church in order to learn how the dynamics of privilege and power are similar to and different from those in White-dominated churches.

The fact that Evergreen identifies with the evangelical subculture makes it a valuable case study for another reason: it affords an opportunity to examine how evangelicals are responding to the growing ethnic diversity in America. While data on religious affiliation is not as precise as one would wish, somewhere between one-fourth and one-third of all Americans identify themselves as evangelical Christians or share the characteristics associated with this group: belief in biblical inerrancy, commitment to spreading the Christian message, personal relationship with Jesus Christ, and the experience of being born again.[8] In the twentieth century, evangelical Christians were not known for their leadership in the area of race relations. They sat on the sidelines during the civil rights movement, while liberal Christians marched in the streets. However, in recent years major evangelical organizations have made race relations a top priority under the name of "racial reconciliation," a term first used in the late 1960s by Black evangelical activists.

In their book *Divided by Faith: Evangelical Religion and the Problem of Race in America*, Michael Emerson and Christian Smith note that since the late 1980s there has been an explosion of racial reconciliation activity, including conferences, books, study guides, videos, speeches, practices by organizations, formal apologies, and even mergers of once racially separate organizations.[9] This promotion of racial reconciliation has had a wide-reaching effect on evangelical churches, prompting some to make minor gestures toward inclusivity and a few churches—like Evergreen—to apply these ideas intentionally to the formation of multiethnic churches. Since this flurry of activity has been well documented in print and on the Internet, I was able to develop a rich understanding of the evangelical context out of which Evergreen's commitment to diversity has grown.

In the simplest terms, racial reconciliation means the reconciling of the races or, to put it another way, the overcoming of racial divisions in society. This innocuous definition avoids the contentious issues that plague the racial reconciliation movement: What causes these divisions? How do we overcome them? Who needs to do the reconciling? Is racism a personal sin or a societal injustice? Can't we just be color-blind? Are all ethnic-specific churches bad?

Why can't we just be Christians? Given the diverse ways these questions are answered by those committed to a theology of racial reconciliation, there is no single approach to racial reconciliation among American evangelicals. While it has become common to speak of the growing interest and efforts being made toward racial reconciliation as a movement, I use the term "movement" loosely in the following pages. The racial reconciliation movement is not a unified agenda but rather an umbrella under which evangelical Christians are addressing racial tensions and striving for racial integration in—and beyond—their institutions.

While many evangelicals have heard of racial reconciliation in one context or another, it is unusual to find a church that embraces the racial reconciliation theology as explicitly as Evergreen.[10] What makes Evergreen even more unusual among evangelical institutions focusing on racial reconciliation is its Asian American majority. Because the movement has focused primarily on the reconciliation between Blacks and Whites, little is known about how Asian American or Latino evangelicals are involved in it. This is not surprising, since there has been little published on the relationship between evangelicals of color and the White, mainstream, evangelical subculture in general. Though I did not set out to study how Asian American evangelicals relate to White evangelicals, it became obvious in the course of studying the racial reconciliation literature that the Asian American members of Evergreen Baptist Church do not share the racial attitudes of their White evangelical coreligionists.

As a predominantly Asian American, evangelical church, Evergreen should not be taken as a "typical" multiethnic church, if indeed there is such a thing. Nonetheless, this congregation provides a fascinating case study and starting point for trying to understand the multiethnic church as a unique social institution emerging in diverse urban social contexts. Through this growing, young, vibrant church east of Los Angeles, we can learn a great deal about the challenges multiethnic churches must contend with to form an ethnically diverse, inclusive community, and about the social and theological values that compel members to face these challenges. While there are many things that I, as an outsider to the evangelical subculture, came to admire about Evergreen, I do not perceive it as an ideal multiethnic church, nor do I present it as a model for other churches to follow. In fact, throughout this study I wrestle with the very idea of what it means to be a "successful" multiethnic church or, for that matter, a successful multiethnic institution of any kind. By allowing themselves to be studied, the members of Evergreen offer us an opportunity to grapple with what an ideal multiethnic community ought to look like, while examining the challenges that a real multiethnic community faces.

Race Relations Have Never Been Better . . . or Worse

Bishop Caldwell is not the only person who thinks the current social climate is fertile ground for the multiethnic church. In the course of my research, I was told many times by both Christians and non-Christians that multiethnic churches make sense now, given how tolerant Americans have become regarding diversity. There is a strong connection between the desire for multiethnic churches and the belief that the current climate in the United States is conducive to their success. To understand the social factors compelling churches to make diversity a priority, we need to begin by examining the social context out of which this movement is emerging. Have Americans really reached a new level of racial tolerance and equality, or does racism continue to profoundly impact one's life opportunities in the United States? There is no simple answer to this question. The current climate looks very different from the vantage point of the Asian-majority San Gabriel Valley, where Evergreen is located, or the crime-ridden neighborhoods of East Los Angeles, than it does to racially privileged, middle-class Whites. The supposed tolerance of Americans may not be so visible to a new immigrant, a non–English speaker, a person of color, or a person struggling to survive economically. As I wrote this book, I grappled with the disparity between these vantage points, as well as how my own vantage point has shaped my optimism for the future of ethnic relations in the United States.

From where I stand as an educated White woman, married to an immigrant from the Philippines and raising two multiethnic children while living in a very diverse, middle-class neighborhood in Southern California, the climate for ethnic relations looks encouraging. While doing this research I lived in Oxnard, located on the coast fifty miles north of Los Angeles. According to the 2000 census, Oxnard is 66.2 percent Latino, 20.6 percent Anglo, 7.4 percent Asian, and 3.8 percent African American. My neighborhood is home to extended families of immigrants from Mexico, Korea, India, and the Philippines, as well as a number of American-born Latino families, Anglo families, and multiracial families. A trip to the local park reveals children of all shades speaking various languages while playing side by side and occasionally, if they can overcome their shyness, interacting. In many ways diversity in Oxnard is "working." That is to say, people mix here. Many neighborhoods, schools, and families are ethnically mixed. Latinos are in positions of power in all aspects of city life, from the mayor to school principals. Oxnard does not have racially-motivated hate crimes or race riots. I am often surprised that there is not more racial tension in Oxnard, but I attribute this to the large number of bilingual/bicultural people who serve as cultural mediators and to the many decades residents here have been "practicing" diversity.

These are all encouraging signs, but even from my comfortable middle-class vantage point it is not hard to see the ways in which Oxnard falls far short of a multiethnic utopia. For example, the children at the park near my house are blissfully unaware that they are the source of the most cantankerous race issue in Oxnard—bilingual education. Although California voters rejected statewide bilingual education in 1998 by passing Proposition 227, support for it is strong in largely Latino districts like Oxnard. The majority of Latino parents sign waivers to exercise a clause under Proposition 227 to have their children taught in a bilingual class. At the same time, both Anglo and Latino parents express concern that students are not learning English fast enough and that Spanish is being promoted in the schools. Headlines are made from the rare occasion when an English-only child is placed in a bilingual class because there is no room for him or her in the few English-only classes in this overcrowded district. The many Latino gangs in the Oxnard area are an equally significant source of racial tension. Fear of crime and gang violence has clear racial overtones, and charges of racial profiling by the police are often in the news.

These conflicting views of race relations in Oxnard became apparent to me as I did much of my writing on a laptop in public spaces. The two places I frequented, a local Starbucks and the Oxnard Public Library, provide contrasting vantage points for gauging how well diversity is working here. Like many pubic libraries, ours has a special mission to help immigrants through English classes, computer training, a passport center, and free legal and tax help, in addition to an ample supply of books in English and Spanish. Libraries seldom encourage conversation, but it seems especially the case that people at the Oxnard Public Library are reluctant to interact. Reflecting the obvious ethnic and class differences between library patrons and library employees, there is little cross-cultural interaction, and ethnic boundaries stay firmly in place. On the other hand, the Starbucks near my home attracts quite a different mix of people, many of whom work in the adjacent financial center. Well-dressed Black, White, Asian American, and Latino customers relax and do business to the eclectic sounds of the Starbucks' CD mix. Conversations among strangers are common here amidst the trappings of the educated middle class: laptops, cell phones, music, and frappuccinos. From this vantage point of economic opportunity it is easy to imagine a multiethnic America that works.

The drama of ethnic relations is played out in libraries and coffee shops like these across the country. The perception among some Americans that the climate is ideal for multiethnic churches is based on a positive experience of increasingly diverse schools, workplaces, neighborhoods, and families. These are the public and private spaces in which people of diverse ethnic backgrounds interact in civil, often egalitarian ways on a daily basis. Sociologist Penny Becker describes such arenas of interaction and discourse as inclusive public spaces.[11] In these spaces, diversity is not merely a fact of life to be tolerated; it is a source of cultural dynamism to be valued and pursued. From a different vantage point, however, the climate looks much bleaker. This is the picture drawn from the increasing disparities between Whites and people of color in educational and economic achievement. Race continues to matter profoundly in determining life opportunities in the United States. The social processes of racialization that privilege White Americans and penalize people of color continue to create a divided society that is far from being racially just.[12] Even Bishop Caldwell, who believes the time is ripe for multiethnic churches, notes that "racial divisions have never been as bad in this country as they are right now."

Depending on how we assess the current climate, multiethnic churches are either the natural fruition of a general trend toward a more racially tolerant society or a progressive social force breaking new ground in forming racially inclusive public spaces. Churches are either catching up with a progressive, tolerant society, or they are a countercultural force challenging entrenched social patterns of ethnic divisions. I argue in the following pages that they are in some ways both, depending on the vantage point we choose to look from.

American attitudes toward diversity have changed dramatically in the last fifty years, but not uniformly. Among young, urban, college-educated Americans, a "cosmopolitan ethos" is particularly apparent. I attribute this to the combination of being educated in the ideology of multiculturalism and being surrounded by diversity during formative years in urban environments. The insistence on embracing diversity in the schools and in the culture at large has instilled in these young people a high value for diversity. When young adults join churches, they look for congregations that reflect the diversity in which they live, work, and go to school. Multiethnic churches do not seem countercultural to these young people who have been reared in diverse settings, but within the larger United States few voluntary institutions have managed to create inclusive communities across ethnic boundaries.

Pushing for the development of multiethnic churches are young adults who have been raised in diverse cities in the climate of multiculturalism with a strong value for diversity. At Evergreen Baptist Church, the most enthusiastic supporters of the church's mission are indeed the cohort of recent college graduates. Like other cosmopolitans, Evergreen's young people have grown up in diverse social settings, move in diverse social networks, and strongly value diversity. While ethnic churches served as a haven in an inhospitable world for their parents, these young people view such churches as at best boring and at worst implicitly prejudiced.

Unlike other cosmopolitans, however, Evergreen's young people are thoroughly committed to the biblically-grounded theology of racial reconciliation. Many are exposed to racial reconciliation in their college years through Bible fellowships like the InterVarsity Christian Fellowship and the Asian American Christian Fellowship, and it is through such evangelical organizations that they learn to think about diversity in theological terms. To understand how young evangelicals are becoming "convicted" with racial reconciliation and taking their convictions into evangelical churches like Evergreen, we need to look at both their secular education in multiculturalism and their religious formation. Because so many Evergreeners were involved with InterVarsity in college, I have included some detail on this organization's approach to racial reconciliation, as well as insights from interviews with staff and student members of InterVarsity in Los Angeles and the national InterVarsity office. This secondary focus on the college formation of evangelicals through InterVarsity proved to be especially useful for understanding how the secular ideology of multiculturalism is reframed and recast in the college Bible fellowship into an explicitly evangelical response to diversity.

The Church and Society

There is in the pages that follow a dialectic between micro-level questions concerning how Evergreen as a multiethnic church "works" and macro-level questions concerning what it means for a multiethnic institution of any kind to "work," and how perceptions of success reflect contemporary American attitudes toward diversity. In asking these questions I am addressing a perennial issue at the foundation of the sociological study of religion: the relationship between church and society. Religious institutions are far from the private shelters isolated from the public sphere that they are often taken to be. Sanctuary walls are porous, and ideas, values, and practices pass in both directions. In the case of multiethnic churches, these exchanges between church and society are clearly afoot. Changing demographics and social attitudes toward diversity prompt the members of Evergreen to ask the same question as civic leaders, educators, neighborhoods, and interracial families: How can we all get along?

As arenas of interaction and discourse, multiethnic churches are intentionally and unintentionally engaging this question, beginning with the meaning and significance of ethnic, racial, and cultural identity. Even the choice of the label "multiethnic" rather than "multiracial" or "multicultural" requires churches to enter into the larger social debate about how to talk about diversity. How much diversity does it take to make a multiethnic church, and what kind of diversity counts? How are African American and Korean American similar but distinct kinds of identities in the racialized context of the United States? What is the relationship between culture, race, and ethnicity? Is ethnic identity even important in a Christian context? Is American culture the same thing as White culture? These are difficult questions to answer, and multiethnic churches often struggle to determine how to frame their desire for diversity.

Not surprisingly, there is a good deal of ambiguity and inconsistency in how church leaders and members talk about these issues, but one approach to diversity is quite common among White evangelicals. Emerson and Smith call it the color-blind approach. Churches that use this strategy rely on a shared Christian identity to form the basis of community, and to varying degrees they ignore or reject the significance of non-White ethnic identity and culture. However, color blindness is not the only approach to diversity that evangelical churches may choose to follow. Evergreen is among those churches that insist on the value of ethnicity, openly address the tensions that arise in an ethnically diverse context, and strive to be intentionally inclusive of those outside of the ethnic majority. There are no doubt more than these two strategies for "managing" diversity available, but as the two most common approaches they lend themselves to comparison. How do the color-blind and color-conscious strategies encourage and limit dialogue about the significance of ethnicity and race in multiethnic congregations?

While it has been well documented that ethnic churches serve to strengthen ethnic identity, it is not clear how ethnicity functions in a multiethnic context like Evergreen Baptist Church. Do multiethnic churches necessarily undermine ethnicity as individuals seek to create shared cultural patterns? Can a multiethnic church actually strengthen the diverse ethnic identities of its members? Is ethnicity reproduced in this context through interaction with co-ethnics, as it is in ethnic churches? Do internal ethnic subgroups form within the multiethnic church in order to maintain ethnic identity? These questions have obvious relevance to the study of ethnicity in American society at large. Evergreen's insistence that it can form an inclusive community without undermining ethnicity challenges the presumption that diversity inevitably leads to assimilation, as well as rigid ideas about what it means to be an "ethnic" American. Rather than forcing a choice between being "ethnic" or being "American," Evergreen promotes a flexible and adhesive sense of identity and encourages members to live out their ethnic identities in their own ways.[13]

A final sociological question addressed in this study is that of institutional change. Given the pattern of ethnic homogeneity in church life, how does a church become multiethnic? How does a congregation decide to take on the goal of ethnic inclusion, and how does it implement that goal? What does a multiethnic church look like in terms of theology, programs, sermons, worship style, leadership style, architecture, food, and so forth? Which members sacrifice the most to make the multiethnic church work? Because Evergreen began this process as an Asian American church, it is the non-Asian members who bear the burden of being in the minority. They are the "boundary crossers" who have literally entered into a space where they are ethnically displaced. By looking closely at the kinds of tensions that arise at Evergreen and how they are addressed, we learn a great deal about the challenges of forming an intentionally inclusive multiethnic community and the kind of cross-cultural skills and attitudes that are needed to make it work. Even more important, we begin to understand the strength of the convictions that compel individuals to bear the costs of social change.

In many respects Evergreen Baptist Church is a microcosm of the larger social struggle with ethnic diversity and integration. While it is clear that Evergreen is adapting to the changing racial attitudes and social networks of its members, its decision to take on a multiethnic mission has the potential to conversely influence how American institutions and individuals adapt as well. At times in U.S. history, churches have been fertile ground for radical change, as well as the power base of the status quo. In the civil rights movement of the 1960s, for example, they played both of these roles with vigor. Intentionally or not, multiethnic churches are participating in a much larger social dialogue about diversity, ethnic identity, and racialization. The important question is *how* they are participating. Sociologist Penny Becker argues that whether local voluntary organizations are to be players in the struggle for racial equality depends on their ability to foster civic habits of tolerance and caring across traditional social divisions.[14] Becker offers two questions for assessing the potential social impact of multiethnic churches: Are multiethnic churches arenas for serious reflection on social divisions, and do they frame and address social divisions in a way that encourages mobilization for social change in the larger society? In the conclusion, I pose these same questions in the case of Evergreen. Clearly Evergreen has been shaped by the cosmopolitan ethos of Southern California, but is this church conversely shaping the larger society?

Plan of the Book

This study begins with the story of Evergreen and its transformation from a pan-Asian church to a multiethnic one. Chapter 1 identifies the factors that influenced the church's pastor, Ken Fong, to take Evergreen in this direction and the tools he has used to frame the church's new identity in appealing ways.[15] While Pastor Ken has been very successful at this task, the work of selling his vision to the congregation is ongoing. In chapter 2, I examine the theological foundations of the racial reconciliation movement, which has played such an important role in Evergreen's development. After discussing the biblical basis of racial reconciliation theology and its development into a larger movement within mainstream evangelicalism, I reflect on Evergreen's unique approach to racial reconciliation, an approach that differs significantly from the color-blind model.

Chapter 3 explores the role young adults are playing in the push toward multiethnic churches and the converging factors, both secular and religious, that have contributed to their value for diversity. Because InterVarsity has played a key role in the lives of many young people at Evergreen, I closely examine how InterVarsity in Los Angeles addresses diversity and racial reconciliation. While many White evangelicals appeal to a color-blind, individual reconciliation approach to diversity, InterVarsity in Los Angeles has stressed ethnic diversity and, increasingly, social justice in its teaching on racial reconciliation. With this foundation, it is no surprise that at Evergreen young adults are the strongest voice for greater attention to racial reconciliation and social engagement in general. The fourth chapter grapples with what it means to call a church "multiethnic." I distinguish the multiethnic church from other institutional forms that urban churches have developed to "manage" diversity by defining the multiethnic church as *an inclusive, ethnically diverse community*. In practice, such churches are often criticized for ignoring or overemphasizing diversity. The challenge for the multiethnic church is to both affirm the unique ethnic heritage of its members and create a shared sense of community. In this chapter I examine how Evergreen has institutionalized its commitment to inclusion of diversity and how the significance of ethnic identity is understood in this multiethnic setting.

Chapter 5 shifts the focus from Evergreen as an institution to Evergreen as a community of individuals. All churches have areas of tension, but multiethnic churches must also contend with conflicts that arise from ethnic differences. In chapter 5 I examine the fault lines along which tensions arise most frequently at Evergreen: communication, food, and family. Underlying these tensions are conflicting views on the role ethnic diversity ought to play in this church and whether it is even possible to be ethnic in a multiethnic context. Influenced by ethnic pride movements and fluid constructions of identity, the young people at Evergreen are optimistic that they can retain their distinctive ethnic identities in multiethnic settings. The sixth chapter considers the costs of participating in a multiethnic church and how Evergreeners find meaning in, or at least learn to live with, their discomfort at Evergreen. Pastor Ken has purposely shaped a "culture of discomfort" that imbues the challenges of the multiethnic church with eschatological significance. Yet diversity is more than a burden for Evergreeners, who also enjoy these challenges and find humor in them.

In the concluding chapter, I speculate on the future development of multiethnic churches by looking at the factors that propelled Evergreen Baptist Church to its new identity. I argue that the new Evergreen reflects changing American attitudes toward diversity and a shift toward local engagement within evangelicalism. I predict that young adults will continue to play a pivotal role in the success of multiethnic churches. Lastly, after having argued throughout this volume for the influence of society on the development of multiethnic churches, I consider the potential significance of multiethnic churches for societal race relations in light of the Evergreen case study.

Two appendixes can be found at the end of the book. Appendix A provides a detailed explanation of the ethnographic methods used in this study, namely in-depth interviews, site visits, and archival research, and my rationale for proceeding as I did. Appendix B discusses the similarities and differences between the multiethnic church and three common institutional structures churches use to bring diverse peoples together: the space-sharing church, the multilingual church, and the pan-ethnic church.

Finally, a word must be said about the use of particular words in this study. There are no agreed-upon categories with which to talk about diversity, and I am treading here on highly contested ground. Though the terms "race" and "ethnicity" have distinct meanings, they are often used interchangeably in common discourse, much to the ire of scholars. Similarly, the terms "ethnicity," "race," and "culture" are often used synonymously (as are "multiethnic," "multiracial," and "multicultural"), or else combined, as in "ethno-racial" or "ethnic culture." Many of those I interviewed for this project had a clear preference for speaking of "ethnicity" rather than "race," as do I. This preference reflects the perception that ethnicity is a more flexible and freely chosen category, and one less tainted by negative associations, than race. Though few Americans today believe racial categories are biologically based, they are far too often reified as more than socially constructed categories. It has been argued that only White Americans have the privilege of adopting ethnicity discourse, but the reality of racialization does not stop the members of Evergreen from rejecting racial categories.[16] The preference for speaking in terms of ethnicity rather than race may also reflect a desire to avoid recognizing and responding to the reality of racialization, as race theorists have repeatedly pointed out.[17] In the following pages I do examine racism, racialization, and racialized identity, but

I do not use the terms "race" or "racial identity" to categorize people, unless that is how they identified themselves to me.

Because this book is based on ethnographic research, I have chosen to reflect the way the individuals I interviewed talk about diversity and their own identity. However, the categories Americans use to talk about diversity change frequently, so I, too, am flexible in my usage and am sensitive to the ways in which others use terms differently than I do. For example, I prefer the term "multiethnic" or "persons of mixed heritage" but have used the term "biracial" when that is how people described themselves. Likewise, while I generally use the term "Latino," if an interview subject refers to herself as "Hispanic," this is the term I use to identify her. When speaking of ethnic groups I have chosen to use the most common terms interchangeably: Anglo, Euro-American, and White; Black and African American; Asian and Asian American. I prefer the term "multiethnic church" to "multiracial church" because it recognizes the diversity of those subsumed into a single racial category such as Asian American; however, when discussing the work of other scholars who use the term "multiracial church," such as Emerson and Smith, I use their terminology. This instability of categories will surely irritate some readers, but I see no other way to accurately reflect the variability, confusion, and ambiguity of the current diversity discourses. Lastly, as the reader has already seen, I capitalize the terms White and Black when referring to members of these ethnic groups. While this is not the standard practice, it ought to be; when they refer to persons these terms are obviously not meant as adjectives but rather as group identifiers functioning as shorthand for the more formal terms "European American" or "African American."

I

For the Healing of the Nations

When I first met with Pastor Ken Fong of Evergreen Baptist Church in January 2002, he was excited about showing me the new church logo, a leaf.[1] The old logo featured three evergreen trees, but in the new logo the single leaf is not attached to any tree; it is falling to the ground. The vein of the leaf is in the shape of a cross, and the stem touches down on a pool of water, sending ripples outward. The image comes from a passage at the end of the New Testament that describes how Christians are sent out to bring healing to all: ". . . and the leaves of the tree will be for the healing of the nations."[2] Just as the leaf in the church logo sends ripples along the water, Pastor Ken hopes that Evergreen will have an impact far beyond the church walls. Since becoming senior pastor in 1997, he has led Evergreen through a significant transformation from an Asian American church to one building, in the words of the church vision statement, reconciled communities: "remarkable montages of cultures, classes and circumstances."

Since its founding, Evergreen's pastors have shaped many different identities for the church, and its current incarnation is no exception. Pastor Ken has worked diligently to bring the congregation onboard with the new vision. This chapter focuses on the factors that contributed to the church's transformation, including Pastor Ken's ongoing efforts to shape the congregational culture around this new vision, and how the staff and congregation have responded to his challenge.

Evergreen Baptist Church

In 1925, the Los Angeles Baptist City Mission Society founded Evergreen Baptist Church, originally called Boyle Heights Baptist Church, as a small mission to serve Japanese-speaking immigrants. In the mid-1930s, a part-time English ministry was added for the growing second generation, but the congregation was forced to close its doors during World War II, when members were sent to internment camps. After the war, returning members began to rebuild with a predominantly English-speaking Japanese American membership. In just three years the church, which was now called the Nisei Baptist Church of Los Angeles, tripled its membership and had 270 children enrolled in the Sunday school. The name was changed in 1949 to Evergreen Baptist Church of Los Angeles, and a few years later the Japanese-speaking members formed a separate congregation across the street, allowing Evergreen to devote itself entirely to English-speaking ministry. After a period of postwar vitality the church fell into decline, and by the late 1970s Evergreen, with only eighty-five members, was struggling to survive.

The future of Evergreen changed dramatically when the church called a third-generation Japanese American, Cory Ishida, as pastor. Pastor Cory attracted many new members, including Chinese Americans. Ken Fong, a third-generation Chinese American, was called as the assistant pastor in 1981 to further the transition from a Japanese American church to a pan-Asian church. As the Boyle Heights area of East Los Angeles became increasingly Latino and members of Evergreen moved east to the San Gabriel Valley, the church decided in 1982 to relocate to the Valley, on a larger site in the city of Rosemead, with the goal of reaching the growing Asian American population there. They moved into a newly constructed church building in 1988 and grew quickly into a nation-ally recognized Asian American church with a weekly attendance of twelve hundred.[3]

Like many evangelical ministers of his generation, Pastor Ken was trained in seminary in the homogeneous unit principle of church growth. Donald Mc-Gavran, the director of the School of World Missions at Fuller Seminary in Los Angeles, developed this principle in 1936. McGavran taught those preparing for foreign missions that forming homogeneous congregations was the most effective method of evangelization, because crossing cultural barriers is too great an obstacle for potential converts. As he explained it simply, "men like to become Christians without crossing racial, linguistic, or class barriers."[4]

In the 1970s, one of McGavran's Fuller students, Peter Wagner, applied the same principle to church life in the United States in the wake of the civil rights movement and the increasing number of immigrants from Latin America,

Asia, and Africa. Rather than support the integration of churches, Wagner provided a justification for maintaining ethnic separation: because people prefer to be with their own kind, homogeneous churches will grow faster. As the back cover of his 1979 book *Our Kind of People* explains, "Wagner transforms the statement that 'II A.M. on Sunday is the most segregated hour in America' from a millstone around Christian necks into a dynamic tool for assuring Christian growth."[5] Pastor Ken studied under Peter Wagner as a student at Fuller Seminary, and became, in his words, "a conspicuous disciple of the church growth movement."[6]

After working at Evergreen for a number of years, Ken decided to write his Doctor of Ministry dissertation on the application of the homogeneous unit principle to a new target population he called American Born Asians or Americanized Asian Americans. In his dissertation Ken describes this "unreached people group" as third-generation immigrants who are highly assimilated in American society while still maintaining a strong ethnic identity as Asian Americans. Americanized Asian Americans had not completely assimilated into the mainstream White culture as the prevailing sociological literature had predicted they would. Consequently, they are not comfortable in either immigrant churches or in the so-called "American" churches dominated by White Americans. Because the church growth movement assumed that one was either "ethnic" or "American," there was no place in the existing evangelical map for Americanized Asian Americans.

Ken's belief that Americanized Asian Americans have enough in common to be considered a homogeneous unit reflected the growing political mobilization of Asian Americans, which he had encountered as an undergraduate at U.C. Berkeley in the 1970s. The 1980s and 1990s saw the emergence of numerous pan-Asian churches along the West Coast, and many Asian American pastors turned to Ken's dissertation for guidance.[7] This manuscript was eventually published in 1998 by Judson Press under the title *Pursuing the Pearl: A Comprehensive Resource for Multi-Asian Ministry*, further spreading Ken Fong's reputation as a founder of Asian American ministry. Ironically, by the time his dissertation was reaching a wide audience, Ken was no longer a proponent of church growth based on the homogeneous unit principle, and his own ministry had shifted in a dramatically new direction.

Through the charismatic leadership team of Cory Ishida and Ken Fong, Evergreen became known as a successful pan-Asian church, though in practice it was largely attracting those of Chinese and Japanese ancestry. As he explains in *Pursuing the Pearl*, these two groups have naturally formed alliances because they have been in the United States the longest and thus are the most Americanized of the Asian Americans.[8] The mission of Evergreen in its pan-Asian

stage was to reach "unconvinced" English-speaking Asian Americans; however, over the course of its history a handful of non-Asians had become members of Evergreen, primarily through intermarriage. While they were never excluded from membership, it was clear that the mission of the church was not to
serve them, or, in the language of church growth, not to dilute the target population. When non-Asians would question Ken on this exclusive focus, he gave
this reasoning: "You would not go to a Japanese restaurant and expect to be
served tacos just because you are Mexican." Looking back on this period of
Evergreen's history, Ken now acknowledges that he was never entirely comfortable with the way his efforts to reach Americanized Asian Americans excluded
others.

In 1990, Ken was asked to join the national board of InterVarsity Christian
Fellowship and to be a main speaker at the annual Urbana conference for
twenty thousand college students from the United States and abroad. He says
that it was at Urbana, in the face of the global picture of God's heart and God's
purpose, that his "ruination" as a leader of Asian American ministry began.
Learning about racial reconciliation through InterVarsity and experiencing it
firsthand at Urbana made Ken feel tremendously guilty about writing off
ninety-nine percent of the world. He explains: "I just ran into my own prejudices. I ran into my own biases and God was challenging me right and left, saying, 'Okay, I understand the initial reason why you're trying to be so narrow in
your focus, but it's not supposed to stay narrow.'" Prior to the Urbana conference, Ken was convinced that the homogeneous unit principle was the best way
to spread the Gospel, but having experienced the tremendous diversity at Urbana, he wanted to be part of a church that included all kinds of people.

Like many of those committed to racial reconciliation, Ken's attraction to
this new theology was intensified by changes within his own family. The Fong
family had become increasingly diverse in the 1990s, through marriage and
the addition of biracial children through adoption and birth. Ken's wife is Japanese American, and they adopted a Chinese American child in 1999, a few
years after his brother adopted an African American child. The first time I met
Ken, he described watching his Chinese daughter and African American nephew
learn to use chopsticks in their adjoining high chairs. The Fong family also includes Korean, Guamanian, Filipino, and European heritages. In light of this
diversity, Ken has posed a difficult question to his parents and siblings: When
do we stop thinking of ourselves as a Chinese family? Painful as it is to lose
that identity, Ken believes that continuing to think of themselves as a Chinese
family clearly excludes family members that they love dearly. It bothers Ken
greatly to think that his Black nephew may be ostracized in Asian American
Christian circles, which he has spent years developing. Reflecting on this

identity problem in light of his InterVarsity experience, Ken became even more convinced that ethnic inclusion ought to be part of all families, including church families.

Rejecting the Asian American focus that had defined his career in ministry up to this point left Ken in a difficult position within his own church and his larger network of pan-Asian church leaders. As Ken put it, "I helped to create a ministry that has blinders on, and I'm literally the person who wrote the book about this." His conviction for racial reconciliation was not the only reason that Ken began to feel ill suited to leadership at Evergreen. It was one piece of a larger vision to develop what he calls the postmodern church. Ken describes the postmodern church as a counter-cultural, outward-looking church that is doing "redemptive" things like serving the poor and breaking down ethnic barriers, as opposed to an inward-focused "Christendom church" that is culturally comfortable. As the assistant pastor Ken had limited power to shape the culture of the church in this direction. By the mid-1990s, his discomfort with Evergreen's inward focus was strong enough that he began to think privately about leaving. While it would have been nearly impossible to convince the senior pastor and the entire membership to move in this challenging direction, an unexpected and drastic change in membership provided an opening for far-reaching change.

In 1996, Senior Pastor Cory Ishida made the decision to split Evergreen into two congregations, forming Evergreen San Gabriel Valley and Evergreen Los Angeles. The split, or "hive," as it is called, was a defining moment in the life of the church. Members now talk about the history of Evergreen in terms of its pre-hive and post-hive periods, but they give conflicting versions of how this split came about. The most positive version is that the church was so large and flourishing that the time was right to divide and plant another new church. In *Pursuing the Pearl* Ken gives a different version of events: the church was in a period of malaise and was losing members.[9] Some Evergreeners believe that the church's ethnic focus lay behind the split, but the hive actually occurred before Ken made public his desire to create a multiethnic church.[10] When he looked back on the hive in 2004, Ken told me he believes the crux of the split was an incongruence between the vision and approach of the lead pastor, Cory Ishida, and himself. With the hive, each pastor was able to focus on his particular vision for Evergreen.

Told about the hive in 1996, members had a short time to decide which pastor to follow. Both were very well liked, and this was a difficult decision for many members. One longtime member told me that being unable to decide, she let her husband choose, as Pastor Cory had instructed couples to do. For almost a year the two Evergreen churches continued to share the Rosemead space by holding services at different times, and this was the most painful period for Ken, who remembers vividly "the human dynamic of seeing people not look you in the eye anymore because they've decided to go with the other pastor, even though you did their wedding, even though you baptized their children, even though you worked together for years, but philosophically you've grown apart—it was horrible." When the legal separation was complete, Cory led his congregation to a rented space east of Rosemead and continued to focus on English-speaking Asian Americans, while Ken stayed at the Rosemead site to pursue his vision of a postmodern, multiethnic church.[11]

Those who chose Ken were attracted to his postmodern paradigm of pushing beyond the status quo. He describes them as people who were coming to church regardless of ethnicity but were more postmodern, messy, outside-the-box. Those who preferred the Asian American family focus chose to go with Cory. Looking back on that painful period, Ken says he can now see God's hand in it, because it served to "out" a division that had been festering for many years between those who wanted a family-focused church and those who wanted to be more socially engaged. While it would have been quite difficult to sell his vision to the whole congregation, the hive served to narrow the membership to those willing to explore new directions. When Evergreen split, Ken was left with the church building in Rosemead, 20 percent of the families, most of the single members, 30 percent of the donating members, and a handful of Sunday-school teachers. They had enough money in the bank to operate for six weeks. Though he had few resources besides the church building, Ken now had the authority as senior pastor to create a new Evergreen, and members that were ready to follow his lead.

The New Evergreen

Some months after I first met Pastor Ken, I was at a Sunday service when he talked at length on the theme of reconciliation, beginning with the church's new logo:

> It comes from Revelations 22. At the end of it it says we will be the leaves that God uses for the healing of the nations. We aren't Christians just to kind of have our own sins forgiven and not go to hell. We are Christians for God to be able to use to extend the boundaries of his Kingdom. . . . That tree is the cross of Jesus and those leaves are every one of us in different shapes, colors and sizes, experience, diversity, variety, all brought together for healing.[12]

In addition to the leaf touching the water, there are other falling and floating leaves, sometimes printed in fall colors of red, yellow, and orange, that grace the cover of the order of service and the telephone directory. Leaves show up on PowerPoint slides during services and in a Flash animation on the church's Web site. They are a frequent reminder that, like leaves falling from the tree and Jesus dying on the cross, the members of Evergreen must allow themselves to be led by the Holy Spirit and used as "ministers of reconciliation, healing, and transformation."[13] The new leaf logo was not Ken's idea. To mark the fifth anniversary of the hive, the church's Information Resource Ministries developed the image based on suggestions from members. In a newsletter article, the workgroup's leader gave her own explanation of the logo: "The leaf shapes will represent different trees, again representing diversity. However, we are united in getting our nourishment from Christ."[14] Coming from church members, rather than from Ken, the new logo is a good indication that within five years Ken's vision for Evergreen had been embraced by the people in the pews.

It was in the midst of the hive transition that Ken began to articulate publicly his dream for a new Evergreen. One of the first things he did was to change the church vision statement: "Evergreen will become a multi-Asian/multi-ethnic, multisocioeconomic, multigenerational congregation." The "multi-Asian" in this statement meant that foreign-born and American-born Asians would be welcome, and the "multi-ethnic" meant that non-Asians would also be welcome. When I asked Ken what the process was for developing the statement, he laughed; one of the benefits of being senior pastor at Evergreen is the power to make top-down decisions. He thought it was important to make this statement publicly, like hanging out a new shingle, so that people who came to Evergreen would be intentionally choosing to be part of this vision.

Casting the Vision

Like all vision statements, Pastor Ken's was an exercise in imagination. As senior pastor, he has the authority to publish a new vision statement, but bringing all the members into agreement with it and getting them actively engaged in making it a reality is quite another matter. Shaping the corporate culture, as Ken puts it, takes a good deal of work. Indeed, sociologist Ann Swidler calls the process of manipulating culture to achieve a new institutional goal "culture work."[15] In the context of a congregation, culture work involves mining the religious tradition and unique history of the congregation for metaphors that can frame the new vision in legitimate religious terms and then institutionalizing the new vision in the church culture.[16] At Evergreen, Ken began this work by casting a vision that would capture the enthusiasm of the congregation.

Ken's new shingle, proclaiming Evergreen a multi-Asian/multi-ethnic, multisocioeconomic, multigenerational congregation, was short-lived. People complained that it was too much of a mouthful and, more important, it sounded too politically correct. As evangelicals, Evergreeners want their church to reflect biblical, not political, values. So in 2000 Ken created a second vision statement centered on the biblical concept of *sedaqah,* the Hebrew word for "righteousness" or "right relationship": "Evergreen Baptist Church of Los Angeles will demonstrate the passion Jesus had for reconciled relationship through our building 'Sedaqah Communities'—remarkable montages of cultures, classes, and circumstances, brought to complete unity by Christ to serve God's eternal purposes in the world.[17] Framing the vision in terms of sedaqah clearly distinguishes what Evergreen is trying to do from secular efforts to integrate institutions. This version of Evergreen's vision statement has stuck and become the foundation for all the church ministry programs, but that could only happen if Ken cast the vision in concrete ways that invited members to take ownership of it.

The primary tool a minister uses for culture work is the Sunday-morning sermon. Pastor Ken also teaches through articles in the monthly newsletter and on the Web site. In the years since the hive, he has spoken frequently on the vision statement through these public media. His first task was to show the biblical basis for reconciliation in order to convince members that "this is not my crazy idea but God's idea." Using both Old and New Testament texts, Ken has shown the theme of reconciliation to be central to the Christian story. For example, in a November 2002 sermon titled "A Church Empowered to Reconcile," he talked at length about the cultural conflicts between Jewish and Gentile Christians described in the Book of Acts. By framing the vision as a modern application of biblical values, Ken establishes reconciliation as a legitimate Christian project. As he puts it, "Reconciling people is something that if you're a Christian for any length of time you can't have a problem with it."[18] He also makes clear that Evergreen is not pursuing diversity for its own sake—as evangelicals believe secular institutions do—but pursuing a "redemptive community" in which social barriers are broken down because that is God's intention for humanity. This important distinction between secular goals and Christian goals is cleverly summed up in one of Ken's catchphrases: "What we are doing is not PC; it's JC."

Using the tools available to him, Ken has skillfully introduced the concept of reconciliation in ways that appeal to members. Everyone I spoke with at Evergreen accepted his claim that God wants people of all walks of life to be reconciled to each other as an obvious biblical truth. In the words of one longtime member, "I believe in it. I do think it is the picture of Revelations where every tribe, tongue, and nation will be together before the throne, and so it just makes sense to me that that should start happening before we get there. That's an easy one for me to buy into." Ken has been much less successful in convincing members and staff that their commitment to reconciliation means that Evergreen must change who it is and how it does things.

Gaining Diversity, Losing Their Identity?

When Pastor Ken announced his intention for Evergreen to become a multiethnic church, many members feared the loss of the church's Asian American identity. They assumed that with an increase in non-Asian members they would be forced to give up the Asian American aspects of their church that they loved so dearly. Would they still honor their Japanese American heritage with its painful history of internment? Would they still be able to hold the Ikebana class and sponsor a team for the Japanese American basketball league? After the hive, the remaining members and staff at Evergreen Los Angeles were 98 percent Chinese and Japanese American. Many of the assistant pastors, worship leaders, and Sunday-school teachers who stayed at Evergreen LA had taken on these roles because they felt called by God to serve the Asian American community, and now they were being asked to serve a radically different kind of community. Because Evergreen's identity was so tied to its Asian American ministry, much of Ken's work has been on the issue of ethnic diversity, even though this is only one piece of the envisioned montage of cultures, classes, and circumstances.[19]

In addition to grieving the loss of their church's identity, Evergreeners feared that as a multiethnic church the new Evergreen would not be able to grow. Why would anyone want to join a multiethnic church, when they could be with their own kind of people? Peter Wagner's insistence that people prefer to be in homogeneous churches was widely accepted at Evergreen as a social fact. Ken had, after all, written his dissertation on the subject. Moreover, this axiom of church growth was being taught in seminaries and ministry workshops around the country, making it all the more necessary for Ken to explain his ultimate rejection of the homogeneous unit principle. He did this without disparaging the value of ethnic-specific churches, like the newly-separated Evergreen San Gabriel Valley. Ken argued that ethnic-specific ministry may be a starting point for Christians, but in order to mature the Christian church must learn to go beyond these natural prejudices: "Just because it's much easier to get people to come to Christ and each other without having to tear down barriers, that doesn't mean that Jesus wants to build his Church that way. Jesus doesn't want to see country clubs with religious overtones."[20] Even Wagner accepts this trajectory of Christian maturation, but Evergreeners still questioned whether such a mature and countercultural church could attract the "unconvinced." In other words, the multiethnic church might be the biblical ideal, and the eschatological fulfillment of God's work, but can it really work in the here and now?

In response to fears that Evergreen would never flourish as a postmodern, multiethnic church, Ken stressed the outrageous audacity of the idea. This strategy seems counterintuitive. It is certainly counter to the church growth movement, which seeks above all to attract new Christians through the most practical means available. Instead, Ken stressed the improbability of Evergreen's success:

> Honestly, you don't need the Holy Spirit to do what society is already doing. Now you bring together fourteen kinds of Pacific Rim people and from the Middle East and South America, White, Black, Hispanic, from the hood, barrios, multi-racial, Democrats, Republicans, Libertarians, Five-Point Calvinists, all together, normally that doesn't work. We have put ourselves as a church in such a desperate position that if God doesn't resource us with that same exact Holy Spirit we are doomed.[21]

There are two important arguments being made here. First, Evergreen is going to do something the secular world cannot, and second, this near-impossible feat can only be accomplished through God's grace.

To succeed where secular society has failed is a powerful motivation for evangelicals. It serves as proof of God's power: the more impossible the feat, the more powerful God appears. In his extensive study of American evangelicals, sociologist Christian Smith found that they thrive on a strong sense of mission and embattlement from the secular world.[22] Ken believes that the unconvinced will be drawn to Evergreen precisely because it is doing what no one else has ever done. As a "preview of the coming attractions" described in the Book of Revelation, Evergreen will be such an amazing sign of God's power that it will attract spiritual seekers who are looking for more than what the secular world can offer. Ken believes that Evergreen will also attract earnest Christians who have left the churches that have been co-opted by right-wing and left-wing political issues and are searching for an authentic sign of God's presence in a church community.[23] Like a beacon on a hill, a multiethnic Evergreen will be proof of God for a secular world.

Evergreen's struggle to form sedaqah communities "against all odds" turned out to be an appealing way for Ken to sell the new vision. In addition to framing the vision in theological terms, an essential aspect of culture work is connecting the vision to the church's history so that the new direction is seen as a natural extension of the church's previous identity. From its Japanese immigrant beginnings in 1925 through its pan-Asian heyday in the 1990s, Evergreen has had many identities. A thread that runs throughout these changes, one that members take pride in, has been the church's adaptability and openness to newcomers. They point to the ease with which the church had previously widened its circle to include first the American-born Japanese and later Chinese Americans, as evidence that Evergreen has always been a tolerant, ethnically-inclusive church. This tolerant, easygoing self-image is one that Ken reinforces in his teaching on reconciliation.

In the November 2002 sermon on reconciliation, Pastor Ken told the story of an Evergreen member who was ministering through the Young Life Christian youth organization to a group of Southeast Asian high school students. When these students converted, he took them to a church close to the high school, where they received a chilly reception:

> It was like a mainline church with a lot of old Caucasian folks, and in
> walks these baggy-pants-wearing, spiky hair, colored, pierced holes,
> whatever, and they didn't look like the people who belonged to the
> church. . . . Well, from the stories of what I've been told, even though
> nobody said "get out," it's like people said "you're not welcome," there
> was this kind of wall there . . . so Rick packed them all up in a car
> and drove them all the way over here, and one of the great parts of
> that story is almost all those young people now are involved and
> members of our church.

If Evergreen has always been an exceptionally tolerant place, then the new emphasis on racial reconciliation is not new at all, but a natural extension of values Evergreen has always embodied. Ken both encourages this tolerant self-image and challenges it to push the congregation further. After talking about how much more tolerant Evergreeners are than those "old Caucasian folks," he goes on to say that "it is too easy to think we don't have problems in this area." If Evergreeners are to live up to their tolerant self-image, the next step is clearly to welcome non-Asians, as well as people of all walks of life, into their midst.

Catching the Vision

When monumental decisions are made in a top-down manner, they may not be accepted by those in the pews, and, not surprisingly, there has been a range of responses, from passionate acceptance to lukewarm tolerance to mild resistance.

Even among the three assistant pastors, all of whom are male and Asian American, I heard a mixture of all three responses.

Danny, who joined the church in 1995 and became a full-time staff member in 1999, is unequivocally committed to the mission.[24] He explained, "I like being cosmopolitan, that's why I like this church. I wouldn't want to be in an all-Asian church." Danny is very optimistic that Evergreen will keep diversifying, not just ethnically but in every way. Thomas, who joined the staff in 1994, has always lived and worked in Asian environments and is less optimistic. For him, embracing the church vision is an ongoing process: "I recognize definitely at an intellectual level that what Ken is saying is thoroughly biblical. It's reflected in the scripture, so because of my commitment to scripture I don't shy away from that. On a practical level it's a lot more challenging to implement." It is the implementation of the vision that gives Thomas pause. He wonders if it may be twenty years ahead of its time and perceives in the congregation a disconnect from a vision "that seems like it's too big." The third assistant pastor, Samuel, identifies as an American more than an Asian and is all for Evergreen becoming multiethnic. What he doesn't want is to hear about it all the time. Samuel thinks they should focus on things that they hold in common: Christianity, family values, and sports. Ken is well aware that he has other staff members in addition to Thomas and Samuel who have questions about how to implement the vision and reservations about whether it will work, just as those in the congregation do.

For longtime church members who followed Pastor Ken in the hive, the new vision came as a surprise. Many had a reaction similar to that of Liz, who has been at Evergreen since the early 1980s: "I was not at all opposed to greater diversity, but at first I didn't see the need to focus on racial reconciliation. People are already intermarrying and everything is fine as it is." It took time for Liz to realize the need to work on racial reconciliation intentionally. Another longtime member, Pauline, really struggled with the hive and which pastor to follow but thinks Ken's vision is wonderful and courageous. She knows that not everyone agrees with it, but hopes they can embrace it at least to a certain degree: "Even if it wasn't for yourself to go out and haul in somebody other than your ethnic group, that you would also feel okay that the trend was going in that direction." Her husband, Michael, is one of the old-timers who would really prefer the church to stay Asian American, but he's willing to take up Ken's challenge, unlike others who have left the church. He explains, "To me it seems like, this is what Christians need to do and you can't help it anyway. I mean, this is the world, especially Los Angeles."

Many Evergreeners drew a connection between the church's new vision and the growing diversity in Southern California. Some were experiencing diversity within their own families, as Pastor Ken was. Rates of exogamous (out-group) marriage have been increasing for all Asian Americans, but among the U.S.-born they range between 30 and 50 percent.[25] With this trend came the increase in multiethnic or *hapa* children.[26] According to the 2000 census, 2.4 percent of Americans identify as multiracial nationally, but in Los Angeles the rate is twice that, at 4.9 percent, and among the 11,898,828 Americans who identified as Asian, 1,655,830 also claimed an ancestry other than Asian.[27] Members of multiethnic families wanted their sons and daughters to feel comfortable bringing their spouses and *hapa* grandchildren to Evergreen. After all, where would these ethnically diverse families go if all churches were defined around a single ethnic group? The increasing number of non-Asian members at Evergreen strained the Asian American identity of the church. One member described the discomfort he was feeling before the hive:

> Every time I heard from the pulpit that this was an Asian American church and that is what the church was targeted for it kind of made me a little uneasy, because here we are in this church and we have some real mainstay families who are not Asian, and I am talking about some really supportive and giving type of people, loving people, and I would just sit there and say "Wow, you can't say that and keep that up like that."

The extensive ethnic diversity in Southern California meant that Evergreeners were also increasingly interacting with non-Asians in the workplace and in social settings. This created a practical problem in terms of evangelization, since Evergreeners are supposed to invite those in their social networks—their family, friends, and co-workers—to attend church. Many shared with me how uncomfortable they felt prior to the hive, or at other Asian churches, when they brought their non-Asian friends and family to church. As families and social networks became more diverse for many of those in the congregation, these Evergreeners began to feel out of step with the cultural climate. For them, Ken's new vision is a welcome change necessitated by a changing society.

In addition to bringing the pre-hive members on board, Ken has been able to attract new members who are already committed to the idea of a church for all people. Evergreen has gained a reputation as a progressive, socially-engaged multiethnic church, particularly among the local InterVarsity college students, which helps it attract young people. After the *Los Angeles Times* article in December 2001, the church saw a steady flow of visitors, some of whom had driven several hours to get there. Evergreen's commitment to diversity and reconciliation has been a major draw for new members, as the remarks of an African American woman, printed in the 2003 church newsletter, attest: "What's special about Evergreen-LA is the emphasis on creating racial reconciliation. I've been a member of a black church and yet there's something about a church that's committed to racial reconciliation and is actively working on that by having a church that's multi-racial, multi-ethnic [that] is really significant."[28]

The monthly Evergreen newsletter prints short biographies of new members, which offer some insight into what has attracted them to the church. For example, a bio of a new White member remarks that she "resonates wholeheartedly with the vision and mission of the church, with its commitment to being a redemptive and reconciling community in every way." Between January 2004 and October 2005, twenty-four of the ninety-five new members made reference to the church's vision or its multiethnic diversity in their newsletter biographies.[29]

Through a vision statement, churches imagine their best selves and project them to the world so that they will attract people who share their goals and values, but some visitors who decide to stay are uninterested in the vision statement or join in spite of it. As a full-service church with many types of groups and activities that appear to have little to do with "creating montages of cultures, classes, and circumstance," Evergreen attracts visitors for many reasons besides Ken's teaching on reconciliation. The most common reason I heard and read in the new member biographies was that the people at Evergreen are very warm and welcoming. As with longtime members still unsure if they want to accept the new vision, the challenge for the church leadership is to bring these newcomers on-board with the vision. Pastor Thomas put it well:

> All churches have strengths besides, strengths in addition to, the vision that we've cast, and other people are going to be attracted by that whether it be family ministries, whether it be the large number of singles, whether it's geographical proximity, whether it's the teaching and the Sunday morning worship. . . . Now the challenge for us is how do we help them understand what we want our congregation to become, and for them to recognize that as they come we want them to grow, we want them to be transformed, and part of that transformation is going to be how they see their own identity, how they interact with others—and especially if one of our main values is for them to be sent out, they need to know how they will engage in a role that's far less homogeneous.

After hanging out its new shingle in 1997, Evergreen grew from three hundred to almost seven hundred members in 2004, and the demographics shifted from 98 percent Chinese and Japanese Americans to 25 percent non-Asian and 75 percent Asian American, with seventeen ethnicities represented.[30] Clearly, many people are catching on to Evergreen's new vision. Those who are "disconnected" from the vision, as Pastor Thomas and others put it, have not stopped the church's transformation, but they can create a drag effect, slowing down progress and making change more difficult. So culture work must be on-going in order to bring both longtime and new members to a greater degree of understanding and commitment to the vision.

The message must be presented in new ways to draw the attention of those who would rather not hear it, and, as is the practice of many evangelical churches in Southern California, Evergreen's leaders frequently introduce new themes and catchphrases.[31] For example, the January 2004 newsletter gave the blueprint for "building a model twenty-first century church," which Ken explains does not mean a model in the sense of something to be copied but "a shining example of what God wants to do with and through very ordinary, messy people." This phrase began appearing in the headings of all newsletters in November 2004 and was soon revised to read "Building a Model 21st Century Missional Church," thus emphasizing that Evergreeners are to be sent out from the church on mission to the larger world. Several years after the hive, the need to continually sell his vision would be discouraging to some leaders, but Ken has a much longer timeframe in mind. He does not expect to see his vision of reconciliation come to fruition in his lifetime, but he does hope Evergreen will continue to move toward it.

The story of Evergreen is unusual in many ways. The church hive and the invitation for Pastor Ken to join the board of InterVarsity were unexpected events that enabled radical changes in a relatively short amount of time. Ken's exposure to racial reconciliation through InterVarsity, in conjunction with his own family's changing ethnic makeup, reflecting the growing diversity and integration in society at large, played a catalytic role in his rethinking church ministry. Pastor Ken was not the only person at Evergreen who was increasingly uncomfortable with the church's ethnically-limited ministry, and when he introduced a new vision many in the pews supported it. After having examined more closely who was attracted to the new Evergreen and what kinds of challenges they have faced in creating a multiethnic church, I will return in the conclusion to the issue of institutional change and what lessons can be learned from the story of Evergreen.

As an evangelical Christian, Pastor Ken turned to scripture, as well as to a growing body of literature, for evidence that reconciliation is God's intention for humanity. Racial reconciliation theology is a distinctly Christian response to diversity that sets evangelical efforts apart from secular responses to demographic and attitudinal changes. In other words, Evergreen does not want to mirror the surrounding society; it wants to be a model of reconciliation for society. To understand how racial reconciliation came to play such an important role in Evergreen's transformation, the next chapter looks more closely at the development of this theological discourse into a movement for social change within—and beyond—American evangelicalism.

2

The Racial Reconciliation Movement

For He is our peace; in his flesh he has made both groups into
one and has broken down the dividing wall, that is, the hostility
between us.

—Ephesians 2:14

George Yancey has defined racial reconciliation as "the process by
which we overcome the previous dysfunctional unequal relationship
between the races and develop an egalitarian, healthy relationship."[1]
The term was first used by evangelical Christians in the late 1960s,
but the idea is not new to Christianity. Since the formative years of
Christianity some believers have been inspired by their faith and understanding of scripture to form multiethnic communities, just as
others have used the same sources to oppose these efforts. In the
United States, Christians who pursued integration faced strong and
sometimes violent resistance. Their efforts to form multiethnic congregations have met with varying degrees of success, and most of
these communities lasted only a short time.

The Azusa Street Revival, which was organized by an African
American minister, William Seymour, is perhaps the best known of
these attempts. The services at Azusa Street in Los Angeles from
1906 to 1908 drew Blacks, Whites, and Latinos by the hundreds, as
well as a smaller number of Asian Americans and Native Americans.
Some saw this interracial gathering, marked by speaking in tongues,
as a sign of the Second Coming; others decried it as a terrible

degradation of Christ's church. The offense was not the multiethnic gathering so much as the mixing of Whites and people of color; Seymour's marriage to a White woman was especially vexing to many in the Azusa leadership. The mixing of people of color in multiethnic churches did not draw such rancor from White Christians. Like many interracial efforts, Seymour's was short lived. The revival itself was a great success, spawning the modern Pentecostal movement, but the mushrooming churches formed along strictly racial lines.

Like William Seymour and generations of Christians committed to integration before him, Pastor Ken believes that "breaking down the walls of hostility" is central to the unfolding history of salvation. Because racial reconciliation theology, and the movement for change it has inspired, have served as the theological context for the new Evergreen, it is helpful to understand this distinctly evangelical reading of scripture. In his ongoing culture work, Pastor Ken draws on the growing body of scholarship on racial reconciliation, but Evergreeners, through their own efforts to embody racial reconciliation, are now part of a larger dialogue about racial reconciliation and how best to implement it. In this sense they have both been shaped by and are contributing to this broad movement.

Beginning with the theological arguments for racial reconciliation, this chapter traces the history of the movement from the 1960s to the first decade of the new century. Competing versions of racial reconciliation are apparent. Early advocates wanted to transform both hearts and social institutions; their commitment to social justice continues to flourish in many Black churches. Within the evangelical mainstream, Whites have shunned calls for social justice in favor of forming reconciled relationships at an individual level. As a historically Asian American church, Evergreen's approach to racial reconciliation does not fit neatly into either the individualistic approach of mainstream evangelicals or the more radical approach of social-justice-oriented evangelicals. Instead, the way racial reconciliation is discussed at Evergreen suggests that Asian Americans, as well as other people of color, may be bringing greater race consciousness into the evangelical subculture.

The Great Commission

Jesus' command to his disciples, "Go therefore and make disciples of all the nations," is a central commitment of evangelical identity.[2] Racial reconciliation theology stresses that this Great Commission, as it is called, requires Christians to reach out to people of other "nations," also called "tribes" or "people groups." Church growth proponents have been critical of racial reconciliation theology, claiming that it detracts from the *real* Great Commission of saving souls, but the central message of racial reconciliation theology is that spreading the Gospel must occur across cultural boundaries. Recognizing that a whole generation of pastors was trained in the homogeneous unit principle, the racial reconciliation literature directly addresses the rationale behind this popular church growth strategy by debunking the biblical hermeneutics used to justify growth at all costs.

Though Peter Wagner did not develop the homogeneous unit principle directly from the Bible, he does believe it is in accord with the Gospel: "If Jesus and Paul did not carry out their ministries in accord with this theory, it would not be worthy of further investigation."[3] According to Wagner, not only was Jesus' "inner circle" of apostles homogeneous, but the churches they went on to plant were as well. Those few early churches that did try to be heterogeneous, such as the Antioch church described in Acts 11, faced serious divisions. Even when the Christian message spread beyond the Jewish people to the Gentiles, Wagner insists that it spread along homogeneous unit lines and that the Jewish-Gentile church at Antioch was "in all likelihood two distinct clusters of house churches."[4] He even refers to Paul as "the first-century champion of the homogeneous unit principle."[5] To refute this interpretation of the homogeneous development of the early Christian church, racial reconciliation theology begins with the evidence of Jesus' cross-cultural ministry and the multiethnic gatherings among the early Christians.

Looking first to the life of Jesus, racial reconciliation proponents emphasize his willingness to minister across ethnic boundaries in a region rife with ethnic conflicts. Many Jewish leaders of his time preached ethnic separation as an important strategy for survival, but Jesus insisted that the salvation story went beyond these boundaries. In the stories of Jesus healing a Greek woman and talking with a Samaritan woman, he is seen rejecting exclusivist practices and embodying the values of inclusion and unity. His radically inclusive message is particularly apparent in his willingness to have "table fellowship" with people considered unclean by pious Jews of his day. Racial reconciliation, as well as reconciliation across all differences, is framed as a continuation of Jesus' example. The authors of *United by Faith* draw this connection directly: "Jesus' inclusive table fellowship and vision of a house of prayer that was for all the nations was a precursor to what we call multiracial congregations."[6]

Scripture stories from both the Old and New Testaments may be used to demonstrate God's intention of reconciliation, but the early Christian church serves as the primary model for evangelicals who try to recreate the community structures and practices of these first believers. Theologian Harvey Conn stresses the radical inclusivity of the early church: "Into a world where class, power and ancestry divided rich from poor, free from slave, men from women, came a society that welcomed all who bore the name Jesus (1 Cor. 1:26–29). Into an ethnic-oriented world that isolated Jew from Greek, barbarian from Roman, came a new kind of gathering place (Gal. 3:28)."[7] Racial reconciliation literature points to the frequent descriptions of ethnic tensions in the New Testament stories of the early Christians as evidence that in crossing ethnic boundaries they were trying to do something unheard of at the time.

Two stories of ethnic strife within the early Christian church, which are often cited in the racial reconciliation literature, come from the Book of Acts. The first involves the congregation in Jerusalem, which was forced to deal with linguistic and cultural differences among Jewish Christians (Acts 6:1–7). According to one of the most widely-read books on racial reconciliation, *More Than Equals: Racial Healing for the Sake of the Gospel*, by Spencer Perkins and Chris Rice, this is how the conflict unfolded:

> Greek Jews complained that the native Jewish widows were being favored in the daily "meals on wheels" program (Acts 6:1). The probable cause of this injustice? The believers were together in a close-knit community during the week, but when the Sabbath came, Hebrew and Greek Christians followed standard custom and went to separate synagogues to worship. This separation led to racial cliques and resulting shades of favoritism.[8]

Lisa Harper, InterVarsity Director of Racial Reconciliation in Los Angeles, also offers a contemporary interpretation of the conflict: "The personal sin of ethnic favoritism toward the Hebrew widows had systemic effects and became an organizational sin."[9] The solution, according to Harper, was for Greek-speaking leaders to oversee the distribution to assure that there was no favoritism, after which the congregation flourished. The message for believers, according to Harper, is to respect ethnic differences within a broader multiethnic community that insists on social justice for all.

The second story is of the church at Antioch, which was bitterly divided over the question of circumcision and whether Gentiles must fulfill Jewish cultural practices to be followers of Christ.

> Then certain individuals came down from Judea and were teaching the brothers, "Unless you are circumcised according to the custom of Moses, you cannot be saved." And after Paul and Barnabas had no small dissension and debate with them, Paul and Barnabas and some

of the others were appointed to go up to Jerusalem to discuss this
question with the apostles and the elders. (Acts 15:1–2)

Though "certain individuals" wanted the Jewish and Gentile Christians to worship and eat separately, Paul and Barnabas prevailed; the Gentiles did not need
to follow the Mosaic law, and the unity of the church is more important than
this cultural difference. According to the authors of *United by Faith,* this story is
really about the importance of forming unity in diversity. Rather than requiring
the Gentiles to adopt Jewish practices or allowing the community to separate
into ethnic-specific fellowships, Paul insisted that they remain unified but accept cultural differences: "Each person who joined the fellowship felt affirmed
for the culture of his or her background."[10] The survival of the Antioch community is seen as evidence that all churches should move from being ethnocentric
to being multiethnic, without trying to erase distinctive cultural practices.

A more common interpretation of the Antioch conflict is that ethnic differences should be transcended in the community of Christian believers. This interpretation is supported by other passages in the New Testament, such as the
frequently cited verse, "There is no longer Jew or Greek, there is no longer slave
or free, there is no longer male and female; for all of you are one in Christ Jesus"
(Gal. 3:28). The salience of ethnic differences within the early Christian community is a major point of contention within the racial reconciliation movement.[11]
Did Jesus intend for his church to be "color-blind," or are ethnic differences part
of the eternal plan? As we will see in the next section, such conflicting readings
of key biblical passages are at the heart of disagreements about how to apply
racial reconciliation theology to Christian organizations today.

A final important biblical source for racial reconciliation theology is the vision of the end times given in the Book of Revelation. In this text John tells of a
vision of the future completion of God's Kingdom: "After this I looked, and
there was a great multitude that no one could count, from every nation, from
all tribes and peoples and languages, standing before the throne and before the
Lamb, robed in white, with palm branches in their hands" (Rev. 7:9). Racial reconciliation proponents feel compelled to do their best to embody this vision of
the Kingdom. Multiethnic churches are a human attempt to create the kind of
perfected church that Jesus will complete upon his Second Coming. The sug-
gestion that Christians ought to be actively working to create the New Heaven
and New Earth described in the Book of Revelation has been the source of
much debate within evangelical Christianity.

Widely held among evangelicals is a belief known as premillennialism. As
Emerson and Smith describe it, "The present world is evil and will inevitably
suffer moral decline until Christ comes again. Thus, to devote oneself to social

reform is futile."[12] As an example of premillennial views applied to racial issues, they tell the story of Billy Graham, one of the founders of modern or neo-evangelicalism. Early in his career as an evangelist, when civil rights activists were looking to the churches for moral leadership, Graham refused to integrate revival meetings in the South. He justified his refusal to support the civil rights movement by saying that "only when Christ comes again will little white children of Alabama walk hand in hand with little black children."[13] Emerson and Smith write of this incident, "This was not meant to be harsh, but rather what he and most white evangelicals perceived to be realistic."[14]

In the decades since, Graham has apologized for the apathy of White evangelicals during the civil rights movement and has become a major advocate of racial reconciliation.[15] Premillennialism is still widely accepted by contemporary evangelicals, but it exists in tension with an impulse to publicly demonstrate the truth of the Gospel by creating examples of Christ's reconciling power. Moreover, some evangelicals are moving away from the premillennial position and emphasizing the importance of human agency in the unfolding of the kingdom of God.[16] While still a minority position within evangelicalism, it is this kind of theology that has invited evangelicals to become transforming agents of society, particularly through political activism.[17] The racial reconciliation literature is able to appeal to the waiters and the transformers by framing the multiethnic church as both a powerful sign of Christ's presence in a secular world and a foretaste of what awaits believers when Christ returns.

Making a Movement

In the late 1960s, Black evangelicals involved in the civil rights movement began to preach a message of racial reconciliation. Antony Alumkal notes that the emergence of racial reconciliation theology corresponds to the fracturing of the civil rights movement.[18] While race moderates were satisfied with the success of the civil rights movement and dissatisfied race activists were turning to the Black Power movement, the early proponents of racial reconciliation insisted that it is only through Christ that racial divisions can be healed. Among these early advocates are John Perkins, Tom Skinner, Samuel Hines, James Earl Massey, William Pannell, and E. V. Hill. Emerson and Smith describe these "founding fathers" of the movement:

> They were all black, all well versed—through experience—in the
> racialized United States, all willing to use the term *evangelical* and as-
> sociate with white evangelicals, all influenced by Martin Luther King

(some were personal friends of King), all committed to mentoring future leaders, and all completely sold on the idea that reconciliation
was, in Samuel Hines' terms, "God's one-item agenda."[19]

These leaders outlined a series of steps toward racial reconciliation that included confession of racism, forming friendships across racial lines, and ending the structures of racial injustice. Emphasizing their commitment to social
change, Alumkal calls the early racial reconciliation movement a "radical demo-
cratic project" that went beyond King's work by fusing radical democracy and a
call for integration with the theology of American evangelicalism.[20] Their call
to create a radical Christian movement for racial justice was directed at both
supporters of the Black Power movement and White evangelicals, who, for the
most part, remained unmoved.

While liberal and even some mainline congregations were fracturing over
the issue of integration, White evangelical Christians remained uninterested
or intentionally opposed to the idea. They turned to theological and practical
justifications, such as the homogeneous unit principle popularized by Peter
Wagner, to defend the status quo. Emerson and Smith explain, "Southern evangelicals generally sided against black evangelicals on the segregation issue, and
northern evangelicals seemed more preoccupied with other issues—such as
evangelism, and fighting communism and theological liberalism."[21] Only a
small cadre of White evangelicals was persuaded to join their Black colleagues
in the cause. Billy Graham, for example, had begun to visibly promote integration in his crusades by the late 1960s, and the main evangelical magazine,
Christianity Today, printed more articles on race issues in the 1960s than ever
before.[22] For the most part, however, the growing evangelical subculture paid
little attention to the issue of race until the 1990s, when White evangelicals began picking up the banner of racial reconciliation and running with it, though
not necessarily in the same direction as the Black founders.

Into the Mainstream

Several events in the 1990s drew national attention to the issue of racial reconciliation and gave the movement the influx of energy that continues to carry it
today. In 1993, *Christianity Today* published a collection of articles under the title "The Myth of Racial Progress," which included contributions by many of the
early founders as well as a new generation of racial reconciliation leaders.
These articles were sharply critical of the failure of the White churches to commit
to racial reconciliation and the hegemony of church growth strategies; the leadership of the National Association of Evangelicals was faulted for not making race

issues a priority. Graham contributed an article to this issue in which he boldly claimed that racial and ethnic hostility is the foremost social problem facing our world today and chided White Christians for failing to take the lead in racial reconciliation.[23]

The "Memphis Miracle" of 1994 is seen as the major turning point for the racial reconciliation movement. During their national convention, the leaders of the White Pentecostal Association of North America (PANA) asked the African American Pentecostal denominations for forgiveness and disbanded in order to form a new, multiracial Pentecostal body. Bishop B. E. Underwood addressed the crowd with these words: "We grieve over the eighty-eight years of rebellion against the reconciliation work of the Holy Spirit. We return with all our hearts to the unity of the Spirit manifested during the blazing revival at Azusa Street."[24] Not long after this event, the leadership of the National Association of Evangelicals (NAE) made its own act of repentance.

At a 1995 meeting in Chicago, the newly appointed NAE executive director, Don Argue, asked forgiveness from African American evangelicals. The event was described in *Christianity Today:* "Three top African-American leaders laid hands on Argue. As he knelt before them, they prayed for a breaking down of barriers. . . . Following that, whole loaves of bread were distributed, and a 'breaking the bread of fellowship' ceremony was held amid a rich time of prayer and praise."[25] The NAE vowed to work together with the National Black Evangelical Association, and all in attendance took a personal pledge to form an "accountability partnership" with a person of another race. In the 1990s, other denominational bodies, such as the Worldwide Church of God and the Southern Baptist Convention, also made public statements of repentance and commitments to pursue racial reconciliation in their denominational bodies and congregations.

While these public displays of repentance made big headlines, it was the Promise Keepers organization, under the leadership of Bill McCartney, that put racial reconciliation on the agenda of millions of White evangelicals. One of the seven promises members pledge to keep states: "A Promise Keeper is committed to reaching beyond any racial and denominational barriers to demonstrate the power of biblical unity."[26] Evangelical and secular newspapers carried stories of the emotionally intense rallies in which White men repented of their racism and embraced their brothers of color. Emerson and Smith provide a vivid description of such an event: "All across the expansive domed stadium, small groups formed around men of color. A great murmur of confession rose and reverberated off the stadium top, further amplifying the sounds. Soon, weeping could be heard, first only in pockets, then spreading like an uncontrollable wave, until the entire crowd was shedding tears of lament."[27] Like those who witnessed the manifestations of the Holy Spirit during the Asuza Street Revival, Promise Keepers experienced these events as a radical sign to the world of God's unfolding redemption. From these emotional gatherings, Promise Keepers pledged to take the message of racial reconciliation back to their families, churches, and workplaces, and to form cross-race friendships.

The enthusiasm for both racial reconciliation and Promise Keepers has died down considerably since the mid-1990s. Racial reconciliation may no longer be the "latest thing" within mainstream evangelicalism, but it continues to generate a lot of interest and activity. New books on the subject are published each year by the dozens, and the growing number of leaders and para-church organizations recognized as "reconciliation experts" is too large to track. These experts have developed experiential programs to educate evangelicals about racial reconciliation and teach the skills necessary for reconciliation to work. Churches across the country continue to add racial reconciliation to their mission statements and to address the issue in sermons, programming, and ministry projects.

With the further institutionalization of racial reconciliation has come greater disagreement—not over its basic goal, but over how it is pursued. A common criticism is that despite the pronouncements of major leaders, no real action has been undertaken, and when steps are taken they have been too small and too slow. Theologian Manuel Ortiz spoke poignantly on this disappointment in 1997:

> Many of us have become vulnerable, publicly expressing our pain and rage for all to examine and touch, with many concluding, "That was a nice testimony." Many of us have joined numerous small group discussions, and we have been asked to participate as advisors for church and para-church organizations on the subject of race reconciliation and multi-ethnicity. We are on committees, developing a theology appropriate for reconciliation, with the hope, the biblical kind of hope, that the organization will buy it and move toward healing and wholeness with a capital W. . . . I believe we are buying time and hoping to get by with minimal pain and change, nurturing the "good old boy" syndrome hoping that we will not have to give up much.[28]

Like Ortiz, many evangelicals of color are frustrated that the attention-grabbing gestures of reconciliation in the 1990s have failed to yield concrete changes. The problem, according to Emerson and Smith, is that when racial reconciliation was adapted by mainstream evangelicalism, its integral social justice aspect was "lost in translation."

Defining the Problem, Finding the Solution

While the early founders of the movement recognized the need to change both hearts and institutional systems, the message of racial reconciliation that has made its way into mainstream evangelicalism is one of individual reconciliation. To understand how this came about, Emerson and Smith examined American attitudes toward race and carried out an in-depth study of White evangelical attitudes.[29] They found that while both White and Black evangelicals support the idea of racial reconciliation, they have very different understandings of what this means. At issue is what these groups identify as the source of racial divisions in society and the solution.

White evangelicals believe that racism is the result of personal sin and are much more likely to attribute racial inequities to a lack of motivation rather than to discrimination in educational or job opportunities. Furthermore, they believe that social change does not effectively come from the government but begins with a personal commitment to follow Jesus. The catchphrase "you can't legislate love" is commonly used to express this conviction that Christians should transform society by "changing one heart at a time" rather than by working to change institutional structures. In contrast, Emerson and Smith found that conservative Black Christians are much more likely to attribute racial inequities to discrimination and to support government intervention to rectify racial injustice. Like the early founders of the movement, Black Christians today are more likely to envision racial reconciliation as a social transformation at both the individual and structural levels.

Exacerbating the divide between Whites and Blacks is the presumption on the part of most White evangelicals that ethnic or racial identity is ultimately inconsequential in the Christian community. In other words, since such barriers as race, class, and gender are destroyed through Christ, there is no need to pay attention to these differences, and it is even argued that talking about them actually creates division and conflict. This color-blind ideology is common among White evangelicals and can even exist in organizations that promote racial reconciliation. For example, in his study of the rise and fall of Promise Keepers, sociologist John Bartkowski found that even though race matters in Promise Keepers, since men are required to confess their sins to a man of a different race or color, racial differences are perceived as having no ultimate significance. [30] Bartkowski argues that because of its stress on individual friendships, Promise Keepers seriously limits interrogation of the social character of racism. When framed theologically, the color-blind ideology can be a powerful tool for both ignoring or effacing difference and silencing conversations about the sources of social inequality that lie beyond individual prejudice. Ironically, White evangelicals will cite Martin Luther King, Jr.'s, hope that Americans would no longer be judged by the color of their skin in order to support their individualistic, color-blind approach to racial reconciliation and to foreclose dialogue on race issues.

Emerson and Smith explain the racial attitudes of White evangelicals in terms of both their limited interaction with people of color and their limited "cultural tool kit." The White evangelical tool kit has a long tradition of antistructuralism and individualism that impedes their ability to recognize how social structures privilege White Americans and penalize people of color. Bartkowski, likewise, points to the central place individualism and personal responsibility occupy in the cultural repertoire of American evangelicalism. To challenge the way White evangelicals understand and seek to eradicate racism is to challenge the very basis of their worldview, and, Emerson and Smith argue, their faith in the American way of life. It is not surprising, then, that the mainstream evangelical approach to racial reconciliation stresses personal transformation via confession of sin and repentance rather than a critical response to the social structures that confer privileges on White Americans. The myopic insistence that racial reconciliation must proceed one heart at a time, and from the grassroots, forestalls the ability of evangelicals to fully comprehend and thus successfully combat racial divisions in America.

Emerson and Smith's cultural-tool-kit explanation of why White evangelicals have taken to the "individual reconciliation" message and rejected the more radical social message of the early movement is too benign for Antony Alumkal. While Emerson and Smith assume that White evangelicals are well-intentioned people, Alumkal argues that their good intentions are also shaped by self-interest. The mainstream version of racial reconciliation, which he calls the "centrist evangelical racial project," developed as a response to both White guilt and the rise of neoconservative politics, which is strongly opposed to affirmative action:

> On one level, these leaders appear to be rearticulating the early racial reconciliation theology into conservative form, stripping it of radical democratic components and substituting individual-level action. At another level, the centrist evangelical racial project appears to be a rearticulation of the neoconservative and related center-right projects into an evangelical form.[31]

The result is, as Emerson and Smith would agree, a severely limited understanding of the causes of racial divisions, leading to ineffectual efforts to rectify these divisions. Governmental intervention in the form of welfare or affirmative action is strongly opposed on the grounds that since racism is at its root a spiritual problem it requires a spiritual solution. In Alumkal's assessment of the racial reconciliation movement, Promise Keepers is especially culpable for spreading this individual-level reconciliation message to millions of White evangelicals. He argues that the appeal of the Promise Keepers' individual reconciliation emphasis is that it allows White evangelicals to engage in cathartic acts of repentance, while fully retaining the fruits of White privilege.[32]

Far from its early development in the wake of the civil rights movement, racial reconciliation is now associated with an antipolitical, individual reconciliation model. Emerson and Smith's widely read book, *Divided by Faith,* has certainly contributed to this narrow association. Neither Emerson and Smith nor Alumkal give much credence to the way racial reconciliation continues to operate outside the mainstream evangelical world because they presume the movement has been entirely co-opted by White evangelicals. Not surprisingly, many evangelicals in accord with the radical racial reconciliation message have distanced themselves from the mainstream segment of the movement. For example, when I interviewed two well-known advocates for racial reconciliation, Rudy Carrasco and Derek Perkins (codirectors of the Harambee Christian Family Center in Pasadena, California), they expressed ambivalence about being identified with racial reconciliation.[33] It depends, they told me, on how it is defined. They do not want to be associated with a movement that has been watered down in order remain safely within the comfort level of White evangelicals.

Rudy Carrasco and Derek Perkins are not the only evangelicals working for racial reconciliation outside of the so-called mainstream version of the movement. Emerson and Smith note that although racial reconciliation seemed to erupt into the consciousness of mainstream evangelicals in the mid-1990s, it had been quietly gathering steam throughout a whole new generation of evangelicals. They identify several dozen leaders, including Black, White, Latino, and Asian evangelicals, all strongly influenced by the radical message of the early racial reconciliation activists. When this new generation of leaders pushed the racial reconciliation issue onto the national agenda of White evangelicals in the 1990s, theirs was not a message of neoconservatism. Mainstream evangelicalism recast racial reconciliation as an apolitical, individual movement, but the more radical versions are still evident. Even Alumkal admits that there are social-justice-oriented wings of evangelicalism.[34] Their adherents are certainly marginal to the mainstream evangelical subculture, but they have their own spheres of influence, such as Jim Wallis's magazine *Sojourners*, the Christian Community Development Association, and some segments of InterVarsity Christian Fellowship.

Racial reconciliation as a biblically-grounded theology and a social movement is very much up for grabs today. For many evangelicals it no longer signifies the kind of sweeping social changes the early founders intended, but

it is not necessarily limited to the color-blind, individual-reconciliation approach of White evangelicals. While it is has become common to associate the
movement with the latter, racial reconciliation is more appropriately seen as an
umbrella movement, encompassing diverse, even conflicting positions, on the
causes of racial divisions and the best strategies for overcoming these divisions
in the church and society.[35]

Racial Reconciliation from the Margins

One consequence of the narrow association of racial reconciliation with White,
neo-conservative evangelicals is that little attention has been paid to the voices
for racial reconciliation that lie outside the mainstream. Nationally, there are
dozens of racial reconciliation organizations led by Black evangelicals, often in
conjunction with White evangelicals, which continue to teach the socially radical message of racial reconciliation formed in the post–civil rights era. Furthermore, the movement has become decidedly multiethnic. Asian American and
Latino evangelicals are increasingly invited to join in racial reconciliation events,
especially in urban areas where a multiethnic framework has replaced the original Black/White paradigm. The impact of new leaders such as Rudy Carrasco,
Manuel Ortiz, David Gibbons, and Ken Fong has yet to be assessed in the racial
reconciliation literature, presumably because evangelicalism is still seen as a
White religious subculture. Like the social-justice-oriented wings of evangelicalism, evangelicals of color are perceived as having marginal influence on
American evangelicalism.

Even though Whites continue to make up the ranks of mainstream evangelicalism in terms of both numbers and influence, the term "mainstream" masks
the important rise in the number of evangelicals of color in recent years. By some
estimates, nearly 90 percent of American evangelicals are White, but there are
indications that the growing edge of evangelicalism is among people of color.[36]
Although the relationship between Black conservative Christians and the evangelical subculture has never been strong, some African Americans have been
willing to identify as evangelicals, and the public commitment to racial reconciliation by White organizations like the NAE and PANA may strengthen this association.[37] Asian Americans and Latinos are already a growing force within evangelical Christianity. National surveys have found that 6.2 million, or 85 percent,
of all U.S. Latino Protestants identify themselves as Pentecostals or evangelicals,
and that by the third generation 29 percent of Latinos identify as Protestant
rather than Catholic.[38] Estimates of the number of Asian Americans who consider themselves evangelical are more difficult to verify, since there have been no
national surveys of this group. Journalist Michael Luo's claim that 2.5 percent of

Asian Americans are evangelicals and that most of the three thousand Korean, seven hundred Chinese, and two hundred Japanese Christian congregations across the country are evangelical is one of the few estimates available.[39]

The growing presence of Asian American evangelicals has drawn attention in one arena: college Bible fellowships. Rudy Busto observes that in the 1990s, Asian American students became central players in American evangelical Christianity through these para-church organizations.[40] The immigrant missions founded in the wake of the post-1965 immigration wave to serve Asian and Latino immigrants gave birth to a generation of young leaders who are now taking a more public role in evangelical institutions.[41] Pastor Ken, who has been invited to speak at such "mainstream" venues as Urbana, Promise Keepers, and the massive Willow Creek Church, is a perfect example of the changing face of American evangelicalism.

Just as little research has been done into how Asian Americans and Latinos are changing American evangelicalism, little is known about their attitudes toward race issues and where they fit into the ideological divide that Emerson and Smith identify between Whites and Blacks. Presumably, they bring unique concerns and strategies, born out of their respective histories of racialization in the United States, to the project of racial reconciliation, but these perspectives have yet to be explored thoroughly.[42] One consequence of this myopia is that the racial reconciliation conversation is framed too narrowly. The commitments and concerns of the Asian American members of Evergreen, from whom I first learned about racial reconciliation, are not reflected in the literature on the subject. Evergreeners and, I would suspect, many Asian American and Latino evangelicals do not support the antistructural, individualistic, color-blind racial reconciliation model derived from the White tool kit. Nor do they necessarily fit with the more radical model of social-justice-oriented evangelicals. The way racial reconciliation has been taught and practiced at Evergreen Baptist Church suggests that there is much more to understanding evangelical racial attitudes than has been explored within the current literature.

Racial Reconciliation Evergreen Style

When I asked Pastor Ken where Asian Americans fit in the divide that Emerson and Smith identify between Whites and Blacks, he told me he had very strong opinions on this question:

> I think Asian American, college-educated—I put that in there because I'm not talking about the poverty-level but those who have

"made it"—we are more like the Whites in that study than we are the Blacks because we now, without realizing all the sacrifices our parents and our grandparents made to get us to Harvard or whatever, we start saying it's an individual problem. . . . When I read that book I said, "As much as I hate to admit this, when I look at my old self, and I look at a lot of the attitudes toward this whole issue of multiethnicity and racial reconciliation in the Asian Christian group, the attitudes sound very White."

Ken thinks the older Asian American members of Evergreen are more open to "thinking like a minority" than younger members who have faced significantly less racism and fail to see how they and other people of color continue to be affected by racialization. His assessment that the racial attitudes of Asian Christians align with White evangelicals finds support in much of the literature, which describes Asian churches as largely apolitical, insular, and focused on overseas missions. But the new Evergreen is not like "typical" Asian churches or, for that matter, most White evangelical churches.

In his role as shaper of the congregation's culture around the new vision statement, Ken has worked hard to keep the congregation engaged with issues of "culture, class, and circumstance." He brings up pressing social problems, such as drug addiction, homelessness, and poverty, and has spoken out against the war in Iraq and uncritical loyalty to the American government.[43] During the 2004 fall elections, Ken encouraged everyone to bring their faith into the polling booth—not to vote a party line but to vote as Jesus would, for "the powerless, the voiceless, the weak, and the marginalized."[44] On racial issues in particular, Ken has brought guest speakers such as Carrasco and Perkins and Brenda Salter McNeil, who believe, as he does, that racial reconciliation must occur on both personal and societal levels.[45] From the pulpit and in the newsletter, Ken keeps racial issues on the front burner as he encourages members to greater commitment to the church's vision statement. That vision, as Ken and others have presented it to the congregation, addresses not only the barriers that individuals construct between themselves and others, but the reality of racialization that transcends personal encounters.

One of the most effective ways Ken has raised consciousness about racialization is to urge members to think about current issues of injustice in light of their own, or their ancestors', experiences. Evergreen is a historically Japanese American church, and there is a strong awareness, even among new members, of the anti-Asian history of the United States. One of the first things members often share with me about Evergreen is that several of the "old timers" at the church had lived in the World War II internment camps. There is a living memory at Evergreen of the not too distant past when Asian Americans faced a great deal of prejudice in California. In the *Los Angeles Times* article that first introduced me to Evergreen, Ken connected this memory of racial injustice to the harassment of Arab-looking Americans in the days after the September 11 terrorist attacks. While many churches held prayer services the day after the attacks, Evergreen's was surprisingly political for an evangelical church. At their prayer service, an Indian American member spoke of being verbally assaulted that morning, and a Palestinian American member shared stories about his family's life on the West Bank before praying with a member of Jewish heritage for peace in that region. Ken explained the goal of their testimony: "We needed to sensitize our congregation to the Palestinian Arab American experience, especially because this is historically a Japanese American church." For Ken, it is obvious that his congregation should immediately condemn the post-9/11 racial harassment.

According to the *Los Angeles Times* article, not everyone at Evergreen agreed with this focus. Some church members were angry that the service did not concentrate exclusively on mourning American losses and thought it was too sympathetic to Muslims. In retrospect Ken acknowledges he may have misjudged the needs of the congregation, but, as he explained to the *Times* journalist:

> As an American, I reference what happened on Sept. 11 as a gross, atrocious, evil act. I share your anger and grief. . . . As an American of color, I need to let you know that I could have the biggest flag on my street, I could be singing "Yankee Doodle Dandy" every five minutes, but if next week the North Koreans bombed some American military base, I am going to be looked at with suspicion, too.

Though Evergreen members did not unanimously appreciate Ken's concern for the latest victims of racial profiling, many did. For example, one member wrote in the October 2002 newsletter: "As a Japanese American whose parents and grandparents went through the internment during World War II, I am very sensitive to the feelings that must be going through the hearts and minds of our Arab-American neighbors or Americans who happen to be Muslim or can be easily mistaken for being Muslim and/or Arab." Although Ken thinks Asian Americans share the racial attitudes of Whites, this public discussion about race and other social issues is the first indication that the members of his congregation are conscious of the effects of structural racism in the United States.

My own interviews with Asian American members of all ages at Evergreen reveal a much greater awareness of racialization than Ken gives them credit for.

Many of the younger members took Asian-American studies courses in college and are quite knowledgeable about past and present prejudice against Asians, as well as other minorities. At the same time, as middle-class, well-educated professionals, few Evergreeners have experienced overt prejudice firsthand in Southern California. Only one person I interviewed could recall any incidents worth mentioning, but in the October 2002 newsletter a young man related a recent encounter with a middle-aged White woman in a local parking lot: "What she did after she pulled up behind us was unthinkable. I saw in the rearview mirror that she put her fingers to her eyes make the sign of the slanted eyes. I was shocked. I hadn't encountered racism that blatant since I was a kid." Even though such incidents rarely happen to Evergreeners in Southern California, several told me they have experienced blatant racism in other parts of the country. They are well aware that the "privilege" of social acceptance in Los Angeles does not extend to much of the United States, where Asian Americans face outright discrimination and harassment. Those I interviewed also recognized that their limited social acceptance by White America has not been extended to other people of color, particularly African Americans, who face prejudice in terms of jobs, housing, and education opportunities.

But awareness of racialization does not mean that Evergreeners would comfortably align with what Antony Alumkal calls the social-justice wing of evangelicalism. Like most evangelical churches, Evergreen steers clear of activities perceived as political, and even the term "social justice" is rarely used by Evergreeners, though Pastor Ken has been pushing these boundaries over the years. Evergreen does not sponsor peace rallies, legislation for social reform, protest marches, or petition drives, but it is a socially-engaged congregation working through established social services. The church's Outreach Division, which is responsible for ministry beyond the church walls, sponsors social service programs such as ESL tutoring, drug and alcohol counseling, a soup kitchen, a homeless shelter, a food pantry, visits to seniors at a local nursing home, and the annual day for service projects in the city of Rosemead. International missions to Africa, Asia, and Latin America, rather than domestic social justice projects, are also emphasized as a means to further the church's vision of reconciliation.

While few Evergreeners would count themselves among the socially progressive "evangelical left," it is clear that the church's members do not fit neatly with the profile of White evangelicals presented by Emerson and Smith. This is a congregation that allows for and encourages serious conversations about social issues. Evergreeners do not attribute social inequities to a lack of motivation on the part of individuals but look to their larger social context. They do not insist on a color-blind world but recognize that ethnicity matters, as the story told in the next section illustrates.

Color-Blind versus Color-Conscious Discourse

Near the end of my research at Evergreen, I was asked to lead a discussion on the subject of racial reconciliation with the church's Prime Timers group for the over-fifty crowd. Expecting to find a dozen or so people, I was greeted by nearly one hundred friendly faces on a Saturday morning. After I described my dissertation research, the first response was from an elderly Japanese American woman, who remarked, "As a Christian I just look at people as people and don't see color. I think all this talk abut race can only be divisive." Her comment sounded very much like the color-blind discourse used by the White evangelicals. When many of those present nodded their heads in agreement, I began to wonder what we were going to discuss for an hour if not racialization and ethnic identity.

Fortunately for me, the discussion did continue, and both Asian and non-Asian members of the Prime Timers found a great deal to say about how race and, more often, ethnicity, matters in their lives. One eighty-year-old Japanese American man told the group that he continues to feel like a foreigner in the United States: "My ancestors came to this country more than one hundred years ago, but I still get complimented on how well I speak English." In some cases, the very same people who had earlier agreed that race is not important spoke of their own experiences of racism and how important their ethnic identity is to them. I had heard this narrative progression a few times before in the individual interviews. The same people who said they do not see differences between people would, with a little nudging, proceed to tell me about all the ways in which racialization has affected them and other people of color. How are we to understand this apparent contradiction, and what does it tell us about the way racial reconciliation is pursued at Evergreen?

Since Pastor Ken works hard to bring racial issues into the public discourse of the congregation, it is likely that those members who promote a color-blind approach have been influenced elsewhere by the attitudes of White evangelicals. If a color-blind outlook is part of the White evangelical tool kit, it should not be surprising that Asian American evangelicals would also speak in these terms, given that their churches have been strongly influenced by White evangelicalism.[46] While all churches respond to normative expectations from their institutional fields, pressures to conform are particularly strong within evangelicalism, and Antony Alumkal cautions researchers to be sensitive to issues of self-presentation and the desire of evangelicals of color to appear to be in conformity with the White majority.[47] When Evergreeners reject racial discourse by insisting that Christians should be color-blind, they may be demonstrating a symbolic adherence to mainstream Evangelicalism. Given the pervasive influence of the "centrist evangelical racial project" and normative pressures to conform to White evangelicalism, the use of color-blind discourse may actually be misleading for the purpose of understanding the racial attitudes of Evergreeners or, for that matter, of evangelicals of color in general.

That some Evergreeners give voice to a color-blind worldview while also expressing a color-conscious worldview, or what I have been describing as an "ethnicity matters" discourse, suggests the strong influence of White evangelical norms. It appears in the case of Evergreeners that their own experiences of racialization undermine their complete acceptance of the color-blind worldview. Like White evangelicals, they publicly affirm the unity of all believers in Christ expressed in the New Testament, in Paul's Epistle to the Galatians: "There is no longer Jew or Greek, there is no longer slave or free, there is no longer male and female; for all of you are one in Christ Jesus" (3:28). This is a deeply held truth for Asian American Christians, just as it is for other Christians, but evangelicals of color know from experience that Christians have often failed to live up to that ideal. After all, the failure of White churches to eradicate racism has been a major factor in the continued vitality of Asian American churches like Evergreen. At Evergreen, color-blind and color-conscious discourses coexist, overlap, and compete, making it more difficult for Pastor Ken to push forward with a socially critical vision of racial reconciliation.

When compared with the mainstream evangelical approach to racial reconciliation and the more radical call for social justice, where does Evergreen fit? I would argue this church fits somewhere in between. Though some Evergreeners are as socially progressive as Pastor Ken, most of the congregation is being pulled in this direction by Pastor Ken rather than already being there. The fact that racial reconciliation is so frequently addressed at this church sets Evergreen apart from churches that discourage any talk seen as divisive or as shifting responsibility for social ills from the individual to society. Compared to the color-blind approach, Evergreen's is color-conscious: publicly acknowledging the way in which social barriers are erected on the basis of one's skin color. Even more important than this social critique, though, is acknowledging that ethnicity matters to Evergreeners as individuals. They are proud of their distinctive ethnic histories and cultures and do not want to live in a color-blind world that effaces ethnic differences. The differences between the color-blind and color-conscious approaches will be even more obvious in chapter 4, where we will look at the ways Evergreen has intentionally institutionalized its commitment to racial reconciliation through church structures.

Just as racial reconciliation is broader than a Black/White agenda, the binary juxtaposition of color-blind versus color-conscious approaches, or individualistic versus social-justice reconciliation, is inadequate for understanding the breadth of the racial reconciliation movement today. The case of Evergreen suggests that within American evangelicalism there is a range of racial attitudes and corresponding strategies for overcoming racial divisions in society, reflecting the growing diversity among those who identify as evangelicals. Evergreeners do not agree on how best to eradicate racism or how to bring people together across ethnic divisions. They have conflicting opinions about the priority placed on racial reconciliation. Some are tired of hearing about racial reconciliation, while others think Pastor Ken needs to make it even more central, just as some want the church to be more social-justice oriented and others want nothing to do with activities perceived as political. At Evergreen there are multiple racial discourses, which coexist, overlap, and compete within the congregation, just as they do among American evangelicals in general.

As I listened to Evergreeners talk about racial reconciliation, it became obvious that those who are most supportive of the church's vision to create "remarkable montages of cultures, classes, and circumstances" are the younger members of the church who have joined since the hive. These young people come from many ethnic backgrounds; the majority are Asian American, but they are also White, Black, Middle Eastern, Latino, and multiracial. They are more likely than the older Evergreeners to embrace racial reconciliation as a matter of social justice and to support engagement with the local community. Because they are the real energy behind racial reconciliation at Evergreen, the next chapter takes a closer look at the values and life experiences that motivate these young people and the implications of this emerging generation for the future of the racial reconciliation movement and for evangelicalism as a whole.

3

The Reconciliation Generation

"Energizing a Reconciliation Generation" is the slogan Brenda Salter McNeil chose for her nonprofit organization, Overflow Ministries.[1] Salter McNeil travels all over the country trying to ignite a passion for racial reconciliation among young people, believing that they have been chosen by God for this work. She writes in the Overflow newsletter: "After much time in prayer and observing the work of the Holy Spirit, we believe that God is igniting a fire among our youth for racial and ethnic reconciliation. What adults have not been able to do to heal our world and bring people together, God is going to use our youth to do in a radical, unconventional and powerful way!"[2] Leading the way will be today's college students, trained through college Bible fellowships, such as InterVarsity Christian Fellowship, to be the next generation of evangelical leaders. We will have to wait another decade or two to see if Salter McNeil's prediction is correct, but if Evergreen Baptist Church is any indication of the future of evangelicalism, it looks as if she will be. Aside from the leadership of Pastor Ken, any success Evergreen has found in its mission to become multiethnic is attributable to these young people, both in terms of their commitment to racial reconciliation and the ethnic diversity within this age group.

Who are these "young people," as they are often referred to at Evergreen, and why are they coming to this church? Time and again I was told that the young people at Evergreen have "a value for diversity," meaning that they place a high value on diversity. Their attitude fits the perspective historian David Hollinger calls "cosmopolitanism": the recognition, acceptance, and eager exploration of diversity.[3] Since the young people at Evergreen are urban-dwellers, the label "cosmopolitan" seems all the more fitting. Like other young adults in the United States, their cosmopolitan perspective has been shaped by exposure to the increasing diversity around them and in popular culture, as well as by the promotion of multiculturalism in the educational system. As evangelicals, however, their "value for diversity" has been further shaped through theological education and the theology of racial reconciliation in particular.

The Post-1965 Generations

When I speak of the young adults at Evergreen, I am referring first of all to members in their twenties and early thirties. Because they span the so-called Generation X (those born between 1964 and 1981) and Generation Y, or what Evergreen calls the Millennial generation (those born in 1982 and after), neither of these categories is satisfactory. What really distinguishes these young people is that they have not yet begun families. A few are married and many are moving toward marriage, but they do not have children and, thus, are not involved in the programs sponsored by Evergreen's large Family Life Division.

As we saw in chapter 1, before Evergreen split into two congregations in 1997 there was a palpable tension between those who wanted a family-focused church and those who wanted a socially-engaged church. The "minivan crowd," as Ken calls them, followed Pastor Cory to plant a new Asian American church, and the messy, postmodern crowd followed Ken. Five years later there were again a sizeable number of families at Evergreen Los Angeles who wanted more family-focused activities and a sizeable group of young adults who were coming to Evergreen for the reconciliation vision rather than family programming.[4] This division is by no means impassable, since there are "family people" at Evergreen who are very committed to the church's vision, just as there are older members who share the young people's enthusiasm for reconciliation. Nonetheless, because almost everyone I interviewed identified a clear division between the young people and the rest of the congregation, I take this generational divide to be significant even if it is an over-simplification of the array of concerns and commitments Evergreeners of all ages hold.

One thing the young and old at Evergreen agree on is that young people are living in a different world. But what kind of a world is it? In their study of the impact of generational divisions on congregational life, Jackson Carroll and Wade Clark Roof suggest that we think of a generation as a carrier of culture.[5] They point out that the culture of Gen Xers has been largely shaped by what they have inherited from Baby Boomers, namely a world in which greater consumption, environmental consciousness, and more equitable gender roles are taken for granted.[6] In addition, it is widely noted that today's young people, to a much greater degree than their predecessors, are immersed in technology and popular culture. Theologian Tom Beaudoin argues that Generation X is defined by its relationship to popular culture, which has served as their dominant maker of meaning.[7] Like Baby Boomers, young people are deeply suspicious of institutions, but they are also cynical about the idealism that motivated the activists of the 1960s. As the first American generation to live with widespread divorce and single-parent households, young people yearn for community, and it is this yearning that brings many to church.

Donald Miller, a sociologist of religion, has given churches that engage with postmodern ideas, rather than rejecting them, the label "new paradigm churches."[8] These churches embrace aspects of postmodern culture, especially popular culture and new media technologies, while holding on to traditional Christian beliefs. Evergreen fits this model perfectly: it uses Christian rock music, catchy slogans, and media images taken from popular movies. The 2004 Advent sermon series, "The Message & Messiah Reloaded," was a takeoff on the *Matrix* movie trilogy. Another characteristic of new paradigm churches is that they are willing to engage with epistemological skepticism. Gen Xers are particularly wary of truths taught by supposed authorities and seek truths that can be verified through personal experience. According to social theorist Anthony Giddens, this is in keeping with the reflexivity of modern society, in which all knowledge is subject to doubt and chronic revision in the light of new knowledge.[9] While some religious communities try to create a protective buffer against skepticism, new paradigm churches maintain a strong adherence to traditional Christian doctrines without alienating the critical-thinking spiritual seeker.

Rather than rejecting the seeker mentality, new paradigm churches view it as part of the process of faith development. Evergreen is typical of such churches; for example, it holds classes for newcomers in which they are encouraged to question Christian truths. For these seekers, faith develops not through accepting doctrine but through their ongoing personal experience of Jesus Christ. Since words like "orthodoxy" and "doctrine" are rarely heard in the new paradigm churches, Miller describes them as "doctrinal minimalists." This description certainly fits Evergreen, where the teaching stresses applying lessons from the Bible in everyday life, rather than such evangelical theological positions as premillennialism and dispensationalism.[10] In fact, one cannot find a creedal statement of any kind printed on any of the church materials, but that does not mean that Evergreeners reject traditional Christian beliefs. Instead, the church's documents publicize Evergreen's vision statement, its mission statement, and its values—hope, humility, and hospitality—all of which make it clear that this is a place where people who believe in Christ can publicly proclaim "God's eternal purpose in the world." Beaudoin characterizes Gen Xers as "irreverent," but that cannot be said of young evangelicals, who, by some accounts, adhere to a more conservative religious ethos than baby boomers.[11]

There are also indications that Generation X has a greater tolerance and appreciation of diversity than older Americans. Beaudoin notes Gen Xers' greater acceptance of same-sex relationships and religious pluralism, but more relevant to this study is their appreciation of ethnic diversity. Raised in the post–civil rights era, they are the inheritors of integrated schools, affirmative action programs, and the ideology of multiculturalism. Generation Xers have never encountered antimiscegenation laws, but they have seen the emergence of the multiracial identity movement. Particularly within urban areas, though increasingly all across the country, young people have more encounters with people of diverse ethnic backgrounds during their formative years than previous generations.

Diversity as the Norm

The data collected during the 2000 federal census made it possible to trace the cycles of increasing diversity in the United States. By the year 2050, White Americans will no longer be in the majority—but to Californians this is old news. When the immigration laws changed in 1965, urban coastal areas like Los Angeles and New York were the first to experience a sharp increase in immigration from Asia, Africa, and Latin America. In the 1970 census, people of color made up only 23 percent of California residents, but by 2000 that number had grown to 53 percent.[12] In Southern California, the population is comprised of 40.3 percent Hispanics, 39.9 percent non-Hispanic Whites, 11.3 percent Asians, and 7.6 percent non-Hispanic Blacks. With this growing diversity, the number of racially-balanced cities in Los Angeles County has almost doubled in the last twenty years, even as White residents leave these areas.[13]

The public schools are a key space for cross-ethnic interaction among young people. More than half of those who live in Los Angeles County speak a language other than English at home, and within the Los Angeles Unified School District ninety-two different languages have been specifically identified.[14] But there are conflicting reports of how much mixing actually occurs in diverse schools. Beverly Tatum (author of *Why Are All the Black Kids Sitting Together in the Cafeteria?*) observes that elementary-school students tend to mix across ethnic lines, but by junior high friendships become increasingly racially divided.[15] More research is needed to extend these findings, but one thing is certain: young people in Los Angeles County today have been exposed to more diversity than any previous generation.

While young people in urban areas experience diversity firsthand, those in less diverse areas of the United States encounter ethnic diversity through popular culture. Television, the *loco parentis* of Generations X and Y, has played a strategic role not only in introducing young people to the "ethnically other" but also in portraying people of color in positive ways. *The Cosby Show*, for example, presented a happy, affluent African American family. Music television stations such as MTV introduced suburban youth to the music and hip-hop culture of Black Americans. In the 1980s, children all over America fell in love with Bill Cosby, Eddie Murphy, and Michael Jackson; in the 1990s, they were enamored of Michael Jordan, Will Smith, and Janet Jackson. More recently, Asian and Latino stars, such as Jackie Chan and Jennifer Lopez, have also gained the status of pop icons, and the fame of golf star Tiger Woods has brought more attention to the presence of multiethnic individuals. More than television or movies, advertisers have brought hipness to diversity. From the Benetton commercials of the 1980s and Gap commercials of the 1990s to the new decade's ads for Apple's iPod and Toyota's Gen Y–oriented Scion marque, advertisers have banked on the "diversity is cool" theme to attract the coveted young consumer. While White faces still dominate the media, and people of color are routinely portrayed through demeaning stereotypes, popular culture has played a significant role in both introducing Americans to peoples previously kept separate and promoting diversity as a positive value.[16]

Having grown up experiencing ethnic diversity as the norm, many of the young people at Evergreen come there specifically to be in a multiethnic church. Johnny, for example, is a recent UCLA graduate whose parents immigrated to the United States from very different parts of the world. Having been surrounded by a variety of cultures his whole life, Johnny cannot imagine being at a homogeneous church, and he is certain Evergreen will grow even more diverse: "When there are people like me who are not Asian, or who are and just love the multiethnic environment, it's going to happen because those people have friends of all different ethnicities." Indeed, I did meet many young people at Evergreen who, like Johnny, not only *accept* diversity, they *value* it highly. This appreciative stance has been formed in large part through the ideology of multiculturalism promoted in the schools.

Multiculturalism

Multiculturalism refers to a new vision of America that emerged in the 1980s and early 1990s out of a confluence of the civil rights movement, ethnic pride movements, and the rising number of immigrants from Asia, Africa, and Latin America since 1965. Even before it was given the name "multiculturalism," this ideology was being taught in the public schools, particularly in urban areas where schools faced unprecedented diversity among their students. Multiculturalism is associated with those who want to celebrate the cultural diversity of the United States, as well as those who are highly critical of the triumphant image of a tolerant America. No doubt there are many other agendas also identified with multiculturalism, but what they all share in common is captured well by sociologist Robert Wuthnow: "True multiculturalism takes the position that diversity itself is of value and that genuine diversity respects the value of people's being able to live within their own communities and pass on their own traditions to their children."[17] When I speak of an ideology of multiculturalism, I am referring to this belief in the enduring value of diversity in and of itself.

How influential has multiculturalism been on young people? Nathan Glazer called his book on the subject *We Are All Multiculturalists Now*. His title makes an ironic claim, given that Glazer is no fan of multiculturalism and the book describes pockets of resistance to it.[18] School districts have been the battlegrounds of these culture wars, and in California, during the 1990s, there were contentious debates at the local and state level over the teaching of multiculturalism in public schools.[19] Some of the strongest opponents of multiculturalism are conservative Christians who associate it with liberal secularism and efforts to remove God from the public sphere. Even when particular versions of multiculturalism, or even the term itself, evoke strong negative reactions, Glazer's title remains quite accurate: diversity has become a widely accepted fact of American life.[20] No child in America can grow up unaware of racial categories, since from an early age children are forced, for better or worse, to take their place within the multicultural schema.

Mixed Marriages and Multiethnic Kids

Taking his place in a multicultural world defined by racial categories has always been difficult for Jacob, a twenty-four-year-old member of Evergreen who identifies himself as Mexican, Spanish, Apache, Navajo, and Honduran. In previous generations those of mixed heritage were often treated with disdain and turned into objects of curiosity or pity, but people like Jacob no longer face intense social stigma. Jacob proudly talks about himself as multiracial. Rather than a liability, he sees this as an asset helping him thrive in a diverse world. Like many people of mixed racial heritage, Jacob is most comfortable in diverse settings. When he graduated from UCLA with a degree in engineering, he moved to Rosemead to be a part of Evergreen's vision of reconciliation.

Since the founding of the United States, mixed marriages and their "mixed blood" offspring have been a source of scandal, but young people have grown up after federal antimiscegenation laws were eliminated and the remaining state laws were no longer being enforced. Many young people in Southern California would find it hard to believe that the state of Alabama did not throw out a law forbidding Black-White marriage until the year 2000—and even then with only 60 percent support in the state legislature.[21] Though some Americans still object to mixed marriages, polls indicate that younger Americans are much more open to them than their elders. Considering the history of miscegenation laws, legal scholar Randall Kennedy is optimistic that Americans are becoming increasingly multiracial in their tastes, affections, and identities. Kennedy credits this development largely to the efforts of multiracial individuals who have challenged the rigidity of racial categories.[22]

In the 1980s, a multiracial identity movement began to challenge the inadequacy of these categories as encountered in countless institutional forms. By 2000, half a dozen states had passed legislation to include a multiracial category on school and employment forms, and for the first time in sixty years Americans could identify with multiple racial categories on census forms in the year 2000.[23] According to the 2000 census, 2.4 percent of Americans identified with more than one race, and 42 percent of these individuals were under eighteen. California has the third highest percentage of multiracial persons in the country, 4.7 percent, and in Los Angeles country that percentage rises to 4.9 percent, more than double the national average.[24] Evergreeners Johnny and Jacob are proud to be part of this growing number of multiracial individuals. At Evergreen they find many other young people who, even if they are not part of the relatively small population of Americans who identify as multiracial, also want the freedom to develop and assert a holistic, complex identity.

Fluid Ethnic Identity

Recognizing the instability of identity is part of the epistemological shift of our times. Talk of the constructed self, the protean self, the negotiated self, and various other unstable selves is common in the halls of academia, but Tom Beaudoin sees this phenomenon also reflected in the relationship of Gen Xers to popular culture and cyberspace: "Both our experience and our imagination of our selves are characterized more by incoherence than coherence, more by fragmentation than unity."[25] Though Beaudoin does not link this notion of flu-idity to ethnic identity, ethnic studies scholars certainly have. But this has done little to change the way most Americans think of ethnicity: as something peo-ple either have or do not have, as if one is either "ethnic" or "American."[26] I heard echoes of this either/or thinking in interviews with some Evergreeners who described themselves as "basically American" or "a diluted Asian."

A more helpful way to capture the complex and fluid nature of ethnic iden-tity is suggested by ethnicity theorists Stephen Cornell and Douglas Hartmann. They speak of ethnicity as being "thick" or "thin," with the key factor being the degree to which it serves as an organizing force in one's life.[27] Some people are more thickly connected to their ethnic culture than others, but this connection also changes depending on life events and context. For example, life passages like births, marriages, and deaths often activate ethnic connections that have been dormant. On the other hand, while ethnicity is activated in certain situa-tions, it can also be purposely hidden. Many people of color learn to hide cultural differences in order to be successful in a White-dominated society. Thinking of ethnicity as fluid, constructed, subjective, situational, ambivalent, unstable, and reciprocal makes it possible to avoid essentializing socially constructed racial categories and the confused notion that one is either "ethnic" or "American." This new way of thinking about ethnic identity is welcomed not only by people of mixed ethnic heritage, but by all those who resist what David Hollinger calls the "authority of color and shape."

No matter how appealing this fluid notion of ethnic identity may be to young people, their ability to assert their chosen identity is limited by the reality that others will perceive them in terms of static racial categories. Mary Waters has written poignantly on the freedom White Americans have to exercise their "ethnic options"—that is, the freedom to be seen as "ethnic" when they wish and "just American" when they wish—but people of color, especially African Americans, are rarely afforded this freedom.[28] These limitations have not stopped individuals from asserting an identity contrary to the one assigned to them, as Tiger Woods did when he said on the Oprah Winfrey show that he does not think of himself as Black.[29] Instead, he made a new identity for himself as a child, "Cablinasian," which embraced his Caucasian, Black, Indian, and Asian heritage. Woods was strongly criticized by Blacks for trying to "Whiten," but many rallied behind his right to be identified as he wishes.

At Evergreen, many of the young people of color are also asserting a fluid sense of ethnic identity, despite facing strong social pressure to accept their given place in the American racial system.[30] Ben, for example, is the son of two immigrants from Hong Kong and grew up attending an English-speaking Chinese church. He feels most Chinese on Chinese New Year, but most of the time he thinks of himself as having assimilated into the Asian American melting pot. Elena identifies proudly as Latina, but since she does not speak Spanish she finds most people "don't have a category for that." Shin, whose parents were born in Korea, sees herself as "a little Korean," but thinks that if she marries a Korean man she will become more Korean. Mark refuses to identify as an African American, insisting that race does not exist. Wei, whose parents are both from China, is not sure what she is but thinks her Asian ethnicity is more symbolic than real, a distinction she learned in an ethnic studies class.[31] Like those who identify as multiracial or multiethnic, these Evergreeners are challenging essentialist racial discourse, even though their freedom to fully exercise these ethnic options is limited by the racial categories others impose on them.

It makes sense that cosmopolitan young people, who have grown up in diverse settings and learned to value diversity, would be more skilled at negotiating diverse settings than older Americans. Coming from diverse families, Johnny and Jacob have had to learn these skills at home, but they both believe people of their generation are more adept in cross-cultural settings. It would be a stretch of the imagination to suggest that *all* young people are both enthusiastic about diversity and skilled at living in a multicultural society in which identities are fluid and situational. Less of a stretch is to suggest that there is a cosmopolitan ethos emerging among urban, college-educated Americans, shaped both by their exposure to diversity and their exposure to new ways of thinking about ethnic identity and diversity. Recognizing this new ethos gives Johnny and Jacob great hope in the future of the church, but, more important, they feel called to make racial reconciliation a reality. They are not alone in thinking that young people will play a special role in bringing about a more inclusive society. Within evangelical circles, many of those pushing for racial reconciliation believe that this generation will be the one to break down the walls of hostility.

The Reconciliation Generation

I first heard the term "reconciliation generation" from Brenda Salter McNeil, but the underlying assumption that young people are somehow better equipped to succeed at racial reconciliation I heard from many people. I met Salter McNeil when she came to preach at Evergreen in 2003 on the subject of racial reconciliation, and afterwards I was able to interview her by telephone. After working with InterVarsity Christian Fellowship for many years, Salter McNeil began Overflow Ministries in 1995 in order to concentrate entirely on healing people and healing the nation through the ministry of reconciliation. Overflow Ministries offers such resources as training courses, motivational speakers, tapes, videos, and study guides. While Salter McNeil gets occasional speaking requests from churches, most of her work is done on the campuses of evangelical colleges like George Fox University and with para-church organizations like the International Network of Children's Ministries.[32] She has noticed over the years that fewer people are arguing about the legitimacy of racial reconciliation; now they just want to know how to do it. The answer, she believes, is to encourage the emergence of a reconciliation generation, which she defines as "a host of people from various tribes, nations, and ethnicities who are Kingdom people called to do the work of racial reconciliation."[33]

Like their Gen X and Gen Y peers, young, urban evangelicals are part of the emerging cosmopolitan ethos described in the last chapter, but within evangelical circles they have been raised to be wary of anything associated with liberal politics, and as a result many are turned off by multiculturalism. As one InterVarsity staff member explains it: "The politically correct movement has shoved tolerance down our throats, and therefore Gen X tends to have a naïve and apathetic stance toward racism." When Pastor Ken was asked to join the board of a predominantly White evangelical college in Southern California, he was surprised to find so much resistance to diversity programs among the White students. He told me, "There's a lot of fatigue out there, or just apathy, if not antagonism, to this whole thing." In some racial reconciliation circles, there is a good deal of multiculturalism-bashing that goes on, but this does not mean that young evangelicals have rejected its basic premise. As I was repeatedly told in my interviews, young people today have a strong "value for diversity."

Racial Reconciliation on the College Campus

While it is tempting to see racial reconciliation as a Christian version of multiculturalism, this interpretation is strongly rejected by evangelicals. As one InterVarsity staff person explained it, "We're reworking a lot of tapes from the educational process where the goal is diversity, the goal is sensitivity, and the goal is numbers across ethnic lines. There is nothing wrong with diversity, but that is not the goal. The goal is healing and forgiveness and transformation." Given the resistance among young evangelicals to anything perceived as part of the "liberal, p.c. agenda" of multiculturalism, the challenge on college campuses is to present racial reconciliation as an entirely different, biblically-based way of approaching racial divisions. When twenty-four-year-old Steve started attending Evergreen, he did not want to hear any more about diversity, which he felt was shoved down his throat when he attended a nearby liberal arts college.

Racial reconciliation, on the other hand, excites him because the Gospel is involved: "Without the Gospel involved it takes on a much more self-centered feel. It's more like I want everybody to know about me versus I want to know about everyone and I want to relate to people." This is precisely the point that evangelical college-based organizations try to make when they insist that racial reconciliation is not multiculturalism, but something much more socially and spiritually profound.

All over the United States, evangelical college students are learning about racial reconciliation. I am sure there are some colleges where it is not talked about, but now that racial reconciliation has been accepted by the mainstream, they are the exception. Here is just one example of how evangelical colleges are promoting racial reconciliation: John Perkins, one of the early founders of the movement, has received honorary doctorates from seven evangelical colleges: Wheaton, Gordon, Huntington, Spring Arbor, Geneva, Northpark, and Bellhaven.[34] Many of the most elite evangelical liberal arts colleges have even created administrative positions to encourage tolerance of diversity on campus.[35] Chances are very good that young people who go to an evangelical college will encounter racial reconciliation through school initiatives and mandatory theology classes, but even at non-Christian schools, they can still learn about racial reconciliation through on-campus Bible fellowship organizations.[36]

InterVarsity Christian Fellowship is known as a strong advocate for racial reconciliation, but other national organizations, such as Campus Crusade for Christ, The Navigators, and Asian American Christian Fellowship, along with numerous regional groups, also teach racial reconciliation theology. These organizations exploded on campuses nationwide in the 1970s, fueled, according to religion scholar Rudy Busto, by a generation of post-1960s university students in search of meaning and values.[37] In the years since, much of their growth has come from Asian American students, many of whom arrive on college campuses already committed to evangelical Christianity. These fellowships are meant to foster the spiritual development of young adults so that when they graduate they will be fully equipped to be productive evangelicals.[38] Because they require an intense commitment of time and energy, college groups have an opportunity to influence young evangelicals at a critical, formative time, and they are often the training grounds for future church leaders. In this way, their influence on the evangelical movement as a whole is much greater than one would expect from the number of young people who participate in college fellowships.

Even though racial reconciliation is on the agenda of all college fellowships, only a handful of students will "get convicted" and make the pursuit of racial reconciliation their life's work. For many more, their college fellowship experience will compel them to engage in the kind of "individual reconciliation" that Emerson and Smith found widespread within mainstream evangelicalism. Most will leave college with a high value for diversity, a value learned through multiculturalism, popular culture, or their families, which has now been reframed and legitimated through racial reconciliation theology. To the extent that they seek out churches that promote this value, college fellowships are encouraging the institutionalization of racial reconciliation in congregational life. All the young people at Evergreen that I interviewed had become interested in, and in many cases committed to, racial reconciliation as participants in a college Bible fellowship. Because Evergreen has a strong connection with InterVarsity through Pastor Ken, I chose to learn more about how this organization is turning young people on to racial reconciliation.

InterVarsity Christian Fellowship

InterVarsity is an international organization of college fellowships that was formed in England in 1877 to serve as a nondenominational Christian witness on college campuses. The U.S. branch, InterVarsity/USA, which began in 1941, now serves more than thirty-five thousand college students on over 560 college and university campuses. InterVarsity also produces training materials, camps, books, and media tools for use in churches and para-church organizations. Since the late 1960s, it has been targeting the evangelization of students of color, and in the 1970s ethnic-specific fellowships were formed, primarily to serve the burgeoning number of Asian American evangelicals. Because Inter-Varsity has a grassroots structure run by paid staff and volunteers, chapters vary tremendously across the county, making it difficult to generalize about the organization. At the national level, racial reconciliation officially became a priority for InterVarsity in the late 1990s.

Hampering the implementation of racial reconciliation efforts at the campus level has been a lack of agreement about the meaning of racial reconciliation and how it relates to InterVarsity's evangelization mission. Antony Alumkal, who has studied the role of InterVarsity in the lives of Asian American college students, contends that it has followed in the footsteps of Promise Keepers in promoting an individual reconciliation approach.[39] I have also heard this criticism of the organization from InterVarsity staff members. In response to such criticisms, the national leadership has tried to foster a more sophisticated approach. In 2003, InterVarsity president Alec Hill published a statement on the tenth of the organization's core commitments: Ethnic Reconciliation and Justice.[40] Here he explains that in order to bring about ethnic reconciliation, we need intentionality, repentance, and justice: "Within InterVarsity, our challenge is to build systems that foster personal and systemic justice." Contrary to Alumkal's assessment, some evangelicals think InterVarsity's racial reconciliation efforts—at least at the national level—are in accord with the more radical early racial reconciliation movement. Rudy Carrasco and Derek Perkins, codirectors of the Harambee Christian Family Center, for example, believe that through its focus on the minor prophets of the Old Testament, InterVarsity has a deeper root in justice issues than organizations like Promise Keepers.[41] They find that among the college students who come to Harambee to volunteer, the InterVarsity students are much further along in their understanding of what it takes to make racial reconciliation a reality. Limiting InterVarsity's commitment to racial reconciliation is a longstanding struggle over how much priority should be given to racial reconciliation, or any social agenda, as opposed to evangelism.[42] Some InterVarsity staff members want to see racial reconciliation given equal priority with InterVarsity's traditional focus on evangelism, but that is far from the case today.

Given InterVarsity's decentralized structure, the national leadership has limited influence over what happens on individual campuses, but the annual Urbana conference has been a key opportunity for the national leadership to speak directly to students. Over the last few decades, this conference, drawing some twenty thousand students annually, has evolved from a largely White gathering to a decidedly multiethnic and international one. According to the Urbana Web site, the 2003 assembly was the most diverse in its history, with 38 percent of the attendees being of non-White descent.[43] The goal of the Urbana conference is for students to commit to evangelism and cross-cultural missions and to make concrete decisions about how to integrate their faith into their lives. At the 2000 meeting, 2,947 students committed to "learn about and get involved in a challenging issue such as racial reconciliation, justice or poverty," and 3,396 students decided to "build a friendship with a person from a different ethnic background and/or get involved with a group or church where I am a cultural minority."[44] As a large, emotionally intense, and exciting gathering, Urbana can be a powerful, Pentecost-like experience that compels students to push for multiethnic fellowships on their campuses that will replicate their Urbana experience.

Across the country, the response of InterVarsity chapters to the racial reconciliation cause varies tremendously by region. Some regions have adopted it as a priority, and others have barely paid it notice. Some chapters have grappled with the role of social structures in racial inequities, while others have stressed making cross-cultural friendships. Chapters in the southern United States have focused on Black-White race relations, whereas those in large urban centers have developed out of a multiethnic framework. The biggest area of contention has been the existence of ethnic-specific fellowships and how they fit into a vision of racial reconciliation. Because each region creates its own organization, there are a number of different configurations. Some campuses have so few students of color that a single chapter is formed out of necessity, whereas other schools choose to have a multiethnic chapter instead of ethnic-specific chapters. Ethnic-specific fellowships are quite common on large, urban campuses.

Both those opposed to and those in support of ethnic-specific fellowships acknowledge that these groups are more effective at evangelizing students of color than White-dominated fellowships. In other words, the homogeneous unit principle works just as well on college campuses as it does in churches. In fact, on campuses with few students of color, these fellowships provide a vitally important respite from the burden of being a minority. These co-ethnic groupings can also play a key formative role in what InterVarsity calls "ethnic identity development." This is noticeably different from the color-blind approach used in many evangelical settings. Ironically, even in ethnic-specific ministries ethnic identity may be of little importance. For example, Rudy Busto noted in his study of college Bible-study groups the "curious disappearance of Asianness in the discourses and practices of Bible study groups organized, paradoxically, by and for specific Asian groups."[45]

InterVarsity is also unusual among evangelical organizations in framing ethnic identity development as a justice issue. Keith Hirata, Assistant Director of Staff Development and Training, explained the purpose of ethnic-specific fellowships: "I view us as a hospital helping people heal from racial injustice, and ethnic-specific ministries do this. They value you and embrace your heritage. You need to have a strong sense of yourself to be a part of a multiethnic church."[46] Hirata sees the existence of ethnic-specific groups as a temporary step in a long process toward the ultimate goal of integration. As students grow in their self-knowledge and their understanding of racialization, they will be better able to meet as equals in multiethnic settings. In the meantime, if InterVarsity is able to attract a "critical mass" of diverse students and staff through the use of ethnic-specific fellowships, it will be in a better position to form truly just and inclusive multiethnic communities.

While some members of the InterVarsity staff reject the ethnic-exclusive groups unequivocally, in recent years there has been a growing appreciation of ethnic-specific fellowships and their importance to students of color.[47] Recognizing the value of both ethnic-specific and multiethnic groups, some regions try to institutionalize both structures and give students of color a choice. Periodically all groups join together for worship, study, or fellowship events. Another way to combine the benefits of both structures is to have a single multiethnic chapter on each campus but to bring students of color together regionally for mutual support and ethnic identity development.

In InterVarsity chapters across the country, there is a good deal of experimentation going on in response to the changing ethnic makeup of students and the changing attitudes among them. Few regions of InterVarsity have invested as much energy into racial reconciliation as the Greater Los Angeles division. Home to some of the most ethnically diverse chapters in the country, InterVarsity in Los Angeles has been in the forefront of developing models for implementing racial reconciliation on college campuses. Staff members have written a number of articles for InterVarsity readership on the successes and failures of these efforts, including a comprehensive guide, *Creating an Acts 6 Racially Reconciling Community: How "Race Matters" Works as a Campus Strategy.* These documents, along with the ten interviews I conducted with past and present InterVarsity students and staff, provided me with a valuable picture of the kind of exposure to racial reconciliation young adults receive prior to coming to Evergreen.

InterVarsity in Greater Los Angeles

Though there was a verbal commitment to racial reconciliation in the Greater Los Angeles division in the 1980s, it was not until the late 1990s that it became a high priority and the staff decided to move beyond words and make racial reconciliation a concrete reality in their fellowships. Since that decision, they have developed a number of different programs addressing racial reconciliation, but the one they are best known for in InterVarsity circles is called "Race Matters," a structure they adapted from the Rock of Our Salvation Evangelical Free Church in Chicago. At the Rock, members of this Black-White congregation are encouraged to talk openly and honestly about race at meetings that are called, for obvious reasons, "Fudge Ripple."[48] After studying what the Rock had been able to accomplish, the staff at the University of California–Los Angeles (UCLA) campus started to hold their own version of these meetings in 1995, which they called "Rainbow Sherbet" to reflect the multiethnic makeup of UCLA students. The name was later changed to "Race Matters," after Cornell West's book by that title.

Race Matters meetings are structured around a theme or question pertinent to ethnic tensions or issues the group is facing. Time is given for biblical teaching on the chosen theme before students break into ethnic-specific groups (including a group designated for mixed-heritage students if enough are present) for discussion of the theme. When the groups come back together, they must share with the whole gathering whatever was said in the small group. In both the small and large group discussions, students are encouraged to voice even those thoughts that they are ashamed of. One staff person explained that the first few comments "will be superficial or p.c., but soon enough someone will take the risk of actually being real with the group about their struggles." By getting "real" about racism and ethnic identity, the students can confront their own and others' prejudices and thus move beyond awareness—the goal of "the p.c. agenda"—to reconciliation. While many raw feelings are expressed during these meetings, students make a commitment to reconcile before leaving and to form cross-racial friendships, both within and outside of the group, in which to continue seeking honesty, repentance, forgiveness, and reconciliation.

Doug Schaupp, one of the creators of Race Matters and now director of the Los Angeles division, is passionate about racial reconciliation and believes that conflict is the only way to get there. As he sees it, unless we get into the hard issues of racialization in America, it is too easy to get stuck in a multiethnic trap:

> People are not convicted about racial reconciliation. People are convicted about multiethnicity, and all that multiethnicity means is getting along. That lasts maybe a year until it gets hard. Who is in leadership? Who is in power? How are we going to work this out? That is no longer multiethnicity. Now we are talking about reconciliation dynamics, and those are super difficult.[49]

Schaupp repeatedly hears the criticism that Race Matters is too conflictual, but he is convinced that conflict lies beneath the surface in every multiethnic community and that it is better to be proactive in addressing it than to be ambushed by it later.

Distinguishing racial reconciliation from the secular multicultural approach is an important part of the Race Matters program. In a short period of time, students learn how to get real about racism and how to reconcile with each other—something they do not learn, according to Schaupp, anywhere else. When I asked him if he believed current college students were especially open to racial reconciliation, he answered:

> I don't think it's a college-age thing, but I do think college folks are risk-takers and InterVarsity staff are risk-takers. . . . I think that college is a particular time of intermeshness. We live in dorms together, and because there is a lot of overlap, there is a lot of conflict and there is a lot of ethnic conflict. So you don't have to wait but a year on any campus for there to be an ethnic crisis. You just read the newspapers on any given campus and at some point there was some major racist

thing or major misunderstanding, and then the question is, is the Christian community going to respond to that or not? Nine times out of ten they are not equipped to. On our campuses we are doing Race Matters because that is the venue to air it right there, and you know seekers love this stuff. They come and they say, "We have never seen such a healing environment for honesty, because in class we have honesty but there is no healing."

For both conflict and healing to occur at Race Matters, there must be a diversity of students to perform the roles of challenging, confessing, and forgiving. With a predominantly White membership in InterVarsity, it is the students of color who are often put in the spotlight during Race Matters. In the name of reconciliation, students are encouraged to confess their racism, and those confessed to are expected to forgive. A White staff member shared this story with me: "A friend of mine said it clearly a couple of times that she felt sort of exploited, that once she gets upset enough to have an emotional reaction about something and breaks down in front of the group, then the goal is achieved." In addition to being catalysts for discussion, students of color are also expected to educate their peers about racism. A successful Race Matters session, I was told by many staff people, takes a well-trained facilitator who will speak for the minority students so they are not overburdened. I was able to see this firsthand when I attended a Race Matters meeting with the InterVarsity group at the University of California–Santa Barbara (UCSB) campus.

UCSB is not nearly as diverse a campus as UCLA, and the campus InterVarsity fellowship is made up primarily of White students. The chapter has been struggling for many years to increase the number of students of color and had recently decided to form a Bible-study group solely for Black and Latino students. The focus of this Race Matters was to discuss how students felt about the creation of an ethnic-specific Bible group. The White students did not have strong feelings about this decision, but the conversation did lead to a heated debate over how to make the weekly joint worship service more truly multiethnic. When students of color complained that the music was boring, White students asked why Latinos and Blacks get so emotional during worship. Even though the question was asked respectfully, it still put the students of color in a defensive position of having to explain and, in a sense, justify a charismatic religious style that is stigmatized in White middle-class society. Conflict also arose over whose responsibility it is to create multiethnic worship. The White students were open to new kinds of music and different speakers, but thought the Latino and Black students should be in charge of making those changes. The much smaller group of students of color argued that putting this task on them was unfair and that if the fellowship was truly practicing racial reconciliation, then all the students should help make the worship more inclusive.

This Race Matters meeting went on for several hours as the students tried to come to some agreement about how to vary the style of worship and whose job it would be to implement these changes. Some concrete decisions were made before midnight, and some good intentions for inclusivity were expressed by the White majority. From the perspective of an outsider, this appeared to be a successful session, since students did deal directly with racial issues and did work through some conflict, but it is clear that the burden of this process fell disproportionately on the few students of color.

Several students of color have left the UCSB InterVarsity group in recent years because they were tired of having to constantly educate the White students. It is precisely the frustrating need to explain themselves, and the reality of racialization in America, to the White students, "who just don't get it," that led to creation of a Latino/Black Bible study at UCSB. The staff hopes that this ethnic-specific group will give Latino and Black students a chance to get out of the spotlight, be nurtured, and perhaps, as one staff person said very honestly, "to let go of some of the hatred they have for White people, which is something that probably wouldn't be talked about anywhere else in the fellowship, even at our Race Matters."

As other InterVarsity chapters around the country have borrowed the Race Matters format, they have found mixed results. Unless the leaders are well trained in conflict resolution and very attentive to the feelings of those in the minority, the meetings can fail to elicit serious reflection on race issues, create ethnic rifts within chapters, or alienate students of color entirely. Race Matters, and the Los Angeles division's approach in general, has also been criticized for being too focused on individual feelings and relationships and, like Promise Keepers meetings, for not leading to concrete change. One graduate of UCLA now attending Evergreen commented:

> I always felt like one of the goals was for people to try and say how
> they are racist and repent of that and go through that emotional experi-
> ence and have someone from the sinned-upon culture forgive them
> and give them a hug or something. I guess I am not really into that
> kind of thing in general, the super-emotional without a tangible result.

All the current and former staff members I interviewed shared this concern that Race Matters is not producing tangible results. One former staff member now at Evergreen explained, "If we can have a good conversation and deal with our personal issues that's good, but there are still real issues faced by immigrants, or from the education system, that just aren't addressed. You can't do trickle-down racial reconciliation." As the weaknesses of the Race Matters format have become more apparent, the initial excitement for this new racial reconciliation tool among InterVarsity staff around the country has died down, and even in the Los Angeles division the once-quarterly Race Matters meetings are now held only sporadically.

In response to criticism of their efforts, the Los Angeles division made a more explicit commitment to what it calls the three-stranded rope of racial reconciliation: justice, ethnic identity, and cross-ethnic friendships. To address justice issues, they decided to focus efforts on increasing the number of Black and Latino students and staff. In the 1990s, InterVarsity was on only seven of the sixty-two college campuses in Los Angeles, for the most part on the elite public and private campuses, which have small Black and Latino student populations. The leadership devoted resources to developing programs on the commuter campuses, such community colleges and the California State universities in Los Angeles, where they would have more interaction with Black and Latino students. By 2002, InterVarsity was serving on fourteen campuses with the goal of doubling that number in five years.

This shift from the elite to the commuter campuses brings greater ethnic and socioeconomic diversity into the organization and has consequently raised its awareness of social justice issues. On the elite campuses like USC and UCLA, InterVarsity has also started targeting Black and Latino students through ethnic-specific fellowships. One Black staff member told me how important this shift has been for the organization:

> People's hearts have been really broken over the years and convicted
> and now they have changed their structures because of the heart check
> that God gave them in the course of Race Matters, and they actually
> appointed people to go out and reach out to Blacks and Latinos and
> have Black and Latino Bible studies in small groups. All of that came
> out of the heart work that God did in the course of Race Matters.

As was the case at UCSB, ethnic-specific fellowships have been created to serve as a safe space for Blacks and Latinos who experienced the racially-charged multiethnic fellowship as too exhausting and rarely healing.

The justice strand of the three-stranded rope is most directly addressed through urban projects. These are group excursions into the inner city for one to eight weeks, in which students engage in service projects, scripture study, and worship in order to reflect on their experiences of socioeconomic and ethnic "displacement." According to the national InterVarsity Web site, these projects "share a common commitment to teaching certain values, such as exploring issues of justice, poverty, racism, racial reconciliation, violence, lifestyle, biblical community, and the ministry of the urban church." The Harambee Christian Family Center in Pasadena, led by longtime racial reconciliation advocates Derek Perkins and Rudy Carrasco, is one of many sites where students are placed to learn firsthand about urban issues of poverty, racism, and violence.

In the Los Angeles region, as many as a hundred students spend an intensive six weeks working in an inner-city neighborhood each summer under the auspices of the LA Urban Project led by Kevin Blue. Blue has been a part-time staff member of InterVarsity for fifteen years and has been instrumental in pushing for more focus on social justice. One White staff member felt that the recent emphasis on urban projects is an encouraging step for InterVarsity's racial reconciliation mission:

> To me it made a lot of sense that if you're going to be pressing for-
> ward in relationships you can't just say, it's about me getting to know
> you or eating tamales and going to a quinceañera. It can't just be me
> hearing your pain, but must be me taking that seriously and taking
> action on it, like organizing unions or something. You can't just take
> the parts that feel good but [you] have to ask, what does it take to
> bring justice? A lot of what makes race a loaded issue is social eco-
> nomic discrepancies.

Approximately 25 percent of graduates from InterVarsity in the Los Angeles region relocate to poor neighborhoods and continue in urban ministry.

Changes have also been made in recent years to improve the organization's support of ethnic identity development. With so much stress on forming cross-cultural friendships and on ethnic displacement, there were few opportunities for students to explore who they are among co-ethnics. Though the Race Matters structure provides time for students to break into ethnic-specific groups and talk about issues in the safety of their co-ethnics, it was felt that not enough was being done to "raise up" the students of color through ethnic identity development. In one staff member's view, "I think you're more prepared to come to the table and to talk about racial reconciliation when you understand what you bring to the table, when you understand who you are."

At UCLA, ethnic-specific events are now held once or twice a quarter to provide space for bonding and growth in ethnic identity. These events are usually for a single ethnic group, but when the five Middle Eastern students had their "family" night, they cooked Persian food for the whole fellowship and taught them traditional dances. More recently, weekend ethnic identity conferences were started to bring students of the same ethnic background together from the entire Los Angeles region. Originally called Five-In-One conferences, they are now called Eight-In-One, as the number of ethnic groups that students break into during the conference keeps expanding. Over the weekend, students break into ethnic-specific groups for tailored biblical teaching for two days and join together for a shared worship service on Sunday morning. Johnny, a young Evergreen member who participated in InterVarsity at UCLA, described the conference as transformative: "The first one was the one that really transformed InterVarsity in L.A. I think everybody just got saturated in how much God really loves you as a multiracial person, as an Asian person, and every ethnicity. When we came together on that Sunday the church was like a circle. You had all these faces facing back at you, and it was incredible."

The ethnic identity development strand of the rope has been influenced by Carl Ellis's notion of core cultural issues.[50] During the UCSB Race Matters meeting I attended, Ellis's idea was explained with an apt analogy:: Like an iceberg, we carry an unseen base of core cultural patterns, values, and beliefs that affect how we relate to others, often in unconscious ways. The goal of this teaching is to bring out into the open cultural differences that are obstacles to racial reconciliation and to counteract feelings of self-hatred. Because the idea of core cultural issues relies on an essentialist understanding of ethnicity, I wondered whether anyone in InterVarsity found it constricting to be fitted into a cultural box. While the staff members I spoke with agreed that this is a potential danger, it is not seen as a likely one, since everyone recognizes that ethnic identity is fluid. InterVarsity is not pushing ethnic authenticity tests, I was told.

The efforts of the Greater Los Angeles division to implement racial reconciliation in concrete ways have been recognized throughout InterVarsity/USA as innovative. The Race Matters and Five-In-One formats have been used at large staff development training sessions and by fellowships in chapters around the country, with mixed responses. At least within the Los Angeles division, Schaupp has seen impressive results from their focus on racial reconciliation: "What we were like in 1994 is totally different from what we are like today. Who we are reaching, who we care about, what we ask students to do, what students are able to do, and what they graduate with is phenomenal." When Rudy Carrasco and Derek Perkins run urban work-study projects at their Harambee Christian Family Center, they have noticed that the more recent groups of InterVarsity students are coming in with a stronger biblical foundation, which helps them confront the hard social issues of poverty and race.[51] In addition to the one-quarter of InterVarsity graduates from the Los Angeles division who choose to work directly in urban ministry, many more graduates take their convictions for racial reconciliation into evangelical churches. The move from a college Bible fellowship to a church can be a frustrating experience for idealistic college graduates hoping to find churches as socially concerned and innovative as their InterVarsity experience.

After graduation, InterVarsity alumni are quick to learn how unique their college experiences were. Not only do few churches have the high level of diversity that college students in Los Angeles are used to, few have a strong commitment to either multiethnicity or racial reconciliation. Even for churches that do care about such things, the church as a multigenerational institution cannot easily replicate the intensive, experimental InterVarsity experience. Graduates wanting to continue that kind of intense religious journey often join the InterVarsity staff or other para-church organizations. Some may even start their own multiethnic churches, but InterVarsity does not encourage this. Though there are no records of what kind of churches graduates join, one staff person has noticed a trend of students of color joining ethnic churches after they graduate. She understands this return to the comfort of the ethnic church as a reaction to being out of their comfort zones for four years. Regardless of their destination, InterVarsity students are encouraged to raise awareness of the need for racial reconciliation wherever they find themselves. Alumni often discover that while they are newcomers to church life, they are much more advanced in their education and experience with racial reconciliation than other laity and even seminary-trained church staff. Given the few choices available to them, it is not surprising that Evergreen has become a popular choice for InterVarsity graduates in Los Angeles.

The Reconciliation Generation at Evergreen

New members at Evergreen are officially welcomed at a quarterly congregational meeting, and each one is introduced with a few words about why he or she wants to join the church. Two things struck me during the meeting I attended in October 2002. First, apart from one Japanese American couple in their thirties, all the new members were in their twenties, and second, they all pointed to the multiethnic makeup or racial reconciliation vision of Evergreen as a reason for joining. In the words of one Asian-Latino couple who had started dating through InterVarsity, "This is the kind of place we can be at home."

Evergreen has become a common destination for InterVarsity alumni and is home to at least eight InterVarsity staff members. Pastor Ken's address at Urbana 2000 brought him a lot of attention in InterVarsity circles, and he is well known to the staff of the Los Angeles division. Alumni at Evergreen find a lot of resonance between Ken's teaching and their InterVarsity experiences, not just in terms of racial reconciliation but also in terms of promoting women in leadership positions and engagement in social outreach. One young woman explained that she found a subculture at Evergreen that is very close to what InterVarsity stands for. Indeed, there is a kind of InterVarsity subculture at Evergreen. Like many intergenerational churches, Evergreen has had a hard time integrating new young adults into the church. They are not, in the words of Pastor Ken, the primary owners of the corporate identity and culture of the church. Many more come as visitors than join as official members. The 2004 church survey revealed that the proportion of those who attend services but are not involved had increased from 12 to 42 percent since the previous survey in 2002.[52] Those young adults that do join officially often stay on the margins of the decision-making circles of the church until they are older.

Several people spoke of the generational divide at Evergreen as if there were really two churches: a family-oriented, Asian-American church and a younger, outward-focused, multiethnic church. Holding these two churches together is Pastor Ken; he is the bridge between the older and younger generations. Ken does not agree that the divide between young and old at Evergreen is really so stark, and in interviews I heard considerable crossover in the values and priorities of younger and older members. Many of the older members fully support Ken's vision for Evergreen to become a model twenty-first-century church. They are the ones who put the money into the church envelopes to pay for the programs that give Evergreen its reputation as a dynamic, progressive church.

Still, it is the young people who are more diverse as a cohort, more comfortable in diverse settings, more educated in racial reconciliation theology and more committed to making it a reality. They are the ones who, in Ken's words, are foaming at the mouth for social change. One older member told me that he believes that until the young people become part of the 20 percent of the church that does everything, the church will never become truly multiethnic: "I think one of the signs that it will actually be working is when the people who are ethnically diverse join as members, stop putting their money in the tithing plates and start being involved in the ministries on a leadership basis." There is no getting around the fact that the future of Ken's vision for Evergreen is dependent upon the successful integration of these young members into the church culture.

Though Evergreen's social mission and racial reconciliation focus appeal to young people, these are not the only draws. Evergreen is a full-service church with good worship, challenging teaching, friendly people, a beautiful sanctuary, and plenty of programs to choose from. Young people come to Evergreen because they believe this is a church where they will be challenged to make a difference *and* where they can feel at home. For a few, the Asian American setting may be quite comfortable, but most of the young people at Evergreen grew up in diverse settings and have diverse social networks. The ethnic church of their parents does not appeal to this cosmopolitan cohort, and when they graduate from college, they look for churches that are multiethnic. They bring with them not only a high value for diversity and experience in diverse settings but also skills for living in a diverse world, such as an awareness of the complexity and fluidity of ethnic identity, that many older members of the congregation lack. These skills make them the boundary crossers, bridging ethnic divides in families, friendships, and religious congregations.

The success of the racial reconciliation movement depends greatly on whether young people will continue to push at the boundaries of the current church structures. There is a good chance that their commitment to racial reconciliation may never get beyond the superficial, and that as they age they will become more conservative on social issues. Dr. Samuel Chetti, executive minister of the American Baptist Churches of Los Angeles and an Evergreen member, reflected on the coming generation:

> There is a space in the university where we allow ourselves the permission to push the boundaries and stretch the complexity and chaos, but the moment we become adults, earning, married adults, we end up reeling in those boundaries to a much closer level . . . . The percentage that experience racial reconciliation and enjoy it is very high, but five to ten years down the road, now it becomes a competitive issue—I'm now competing with Hispanics or Blacks or Asians—then [the students] are no longer in the Bible studies and in the dormitories talking about these issues.[53]

Ken agrees that, for most of us, growing older means a shifting of priorities. Perhaps as they grow older, start careers, and begin families, Evergreen's young people will lose some of their zeal for social change and put their energy into family programs, as have generations before them. However, Ken believes that even as concerns and interests shift, the biblical teaching of racial reconciliation will still prevail upon them to make ethnic inclusion a priority. For the moment, youthful zeal for diversity and social change is strong enough to catch the attention of churches intent on attracting this demographic. Reconciliation of racial divisions has become one way for churches to also reconcile the generations and make sure that the next generation of evangelicals is successfully integrated into the fold.

4

Becoming a Multiethnic Church

Graduates of InterVarsity looking for a multiethnic church are often sorely disappointed to find that while many churches claim they value diversity or racial reconciliation, few have much diversity in their pews. The Multiracial Congregations Project, funded by the Lilly Foundation, set out in 1999 to learn just how racially divided congregations in the United States are.[1] Defining a multiracial congregation as one in which no single racial group constitutes over 80 percent of the total, the research team found that only 7.5 percent of all congregations and only 5.5 percent of Protestant churches are multiracial. That Sunday morning continues to be, in the words of Martin Luther King, Jr., "the most segregated hour in America," is a source of great embarrassment for many Christians.[2]

Like Bishop Caldwell of Greenwood Acres, Pastor Ken decided it was time for change. Rather than pay non-Asians to come, though, he hung out a new shingle announcing that Evergreen was a church embodying reconciliation. Casting the vision was followed up with work, culture work, to form a community committed to the vision. In the first chapter, we looked at how Ken worked to sell his vision to the congregation and the resistance he faced. This chapter considers whether Evergreen has reached its goal: is Evergreen a multiethnic church? This is far from an easy question to answer. We first have to grapple with what it means to describe a church as multiethnic. Demographic definitions are a useful starting point, but there is much more to a multiethnic church than numbers. This chapter explores how the goal of multiethnicity is institutionalized in Evergreen's church structures, and what ethnicity means in the context of this multiethnic community.

Evergreen in Transition

When I began my research at Evergreen, five years into its new mission, I knew from internal church surveys that Evergreen had made significant progress in attracting a more diverse membership. By 2002, the church was only 75 percent Asian American. Using the 80/20 definition developed by the Multiracial Congregations Project, Evergreen qualifies as a multiracial church, but I wondered to what extent the congregation thought of itself as a multiethnic church and, if they did not, how it would know when it had reached this goal.

Despite its demographic diversity, there are many signs that the boundaries at Evergreen have barely budged. With 75 percent of its members and almost 100 percent of its staff of Asian ancestry, Evergreen still feels very much like an Asian American church. As one member put it, "Just in terms of gut feel, it is probably still an Asian church, but I can see that changing." Evergreen is also still perceived as a pan-Asian church within its institutional field, the churches and organizations that Evergreen is in dialogue with. In fact, many of the pastors I spoke with in Los Angeles who knew of Evergreen were surprised I would study it as an example of the multiethnic church phenomenon.

My confusion about how to describe Evergreen was not helped by the January 2004 newsletter, which included the biographies of two new members, both of whom looked to be in their late twenties. An Asian American member, who had been with Evergreen a little over two months, called it a "wonderful Asian-American church where he feels right at home." Just below this, a new Latino member described the church as a "family-style, multi-generational church seeking to become the embodiment of Christ's call for racial reconciliation." As I read these Evergreeners' descriptions of their church, I wonder if they are really talking about the same place: is Evergreen an Asian American church or a multiethnic one?[3]

In *Congregations and Conflict*, Penny Edgell Becker argues that conflicting ideas about *who we are* and *how we do things here* are at the root of church conflict:

> Identity conflicts involve both power and symbols; they can be understood as conflicts over the power to symbolize different understandings of the congregation's identity and to institutionalize these understandings in very concrete ways, including the liturgy, the programs,

the ways of making decisions, and the norms of interaction that, taken together, form the overall tenor of congregational.[4]

Evergreeners clearly have conflicting ideas about who they are as a congregation. To some members it is a comfortable, Asian American, family church, and to others it is a progressive, missional church *becoming* multiethnic. Those who fall into the latter group stress that the church is in transition and see its growing diversity as central to Evergreen's identity, but few describe the church as unequivocally multiethnic. Most members see the church, as Ken does, as still growing into its new vision.

A number of years after the 1997 hive, Evergreen is still predominantly Asian American—a fact that is a great disappointment to some and a relief to others. As we saw in the first chapter, not everyone at Evergreen is sold on the multiethnic vision, and many people I spoke with believe a large portion of the church membership is simply disconnected from it. What bothers those who want Evergreen to become a multiethnic church is the extent to which those who identify Evergreen as an Asian American church are choosing not to acknowledge the growing diversity in their midst. If describing Evergreen as a multiethnic church is a stretch, so is describing it as an Asian American church, given that 25 percent of its members are non-Asian. Evergreen's identity is currently contested and in transition. Those who share Ken's vision wonder how much longer it will take for Evergreen to become *truly* multiethnic. My question is, how will they know when they get there?

Defining the Multiethnic Church

What is this new kind of church that some believe holds the key to ending racial divisions but is so difficult to achieve? What is it that people are looking for when they say they want a diverse church, and what does it look like in terms of institutional structures? As a researcher, I found it difficult to track the incipient phenomenon of multiethnic churches without a clear sense of what it is they look like. With a growing number of young Christians seeking multiethnic churches, the term has taken on a marketing appeal, which makes it all the more important to be wary of how it is used.

It may seem easy enough to use a demographic definition, like the 80/20 racial split of the Multiracial Congregations Project, but this approach has several limitations. First, using the traditional racial categories to identify diversity ignores all the other ways in which Americans choose to identify themselves, especially multiracial individuals but also those who prefer to identify with the country of their ancestors rather than an ascribed racial category. Insisting that only racial diversity matters excludes all those who do not neatly fit into these categories and ignores the significant diversity within them. Second, the 80/20 definition pays attention only to demographics and does not take into consideration the dynamics of interaction within the congregation. Churches have developed an array of institutional structures for managing diversity, such as holding separate services for each group. It is not always clear when a church is really a church and when it is an aggregate of groups sharing space.

Whenever I learn about a multiethnic church, my first question is always *what are the demographics?* The racial *and* ethnic makeup of the membership is a good place to start, but numbers alone do not define the multiethnic church. Numbers matter, to be sure, for without cohabiting we cannot form relationships, but it is quite possible for an institution to be inhabited by people of diverse ethnic identities without engendering any substantial crossing of ethnic boundaries or creating a community of equals. The mere presence of diversity, after all, does not necessarily lead to integration, substantial cross-cultural interaction, racial reconciliation, celebration of differences, or ethnic inclusion in any meaningful sense.

Public high schools are a case in point. The way students gather in ethnically-defined clusters across the quad during lunch reveals that ethnic identity is a powerful subgroup boundary. Though students are required to interact to some extent in the classroom, they are free to form friendships on the basis of ethnic similarities, and the resulting ethnic divide is conspicuous. Churches have so far avoided this problem. They are rarely as internally divided as Los Angeles high schools, not because they are more inclusive but because they have too little diversity for minority members to form subgroups. The contrast between the diversity in public, urban spaces and the homogeneity of congregations is stark. But church leaders are quick to point out that forced integration has not succeeded in creating genuinely inclusive communities.

As religious organizations around the world work to overcome social divisions, one thing they all share is the conviction that the goal is not numerical diversity. Theologian Michael Mata explains, "There exists a qualitative aspect to the notion of a multiethnic congregation."[5] Because of this qualitative aspect, churches that are demographically diverse, like Evergreen, still do not *feel* multiethnic to some of their members. As I spoke with evangelicals across the country, I was surprised how many of them doubted that there are any churches in the United States that are *truly* multiethnic. In their eyes, so-called multiethnic churches are lacking in some significant way. The two criticisms I heard most often are that these church are too internally fragmented by diversity to be considered a single community, or they are too homogeneous in terms of culture to be considered ethnically diverse. Fragmentation and homogenization are the traps that churches fall into when they overstress either diversity or unity. Whatever the quality is that sets the multiethnic church apart, it must lie somewhere between these two poles.

Besides having demographic diversity, multiethnic churches must find ways to affirm diversity while still building a sense of shared community. One word that captures both of these goals well is *inclusion*. When people think about joining a church, they often think in terms of being included. They ask, "is this a place where I will be accepted for who I am with my complex identity and unique cultural practices?" If inclusion is the key quality that makes a multiethnic church, then we could use it to define the "successful" or ideal multiethnic church as follows: *the multiethnic church is an inclusive, ethnically diverse community.* This working definition can serve as a starting point to understand what the ideal multiethnic church is all about.

Inclusive of What?

When people talk about wanting more diversity in their church, it is often not clear what kind of diversity they want to include. The first thing people point to when talking about diversity is how many people of each group they have, but they may categorize these groups in any number of ways, such as racial, cultural, generational, linguistic, or country of origin. Which of these is the best measure of a church's ethnic diversity?

This issue of how to talk about diversity arose at Evergreen shortly after the hive in 1997, which separated the old Evergreen into two churches. In his first formulation of the new church's vision statement, Pastor Ken used the phrase "multi-Asian/multi-ethnic," but people found this too much of a mouthful. On the other hand, "multiracial" is not a popular term at Evergreen. Many Evergreeners told me they find racial language harsh and stifling. To them, race connotes an imposed identity rather than a chosen one. The older members, and those who have immigrated recently, do not want to be subsumed into the racial category "Asian American" and insist on their distinct ethnic identities as Japanese Americans and Chinese Americans.

They are not alone in perceiving ethnicity as a more specific, more flexible, and gentler way to talk about diversity than race. A similar shift in terminology is taking place within much of the literature on church diversity. There are even signs that the term "ethnic reconciliation" is beginning to replace "racial reconciliation" within evangelical circles.[6] This preference for ethnicity discourse can be seen as an example of people of color asserting their "ethnic options" to identify in the way they want to, but it may also reflect a desire to avoid talking about the ways in which racial categories are used to privilege some and marginalize others. In other words, avoidance of talking about race can easily become avoidance of talking about racialization. In an effort to cover all their bases, some churches use terms like "ethno-racial diversity," but others have taken a different tack altogether by framing diversity in terms of cultural differences. This is the approach Ken took in the second version of the vision statement, which refers to "montages of cultures, class, and circumstance."

Churches that frame diversity in terms of cultural difference usually focus on such obvious cultural markers as language, dress, food, and music. Worship services are a perfect opportunity to "showcase" a variety of cultures, and on an individual level churches may encourage members to dress in ethnic garb and bring their own kind of food to church potlucks. This works particularly well in churches that attract immigrants, who often display clear cultural markers, but when the American-born generations act increasingly like their White peers, it becomes much harder to identify cultural differences. In churches attracting American-born members, the presumption is often that everyone has assimilated to "American" culture, which is more accurately identified as middle-class White American culture. Sociologist Robert Bellah, for example, has argued that, aside from a few ethnic enclaves, there are no real cultural differences in the United States thanks to the pervasive forces of the market, mass media, and mass education, which "obliterate the genuine heritage of Anglo-American, European, African and Asian culture with equal thoroughness."[7] Even among his very diverse UC–Berkeley students, Bellah observes that once language goes, so does "in any deep sense" cultural difference.

If Robert Bellah were to visit Evergreen, he might quickly conclude that there are no significant cultural differences here, but that would be a mistake. Cultural differences are not always visible at first glance. They may be quite subtle, such as facial affect and talking with one's hands.[8] More significant are differences in values, communication styles, and ways of thinking and making decisions—differences that reflect what InterVarsity students call their "core cultural issues." Those in the majority group are often blind to the extent to which they assume that their cultural practices are normative and, not surprisingly, unseen cultural differences are a common source of tension in ethnically diverse communities. How churches recognize cultural diversity is made even more complicated by the fact that there is great variation in the ways individuals relate to ethnic identity and ethnic culture. After all, ethnicity is not static but fluid, and when given the freedom individuals will vary the extent to which they assert a particular identity among the many identities they have an affinity with. And we should not forget that the ability to perform "Whiteness" is highly rewarded in professional America, which may explain why Bellah saw no significant cultural differences among his ethnically diverse Berkeley students.

When church members claim they want to be in a diverse church, they may not really want cultural diversity. They may believe that, regardless of skin color, we all do things the same way: the Christian way or the American way. In this case, newcomers are expected to assimilate into the church culture, which inevitably reflects the culture of those in the majority group. As noted earlier, this color-blind approach appeals to many White evangelicals. Since they are used to being in the majority group, the color-blind approach allows Whites in these churches to remain culturally comfortable, while people of color must assimilate to an Anglo American church culture. The authors of *United by Faith* identify this institutional pattern as the "Assimilated Multiracial Congregation" and point out that this model is not limited to White-dominated churches.[9] It can be found in any church where there is one racial group whose power and culture is imposed on the entire church, including Evergreen Baptist Church.

While the potential clearly exists for the majority to force their culture on the rest, one can certainly imagine a multiethnic church in which those in the majority choose to recognize and affirm the cultural values and practices of those in the minority. In his definition of the multiethnic church, theologian Roger Greenway stresses this aspect of inclusivity: "A true [multiethnic] congregation blends distinctive elements of various ethnic traditions in such a way that no single tradition predominates or suppresses others. Nor is the outcome such an 'osterized' mixture that nobody can tell one element from another."[10] There is an explicit rejection of forced assimilation in much of the multiethnic church literature, but how cultural differences are best incorporated into church life is very much an open question. Churches that are too formulaic in their attempts to "affirm" cultural diversity are perceived as fake or only superficially diverse. In a reversal of the color-blind approach, they may even pressure members to "be ethnic" in stereotypical ways for the sake of presenting a culturally diverse community. These efforts to be inclusive of diversity often fail, because they are not complemented by nurturing a sense of community that binds everyone together.

An Inclusive Community

The term *inclusive community* is used often and loosely in discussions of multiethnic churches. It seems somewhat redundant, since the notion of community implies inclusivity, but the extra emphasis on inclusion is so common within the literature on multiethnic churches that it warrants our attention.

Robert Wuthnow cautions us against thinking of congregations as communities, despite the frequency with which both scholars and people in the pews use the terms interchangeably. He writes that the term *community* "implies a supportive set of interpersonal relationships that forge a common bond of identity and caring among people. It requires interaction, give and take." In Wuthnow's view, a congregation is more properly thought of as a gathering of people who share a corporate identity rather than a community, since it is quite unlikely that everyone in a congregation would have such relationships, especially in churches that have more than one service. There is something peculiar about calling a church a community when many people in the pews may not know each other at all and certainly do not share "a common bond of identity and caring."[11] Still, I think there is more to the idea of the church as a community than Wuthnow believes.

Not all churches try to be a community, but evangelical churches typically do.[12] In the hope of attracting those seeking community, these churches put a great deal of effort into the "ministry of hospitality" and the formation of close bonds. At Evergreen, members of the hospitality team, wearing bright blue aprons, wait for visitors in the parking lot and shepherd them to the sanctuary. Given the importance of a warm handshake and a smiling face in making visitors feel welcome, you might say that church greeters are on the front lines of the multiethnic church movement. If the front lines are successful, the visitor will return and begin the much more difficult process of learning the culture of the church, how things work here, and, most important, forming bonds of caring and identity. Jack, a White man in his late thirties, thinks Evergreen does a great job of drawing people in and making them feel part of the family:

> When I first came here, I came early because I didn't know what time the service was, and I just started talking to folks that were here and asked them if there's a singles group, and during that morning about three or four people actually approached me and said, "I heard you're interested in a single's group. Would you like to get plugged in?"
> That sort of sensitive responsiveness and inclusiveness really surprised me.

Many of the members told me it was the friendliness of the community that attracted them to Evergreen, and in the 2004 survey 98 percent of respondents said they feel welcomed there. But forming close bonds requires much more than a warm smile and friendly handshake. How is it that people can attend Evergreen with seven hundred others and still feel they are part of a community?

One strategy that has worked well for evangelical churches is the use of cell groups, such as Bible-study, special-interest, or support groups, which meet outside of the Sunday worship time. A pastor of an Asian American church in northern California explains their effectiveness this way: "[Young adults] are looking for a place to belong. A cell group reaches out to them. BAM! They've got seven, eight friends. You need seven to ten significant relationships to feel like you belong."[13] By forming bonds of caring within a cell group, members feel a sense of belonging in the entire church, since the cell group is a micro-cosm of the larger community. Cell groups are so successful at promoting interpersonal bonds that they are common in churches in such theologically dis-parate denominations as Roman Catholicism and Unitarian Universalism.

In January 2002, Pastor Ken launched a "Building Sedaqah Communities" campaign. At that time, 40 percent of Evergreeners were involved in these cell groups, and the goal was to get 75 percent involved because, according to his ar-ticle in the newsletter, "real Sedaqah community is best experienced with regu-lar, smaller groups of people in homier settings than can be created on Sunday mornings at church." These small group ministries had existed at Evergreen for many years as Bible-study groups, but starting in 2002 they were being trans-formed into "more intimate communities of believers where the Bible is still studied but there will be ample opportunities to practice what we study."[14] In other words, these groups are supposed to do service projects together in addi-tion to Bible studies and social activities. Most of Evergreen's cell groups are called Neighborhood Sedaqah Groups because they are geographically tied to a region of Los Angeles County, but some are targeted at specific groups, such as young adults. At the time of the 2004 survey, 56 percent of respondents be-longed to a Sedaqah group. Sedaqah group members can still make connec-tions with other Evergreeners through other kinds of small groups, such as the Men of the Bible (MOB) or the Prime Timers group for those fifty-five or older. In an effort to create more opportunities for "good, face-to-face connections," Pastor Danny began organizing monthly Sedaqah lunches at the church in July 2003, with more than a hundred people attending.

What makes a church feel like a community is not that everyone is inter-acting with everyone else but that the *potential* exists to form a bond with any member. The experience of being welcomed into a community and the belief that one has formed a bond of identity and caring with others brings many people to churches each Sunday and inspires them to give generously of their time and money. Those churchgoers who do not form such bonds rarely stay or become active in the church. Describing a church as "inclusive" is a way of emphatically stressing that members are open to forming supportive bonds with anyone who walks through the door. It makes clear that that those boundaries, which in the society at large operate to exclude on the basis of race or class, are not operative within this particular church community. Put another way, in an inclusive church there are no boundaries on interactions or forming close bonds.

In practice, of course, saying that a church is inclusive does not necessarily make it so, and the real judge of the accuracy of this claim is the visitor. Almost everyone I spoke with at Evergreen had done some church-shopping before settling on Evergreen and, in the process, had visited churches in which they felt excluded, uncomfortable, marginalized, or invisible because of their ethnicity. For many, there was no single incident or aspect of the church that they could point to; it was simply a sense that they were not welcome. As a newcomer, it is easy to feel excluded and to attribute such exclusion to prejudice. It happens just as Pastor Ken described in his sermon on reconciliation, in the story of the spiky-haired South Asian teens (chapter 1). When these teenagers visited a White church, there was nothing that said they were not welcome, but they heard the message loud and clear. Presumably, if that feeling persists the visitor will look elsewhere for a more inclusive community. It is unlikely that we would find many church members who feel strongly excluded from the community, but many will choose to join even if they do not feel completely at home there. These critical but committed members are particularly helpful in identifying the ways in which the church has successfully institutionalized inclusion and the ways it falls short.

Institutionalizing Inclusion

Though a few churches make statements prohibiting certain kinds of people from membership, and others make statements declaring that they exist to serve a certain clientele, most churches never publicly state the boundaries of who belongs and who does not. Nonetheless, every Sunday visitors make judgments about how welcome they feel in a particular church. Public displays of inclusion are concrete expressions of a church's commitment to the values of tolerance and diversity that are easily observable by newcomers. Vision statements printed on a church's handouts and proclaimed boldly on its Web site are a very public way to show that these values are important priorities, but they cannot assure the quality of inclusion.

Consider what would happen if a White congregation in a neighborhood that is becoming increasingly Latino decided to reach out to these newcomers and developed a new vision statement declaring its inclusive intentions. Through the increase of Latino members and the loss of disgruntled White members, this church eventually reaches the 80/20 split that qualifies it as multiracial according to the Multiracial Congregations Project. As the neighborhood grows increasingly Latino, this demographic shift may bring about a Latino majority inside the church, and it may begin to attract Asian and African American members as well. The church's Web site and brochures proudly feature a mix of smiling Asian, Black, Latino, and White members. As news gets back to the denominational leadership, this church is widely trumpeted as a successful multiethnic church. The pastor is now officially recognized as an expert in multiethnic church development, and is invited to speak at denominational gatherings on the subject of diversity. But behind the veneer of diversity, the leadership of this hypothetical church remains White, its worship style decidedly White, and its institutional culture White. Such a church may have good intentions to be multiethnic, but it has done little to institutionalize the inclusion of ethnic diversity.

Beyond an inspiring vision statement and warm handshake at the door, multiethnic churches must put their words into action by institutionalizing them in church structures, most importantly the leadership, programming, and corporate worship.[15] In all three of these areas Evergreen has taken some steps to institutionalize its goal of breaking down divisions of "culture, class, and circumstance." Such changes are not welcomed by everyone at the church, while others think they are far too small and too slow in coming.

Leadership

The leaders of the church have the power to shape the institutional culture. If the pastor, the church board, and the office staff are all of the same ethnicity, members may question how inclusive the power structures of the church really are. At Evergreen, the fact that all except one of the paid staff are Asian American was mentioned repeatedly in interviews as a real weakness in the church's efforts to be inclusive. Pastor Ken explains that during the hive he tried to retain all the staff he could, and all the pre-hive staff were Asian American. Subsequently Evergreen needed to hire a new music leader and filled the position with a White man. The problem, as one of the assistant pastors put it so well, is how to diversify the staff naturally rather than just trying to fill a quota. In 2004, an opportunity arose when the Director of Worship Ministries resigned and a White woman was hired as Pastor of Worship Arts, thus breaking two barriers in the church leadership. But since the resigning director was the only non-Asian staff member, the staff remains overwhelmingly Asian. Jacob hopes they will soon hire a Latino staff person who can lead the congregation's outreach to Rosemead's largely Latino population.

It might be quite obvious from noting who is in paid and unpaid leadership positions whether a particular ethnic group dominates or, conversely, is excluded from the inner workings of the church, but power may be unequally distributed in very subtle ways. An inclusive church, then, must be attentive to its leadership and decision-making processes. For example, if positions are filled by a process of self-nomination, those who have been raised in a culture that encourages assertiveness will more readily step forward than those who have not. Some Evergreeners believe that this factor has led to an imbalance in leadership, which will only get worse as the church becomes more diverse.

A pastor of a nearby Asian American church told me that as more Chinese American members joined during the 1980s, they quickly moved into leadership positions because they asserted themselves more readily than Japanese Americans. He explained, "There's a saying in Japanese American culture that says the nail that sticks up gets pounded down. So no one volunteers. Everything is done very relationally, very slowly." In his view, when Chinese American members joined Evergreen, they volunteered freely and were quick to take on leadership roles in the church. Within a few years the church began to be Chinese-dominated, and this imbalance contributed to the church hive. This outsider's assessment was shared by a few members of Evergreen, but others expressed concern that as more White members join Evergreen, they will take over the church because they are more assertive than Asians. One member of the church board noted that even though there are few Whites in leadership positions, their assertiveness gives them a degree of influence far outweighing their numbers.

At this point, Evergreen is delighted to have any non-Asians in positions of leadership, but in the future it may have to be more sensitive to how power is shared.[16] Because subtle cultural practices are largely unintentional and unconscious, opening up the "corridors of power" often requires more substantial changes in the way churches identify and develop leaders than is first realized. One way Evergreen staff members have tried to encourage greater diversity among volunteers is to highlight what diversity there is among the volunteer leadership. Almost every issue of the newsletter includes articles written by or focusing on the service of non-Asian members. For example, the June and July 2003 issues introduced the congregation to the new church moderator and a new deacon, both of whom are White men who have been coming to Evergreen since before the hive.

Church Programs

Since the hive, Evergreen has offered a variety of programs and events that address the vision of reconciliation. One of the first attempts to incorporate it into religious education programming was led by a young biracial couple, Karen and Nate, who had served on the staff of InterVarsity at a college in Los Angeles. After seeing little concrete effort to advance racial reconciliation at Evergreen, they created a course on the subject, which they tried out on their Sedaqah group before offering it to the adult members of the church in 2001. Karen and Nate were surprised that fifteen people showed up to the first class, and, although attendance dwindled, they were pleased that the class had brought together people who also wanted to see racial reconciliation become a higher priority at Evergreen. As Karen told me, "We started to discover that there are these little pockets in the church of people who either had encountered the concept of racial reconciliation on the campus or through InterVarsity or just having different careers."

In 2001, Evergreen also held an open house for its Rosemead neighbors with the theme of celebrating cultures around the world. Several of the Asian members mentioned this event as an example of what Evergreen is doing to become more culturally informed, but not everyone was pleased with the outcome. Karen, for example, was appalled by what she saw:

> This isn't multicultural. This is like "Asian culture day" because there is a Korean booth, a Japanese booth, Hawaiian, Chinese, Hong Kong, all these different things, and then there is an Africa booth and it is all animal masks. There is no exchange. . . . We had people who spent summers in Africa [on missions] and nobody called to find out from them about Africa. . . . There was no attempt to make it real or to have a learning opportunity.

Karen was embarrassed to imagine what impressions Latino and Black visitors would draw from this event about the church's attitude toward them. When I interviewed Karen and Nate in 2002, they were disappointed that Evergreen was not doing more to engender serious discussion of racial reconciliation. They had tried to raise the issue in their Sedaqah group but found little interest. In their eyes, Pastor Ken does a terrific job of getting people excited about reconciliation, but there is no structure to carry that excitement forward. Darren is a White member who is also disappointed to see more lip service than concrete action. He thinks the most important action should be more dialogue: "We should be dialoguing about our fears, our hopes, our desires. We should be dialoguing with people in the context of diversity so that we are forced to deal with things or at least forced to talk about them." This is precisely what Pastor Ken hoped would be accomplished through the annual all-family church camp in 2002 on the theme of racial reconciliation.

Local reconciliation advocates Rudy Carrasco and Derek Perkins were asked to lead the three-day weekend, titled "Peaces of the Puzzle," at Concordia University in Irvine, California. Two hundred and fifty people attended the camp and heard stories about the work Carrasco and Perkins do through the Harambee Christian Family Center to forge reconciliation between Blacks and Latinos in Pasadena. Ken hoped many more Evergreeners would go but ultimately thought the camp was a success because it helped those who came become more conscious of the painful effects of racialization. Karen and Nate also hoped that the retreat would lead to greater awareness of how hard and painful racial reconciliation is. As Karen put it, "We need to learn to think about how other people are thinking. If you are doing [racial reconciliation] right it is going to be hard and really suck and you are not going to want to do it." Afterwards they reported that the weekend met some of their expectations, but did not go deep enough into the hard stuff. This was an assessment shared by many in the congregation who are strongly committed to racial reconciliation and want to see it taken more seriously.

One church initiative does just that. In 2004, a racial reconciliation research group was formed to evaluate the racial climate at Evergreen and make recommendations for educating and training the church.[17] The group reported in the newsletter that while Evergreeners give a high priority to racial reconciliation, they have limited understanding of the concept. As one member of the research group put it bluntly, "Many Evergreeners would have an easier time understanding the laws of physics than defining racial reconciliation." The study group recommended that Evergreen utilize the services of reconciliation consultant Brenda Salter McNeil and form a Racial Reconciliation Resource Team "to begin to model the values of reconciliation." Following these recommendations, Evergreen began a two-year partnership with Salter McNeil in 2005 and launched the Rec'ing Crew, as the Resource Team is affectionately called, with two Asian American and one Latino member serving as team leaders. In January 2006, the Rec'ing Crew advertised a new adult religious education course called "A Journey Toward Reconciliation." According to the brochure, the objectives of the course are:

> To understand the core message of reconciliation throughout the Scriptures, connect with your own ethnic identity and racial reconciliation journey, wrestle with the primary obstacles and barriers to reconciliation, learn to empathize with others through the sharing of

personal stories, and [be] equipped with biblical resources and personal skills to be a minister of reconciliation.

During the same month, the Rec'ing Crew also sponsored a discussion night in honor of Dr. Martin Luther King, Jr.'s, birthday, based on the movie *Crash*, described in the announcement as a thought-provoking movie about the clash of race, culture, and classes in Los Angeles.[18] With this new group charged solely with promoting deeper understanding of what racial reconciliation requires, Evergreeners may see more concrete programming designed to "get real" about racial reconciliation.

Ritual Inclusion

As the focal point and main gathering time of a congregation, the Sunday worship service is the most important arena for churches to make their commitment to inclusion visible. Churches can hire worship leaders or involve laity who visibly demonstrate the church's diversity, but it is much more challenging to reflect inclusion through the content and form of the service. Compared to those churches that highlight diversity in their communal worship, Evergreen has not emphasized public displays of diversity. There are always a few non-Asian faces leading the service, but this has required continual recruitment on the part of the ministry staff. For the non-Asian visitor trying to decide if he or she can fit in at Evergreen, the importance of seeing diversity "up front" cannot be overstated. For example, Karen once observed an African American family walk entirely around the sanctuary so they could receive communion from an African American man. Another example of the importance of connecting ethnically with those up front was related by a young Latino woman. She was very appreciative that Pastor Ken, during a baptism ritual, drew attention to the fact that this was the first Latino child ever baptized at Evergreen.

Conflicts over music choices are often generational, but in the multiethnic church they can also be marked by ethnic boundaries. Churches can vary musical styles in the hope that everyone will find something appealing, or they can rely on the "American-style" praise music popular in evangelical circles. Since Evergreen has used the latter strategy, music has not been an arena for institutionalizing the church vision. The Sunday morning services begin with thirty minutes of lively praise music, often in the Christian pop style popularized by Vineyard churches. Occasionally a more traditional Baptist hymn will be included to make the older members happy. On rare occasions, the services will include a song in a language other than English; for example, a group of young people raising funds for their mission trip to Japan sang a Japanese song. Many of the young people I interviewed would like to hear more songs in other lan-guages, like those they have heard at the Urbana conferences. Pastor Ken has long dreamed of bringing more diverse musical styles to Evergreen, especially gospel music, and in 2005 he hired a choir director for this purpose. The newsletter describes a performance by the Evergreen Gospel Choir: "People of all ages wore bright shirts, stood in formation, harmonized, and even did some synchronized swaying, often inspiring the sometimes rhythmically-challenged Evergreeners to jump to their feet and engage in some clapping and hooting and hollering."[19] In the same article, the new choir director reminds the con-gregation that gospel music is not only about celebration but also about the suffering and perseverance of their African American brothers and sisters. She does not make a direct tie to the church's reconciliation vision, but the ad-dition of gospel music may inspire greater appreciation of African American experiences.

The content of the service, from announcements to testimonies, also pro-vides clues as to the value a community places on diversity. The sermon is the most important opportunity to make explicit the church's commitment to inclu-sion, and Pastor Ken often addresses this theme when he is in the pulpit. The message can come across through sermon themes and the illustrations used, as well as through jokes and personal stories that suggest an acceptance of all people. In some years Evergreen has held a service in January in honor of Mar-tin Luther King, Jr., not only to celebrate the many civil rights leaders who shared the Baptist faith, but also to bring attention to the continued effects of racism in the United States. In one such celebration, an African American member shared her own research on patterns of "aversive racism," and Pastor Ken challenged members to pay attention to the ways they are ignoring the suf-fering of others by refusing to look seriously at the subtle ways they perpetuate racial inequality. Following up on the guest speaker, Pastor Ken told the con-gregation, "Just because in this setting we happen to be in the majority, you have these other settings where you know exactly what it feels like to be mar-ginal or invisible or whatever. And so, it's like 'shame on us because we should know better.'" Few Sunday morning services at Evergreen deal with racial is-sues as directly as this one, but the reconciliation theme is often woven into the content of the service in some fashion.

From crafting inclusive mission statements to appointing trustees and vary-ing worship styles, churches can institutionalize inclusivity within their leader-ship, programming, and corporate rituals. These concrete actions are observ-able and in some sense measurable, but they can only go so far in creating a sense of welcome and acceptance. If individual members are not willing to cross ethnic boundaries to form bonds of identity and caring, the church will have difficulty drawing members from outside the dominant ethnic group. Given the tendency of people to form social bonds along ethnic lines, we should expect to see this pattern replicated in churches unless intentional efforts are made to counteract it.

Strategies of Inclusion

In this chapter I have described the multiethnic church as an institution in which people choose to cross ethnic boundaries to form a group in which everyone feels welcomed and affirmed as individuals as well as part of a shared community. When ethnic boundaries are crossed, what happens to ethnic identity? There is clearly a wide array of strategies churches can use to frame the salience of ethnic identity in the multiethnic church. If we look at the way institutions talk about and act on their commitment to ethnic diversity in institutional structures, at least four strategies are apparent. Some churches ignore ethnic differences altogether, as in the color-blind approach, and impose the dominant group's culture on the church leadership style, program themes, and corporate worship. Others emphasize ethnic diversity publicly as a stated value but fail to institutionalize it in church structures, or conversely institutionalize diversity in structures without making it part of their public values. A fourth alternative is to insist on diversity of ethnic expression in every aspect of the institution. These four strategies for framing the salience of ethnicity in the congregation are represented as ideal-types in Table 4.1.

As with any typology, these categories do not correspond perfectly to the way real churches are grappling with the question of how to frame ethnic identity in their congregation. For example, is Evergreen monocultural or multicultural in its church structures? As an Asian-feeling church with a gospel choir, Evergreen is clearly moving toward the multicultural model, but it is has not yet reached it. The issue of whether ethnic diversity is acknowledged at Evergreen is much clearer. Evergreen is color-conscious, but this term fails to capture the

TABLE 4.1 Salience of Ethnic Identity in Church Culture

	Ethnicity is ignored	Ethnicity is acknowledged
Dominant culture apparent in church structures	Color-blind, monocultural, multiethnic congregation	Color-conscious, monocultural, multiethnic congregation
Multiple cultures apparent in church structures	Color-blind, multicultural, multiethnic congregation	Color-conscious, multicultural, multiethnic congregation

degree to which Evergreeners value ethnicity. Much more than being conscious of the ethnic differences among them, this congregation welcomes diversity and is striving to become more inclusive. Perhaps the best way to grasp the extent to which ethnicity matters at Evergreen is to compare its approach with the way ethnicity is framed within a color-blind, monocultural multiethnic church. Early in my interviews at Evergreen, I learned about such a church, Mosaic, which is also located in Los Angeles. Mosaic is also very popular with young evangelicals, and has recently been the subject of an excellent book by sociologist Gerardo Marti.[20] Despite the many similarities between these two churches, there is an ideological gulf separating the ways each one frames and works toward greater diversity.

Ethnic Transcendence

Before Gerardo Marti published his sociological study of Mosaic in 2005, the church's pastor, Erwin McManus, had already put Mosaic on the evangelical map with his book *An Unstoppable Force: Daring to Become the Church God Had in Mind.*[21] This book strongly criticizes churches that are too comfortable. McManus writes, "The church became a refuge from the world rather than a force in the world. Predictability and stability became dominant themes. The cultural environment became comfortable, and the gospel shifted from a church 'on mission' to a church that supported missions."[22] In evangelical circles, Mosaic is admired not only for its ethnic diversity but also for its innovative worship services, which attract a weekly attendance of fourteen hundred people with an average age of twenty-six, and missional focus.[23] With a membership that is one-third Asian, one-third Latino, and one-third Anglo, Mosaic has also been noted as one of the most diverse churches in the country.[24] Marti undertook an ethnographic study of Mosaic to learn how a church formed in the mid-twentieth century by White Southern Baptists came to be a leading model of a vibrant, multiethnic church. Surprisingly, he found that diversity is not an important aspect of the Mosaic culture and is instead purposely obscured.

Like the young adults described in chapter 3, Mosaic members have very fluid ethnic identities. The church attracts young people who grew up in suburban, Anglo neighborhoods and are part of the "middle-of-the-road, generalized American culture." They think of themselves as Americans or hyphenated Americans and have little competency in their ancestral cultures. According to Marti, Mosaic functions as an "ethnic haven," a refuge for second and third generation "ethnics" escaping ethnic entrapment. Instead of reaching out to immigrants, like the large Latino immigrant population in the surrounding neighborhoods, Mosaic appeals to young people with weak ethnic ties. McManus refers to this as the "principle of the half-step," a term that derives from the field of missiology.[25] Marti explains the principle: "Instead of looking at the most ethnically distant person to reach, church leaders should target ethnics that are only a 'half-step' removed."[26] Mosaic does not entirely ignore ethnic identity; rather it is "co-opted or renegotiated under the guidance of the charismatic leadership of Mosaic."[27] Church leaders purposely manipulate the presentation of their own ethnic identity in order to form connections with potential followers and gain their trust before actively "reconstructing" the malleable identity of these young adults into a new shared identity as dedicated followers of Jesus Christ. Marti calls this process of reconstructing identity "ethnic transcendence" because the divisive aspects of ethnic identity are transcended through shared commitment to Christ.

Ethnic transcendence is, in some sense, built into the evangelical identity through the conversion experience. By being "born again" one takes on a Christian identity as primary, but what this means in terms of the continuing significance of ethnic identity varies among evangelical Christians. For example, InterVarsity staff in Los Angeles have made ethnic identity development a critical part of the three-stranded rope of racial reconciliation. In this case, ethnic identity is affirmed through its relationship to Christian identity.[28] In other evangelical settings, ethnic identity is not only ignored but actively demonized. Russell Jeung writes, in his study of evangelical pan-Asian churches:

> One's Asian American background is more of a negative past from which one has to be healed and a culture that needs to be transformed. By categorizing ethnic traditions and values as, at worst, 'satanically inspired' and, at best, 'unhealthy patterns,' Asian American pan-ethnic congregations discard cultural resources and experiences that might make them distinct from other evangelical Christians.[29]

Mosaic's approach to ethnic transcendence is not nearly this extreme. According to Marti, because it is assumed that the young people who come to Mosaic already value diversity, it does not need to be explicitly stated by church staff. Members often point to the multiethnic makeup of the church as its most appealing feature. Ethnic differences are not demonized here, and they are acknowledged in private conversations, but they are not central to the identity of Mosaic members nor to the congregational culture as a whole.

Marti suggests that we think of Mosaic as multiethnic and monocultural. Its singular culture reflects the White popular culture of middle-class American youth. To say that Mosaic embraces popular culture is an understatement: through its affinity with the Hollywood entertainment industry, Mosaic promotes artistic innovation and the use of media technologies as tools for Christianizing popular culture from within. For the young adults at Mosaic, their shared identification with American pop culture is coextensive with their shared identification as evangelical Christians. Marti concludes that to the extent that White popular culture appeals across ethnic boundaries among young adults, Mosaic is naturally multiethnic, though remarkably homogeneous because it attracts a niche population of educated, middle class, Generation Y, half-step ethnics with a passion for popular culture.

Ethnic transcendence as a strategy for creating a unified, focused congregation is a direct application of the color-blind logic that ethnic differences are ultimately inconsequential for God's eternal plan. Though Emerson and Smith found this color-blind approach prevalent among White evangelicals, it is clear from the successful growth of Mosaic that it also appeals to some Asian American, Latino, and African American evangelicals. The ethnic transcendence strategy attracts those who believe racism can best be overcome by treating people as people. Because ethnic identity is transcended at Mosaic, there is no attempt to institutionalize diversity in church structures. It is presumed that authority and power are equally available to everyone in the congregation, so no special attention is given to diversifying leadership roles. Members are expected to form friendships across ethnic boundaries naturally, without needing any special encouragement to do so. Even without efforts to intentionally overcome these historical social barriers, Marti observes that there is a great deal of diversity and interaction across ethnic groups, at both the leadership and friendship levels.

Mosaic is by all accounts a very successful multiethnic church, yet there is something incongruous about calling it multiethnic; while intentionally inclusive of people as individuals, Mosaic is not inclusive of their ethnic identity. To the extent that ethnic differences are ignored as irrelevant, it is also difficult to see Mosaic as a community in which individuals intentionally cross ethnic divides. While Mosaic certainly promotes acceptance of all members regardless of ethnicity, acceptance is predicated on a framework that denies the social and spiritual significance of ethnic identity. In practice, the members of Mosaic must negotiate ethnic boundaries that in theory are not supposed to exist.

Because attention to ethnic difference is viewed as divisive at Mosaic, ethnic dynamics, racism, and prejudice of all forms are not dealt with openly. Penny Becker noted a similar silencing in her study of two multiracial churches in the Chicago area: "Political discourse, understood as discourse that takes for granted that there are different subgroups with opposing interests, is defined as 'hurtful' here, and those who engage in it are actively sanctioned."[30] Pastor McManus has been intentional about steering clear of this link between multicultural discourse and politics: "Being multicultural isn't our focus. When you make that your agenda you get people with a political agenda."[31] Like those with strong ethnic ties, people with political agendas, including the pursuit of racial reconciliation understood in terms of social justice, will find little support for these commitments at Mosaic.

What is fascinating about Mosaic and other churches in Los Angeles that use this strategy, such as Faith Community Church and Oasis, is that they are attracting a more diverse membership than churches that are intentionally striving to be multiethnic.[32] Much of the literature on multiethnic church development insists that churches must be intentional about diversity to succeed in the endeavor, but Mosaic is a flourishing color-blind, monocultural congregation. Marti concludes from his study of Mosaic's success that intentionally seeking diversity is a poor strategy for gaining it.. He argues that Mosaic's strategy of "ethnic transcendence," coupled with the embrace of popular culture, the arts, and innovation, will be a more effective means for predominantly Caucasian churches to achieve diversity.[33]

As prevalent as color-blind attitudes may be among evangelical Christians, they are not universal, and the ethnic transcendence strategy does not appeal to all evangelicals. Obviously, immigrants to the United States strongly prefer ethnic churches that maintain and replicate ethnicity. But there are many evangelicals for whom ethnicity still matters—personally, as part of their own ethnic identity, culturally, as an exciting dimension of urban life, or socially, as an undeniable reality in the processes of racialization. For these evangelicals, Mosaic's ethnic transcendence approach is unsatisfying and counterproductive. Marti tells the story of a young African American woman at Mosaic who was also active in a para-church organization committed to racial reconciliation. She explained to Marti that she was leaving Mosaic because it was, in her view, a White evangelical church emphasizing values incompatible with the African American experience and because she found the church's unwillingness to "work with broader cultural issues" undermined its ability to work toward racial reconciliation.[34] I spoke with several young people at Evergreen who had similarly tried out Mosaic and found its refusal to engage publicly in diversity issues both personally stifling and inimical to the goals of racial reconciliation.

Ethnic Inclusion

Multiethnic churches that choose the alternative course of acknowledging and affirming ethnic identity use what I call an ethnic inclusion strategy. Some churches take this affirmation a step further and "celebrate diversity," but I rarely heard this phrase used at Evergreen. While this no doubt reflects the negative association of this phrase with multiculturalism, it is also indicative of the strong sense at Evergreen that it is hard work to form an ethnically inclusive church. This is a theme that runs throughout Pastor Ken's teaching on racial reconciliation and has become part of the members' attitudes toward their mission. Instead of celebrating diversity, Evergreeners speak of the value of diversity and of being proud of their ethnic heritage. To be sure, this valuation of ethnicity occurs within an evangelical theology that privileges Christian identity, but unlike evangelical churches that frame ethnic and Christian identity as competing alliances, Evergreen affirms ethnic differences as part of God's eternal plan for humankind.

Like Mosaic, Evergreen attracts a diverse cohort of young people, as well as people of multiethnic heritage and those in mixed marriages. Many InterVarsity graduates try out both churches and may even bounce between the two for a while before choosing one. Both churches appeal to young people with their charismatic pastors, engagement with popular culture, and friendly people. It does not take long, however, for the differences in how they frame and institutionalize diversity to become apparent. Those who choose Evergreen over Mosaic do so because diversity is publicly valued and affirmed and the church is making efforts to move from its pan-Asian culture to become (more) multicultural as it institutionalizes this value in church leadership, programming, and corporate worship. Put more simply, they prefer Evergreen because it is possible to talk about diversity issues there, while Mosaic's ethnic transcendence strategy forecloses such conversations.

While Evergreen's racial reconciliation vision is certainly not framed as political, the way ethnicity and diversity are recognized allows for serious conversations on social issues, such as racial profiling after the 9/11 attacks. It is important to recall, though, that some Evergreeners were not happy with this attention to social issues and would rather not see so much emphasis put on racial reconciliation. Likewise, I expect there are those at Mosaic who are not happy with the lack of attention to diversity issues. As with any church, some people are attracted to Evergreen and Mosaic regardless of the stated church goals or the efforts of the leadership to shape a particular congregational culture. It will be fascinating to watch Mosaic and Evergreen develop in the next few years. Both churches are thriving and show a promising future, as they have found target audiences attracted to their very divergent approaches to the multiethnic church.

Listening to Christians in Los Angeles and around the country talk about their desire to be part of a multiethnic church, I found it clear that they are not all picturing the same thing, even if they are working with the same Bible. One thing all multiethnic churches have in common is that they are engaged with the question of how to frame diversity and inclusivity in their discourses, their interactions, and their institutional structures. There are many churches grappling with diversity that do not, for one reason or another, fit my definition of the multiethnic church as an inclusive, ethnically diverse community, and the reader interested in the various structures of ethnically diverse churches will find a comparison of three common forms (the space-sharing church, the multilingual church, and the pan-ethnic church) in Appendix B.

In talking with pastors and scholars over the last three years about multiethnic churches, I have been struck by how high the standards, or rather expectations, for this new kind of church are. I struggled a great deal with the question of whether I should call Evergreen a multiethnic church before realizing that qualifying it as "becoming multiethnic"—the way that Evergreeners themselves do—makes a good deal of sense, considering where the original vision comes from. Imagined through the lens of the New Testament, the multiethnic church is an ideal community, and because it is an ideal that will not be achieved until the Second Coming of Christ, real churches will always fall short. Evergreeners may never feel that their church is *truly* multiethnic, but that does not stop them from trying to embody this ideal within existing institutional structures.

I have settled on describing Evergreen as an Asian-majority, multiethnic church with a desire to become even more diverse and even more inclusive of diversity. That so many non-Asian Christians are coming to Evergreen, despite an apathy or even resistance toward the changing identity of the church on the part of some established members, speaks volumes to the potential for multiethnic church growth in Los Angeles. At some point, Evergreen may no longer look and feel like an Asian American church, just as at some point Pastor Ken's family may no longer look and feel Asian to his parents and siblings. Until then, it will continue to be in a state of transition, moving away from its Asian American roots to become a truly multiethnic church.

Many Evergreeners believe that becoming a multiethnic church is simply a matter of gaining a critical mass of non-Asians. They assume that if they are surrounded by enough of their co-ethnics, Whites, Blacks, and Latinos will feel comfortable at Evergreen and continue to grow in numbers. They assume that the church's institutional structures, such as the paid staff, will naturally change to reflect the growing ethnic diversity of its membership. The problem with these assumptions is that they ignore the power those currently in the majority group hold in shaping the congregation's future and the very real conflicts that arise in a multiethnic setting. Those in the majority, the owners of the corporate culture, as Pastor Ken calls them, can hinder or advance Evergreen's vision, at both an institutional level and an individual level, by the ways they relate to one another. The next chapter turns to this personal dynamic and examines the areas of tension that individual Evergreeners have encountered as the church has grown increasingly diverse.

5

The Dividing Lines

People call the office and want to know if non-Asians come to
our church because they really want their children to marry an Asian.
—Evergreen staff member

Like all churches, Evergreen Baptist Church has its share of conflicts
and areas of tension. Members disagree over what to spend money
on and what kind of ministry programs to offer. Older members
want more traditional hymns, while the young people think the music is out of date. These are the areas in which sociologists expect to
find congregational conflicts, and Evergreen is no exception. However, in addition to the typical money and worship wars that churches
experience, Evergreen must also deal with conflicts that arise from
its efforts to embody racial reconciliation. In the last chapter, we saw
that institutionalizing inclusion is a common arena for conflict in
multiethnic churches, and we looked at how Evergreen has handled
these issues. Here I focus on what Evergreeners themselves identify
as the areas of ethnic tension. These "disconnective points," as one of
Evergreen's pastors calls them, make it difficult for people to feel that
they are part of a unified community. Not only do disconnective
points make it hard to create a sense of community, but they can also
form fault lines that can, under certain circumstances, erupt into
public conflict.

Fault Lines: Communication, Food, and Family

Evergreen members do not, for the most part, like to talk about the tensions at their church. This is not unusual; people are often reluctant to "air their dirty laundry" in front of strangers, and churchgoers in particular do not like to talk about conflicts in the house of God. With a little prodding, and some help from forthcoming members, I did uncover some areas of tensions at Evergreen that are attributed to its multiethnic makeup. Matters of communication, food, and marriage came up most frequently as a source of disconnective points caused by cultural barriers. The presence of these fault lines is indicative of how strongly many members at Evergreen value their ethnicity. Behind their concerns about food, communication, and marriage is the keen desire to hold on to who they are and to resist assimilation. Churches that use an ethnic transcendence strategy avoid conflicts that arise around disconnective points by encouraging members to discard ethnic commitments. Because Evergreeners value ethnicity so highly, they are trying to find a way to be multiethnic without effacing or undermining ethnic differences.

Communication

Samuel, a Japanese American assistant pastor at Evergreen, explained to me what he meant by "disconnective points" by using language as an example. When people speak in their native languages, it cuts others off. Multilingual churches face this problem every day, but it is a new problem for Evergreen, which has been an English-speaking congregation since the mid-1940s.[1] The number of foreign-born members has increased sharply since the 1997 hive, as has the number of those born in the United States to immigrants.[2] It is a mystery to the church staff why immigrants are attracted to Evergreen, since the church has made no effort to target this group.

One consequence of this influx of recent immigrants is that more members speak English as their second language and prefer to converse socially in their family language. Even when used in private conversation, this behavior can feel exclusive to those nearby. Samuel thinks that the increasing tendency of Chinese American Evergreeners to speak in Chinese is a serious problem: "As soon as they hear Chinese or you hear people talking Chinese into a cell phone, those are points where people feel disconnected. . . . However, if we're all speaking English, it really doesn't matter if you're Hispanic, Asian, White, Black; I'm still connected there some way through the language." The common ground at Evergreen has always been "Americanness," according to Samuel, and when people hold strongly to their own culture, it undermines the fabric of the church.

The way language is used in church events, such as the worship service, also creates disconnective points. When the church saw an increase in Chinese American members in the 1980s, the pastors had to be more sensitive to the ways in which the content of their sermons assumed a Japanese American audience. Two ways to avoid potentially excluding listeners are to rely on "American pop culture" as the lingua franca, or to provide more explanations whenever reference is made to a less-familiar culture. Evergreen's pastors have done some of both. Pastor Ken says that in their sermons pastors try to give a quick explanation when using cultural references that are not widely recognized, but at the services I attended there were frequent references that would be unfamiliar to many non-Asians—and few explanations.

Humor, an important part of the Evergreen culture, is not amenable to explanations. Jokes about Jet Li or Orange County Asians, for example, lose their punch when picked apart. For someone unfamiliar with Asian America, it would be easy to feel left out or even offended by these "inside" jokes. Samuel remarked, "I bring my friends to church and they feel uncomfortable when they hear all these Asian terms and they get upset when they hear some of those jokes." To appreciate the worship services at Evergreen one does not have to be Asian American, but one does have to be Asian American–literate or willing to learn. Not surprisingly, the vast majority of the non-Asians who have made Evergreen their home have prior exposure to Asian American culture through friendships or missionary work.

How people communicate has been just as much a source of tension at Evergreen as what they communicate. When it became a Japanese-Chinese church in the 1980s, members had to learn to work through their different styles of communicating and different expectations about how things should be done. Samuel recalled his first encounter with this issue:

> I remember the first time going to a Chinese restaurant and the guy started just yelling at the waiter and I said, "What are you guys doing, why don't you ease up on the guy?" They go, "Oh that's just the way we talk to them." Or when the food came they were passing it on the lazy Susan and chopsticks are going all over the place and I'm sitting here thinking *aren't you going to save some for everybody else?* and then the reply I got was "you snooze, you lose!" You know Chinese culture is a lot more up-front and straightforward than the Japanese culture.

Both Japanese and Chinese American members spoke of how direct and assertive the Chinese culture is in contrast to the Japanese concern for showing respect and avoiding conflict, and these assumptions were often used to explain why so many leadership positions are filled with Chinese American members. Regardless of the validity of these cultural stereotypes, the frequency with which I heard members talk about the conflicting cultural styles suggests that they have become a paradigmatic example of cultural conflict at Evergreen.

With the addition of members from an array of Asian as well as non-Asian cultures, the number of communication styles has multiplied. Still, tensions in this area continue to be framed in terms of direct versus indirect communication styles. One White woman explained her frustration with what she perceived as an Asian American cultural trait: "I mean if people were angry at you at this church, you wouldn't even know it anyway, because they are so indirect." While many multiethnic institutions address communication issues through what are called cross-cultural communication workshops or diversity training programs, Evergreen's leaders see little need for such intervention because these disconnective points have not erupted into public conflict. Individuals may feel "weird about things," as one person put it, but they do not make it a public issue. Nonetheless, concerns about communication styles are widespread and add to a sense of disconnection within the community.

Food Matters

Non-churchgoers may have a hard time understanding how significant food and communal eating are to the life of a church. People have even been known to choose a church based on the kind of refreshments served after the service. Eating together is a core activity of community-oriented churches. It falls into the broad category of "fellowship" activities, at which church members are supposed to form the bonds of caring and identity that are the basis of community life. Food makes the fellowship flow better, but, more important, shared eating, or commensality, takes on religious significance as a ritual of the congregation.

At the same time, food is also an important marker of ethnic identity and a vehicle for reproducing ethnicity in the next generation.[3] Food preferences can remain long after ancestral language has been forgotten; one senior member of Evergreen remarked, "I don't know why it is but the food continues. Isn't that strange? That's the one thing that just keeps going, keeps passing on. My grandchildren still eat rice for breakfast." Indeed, when I asked many of the younger members at Evergreen what their ethnic identity means to them, food was often the first thing mentioned. While eating together is normally a time of interpersonal bonding, communal eating in a multiethnic setting can become a divisive activity because of the strong link between ethnicity and food.

After hearing from a few members that food has been a source of ethnic tension, I began asking all the Evergreeners I interviewed whether food is a source of friction. Almost all of the Asian American members said no, and almost all of the non-Asian members said yes. For the latter group, there seem to be two related problems when it comes to eating at Evergreen. The first is that the food of choice is always Asian, usually Japanese or Chinese, and there is no give-and-take on this matter.[4] At church events and during those times when members go out for food fellowship together, there is little effort made to be inclusive of other food preferences. The second problem is that the food served is too "foreign" for some palates, making shared eating an unpleasant event and an example of what Samuel calls a disconnective point. Because one person's comfort food is another person's source of discomfort, finding common ground on which to encourage fellowship in a multiethnic church is quite tricky.

When groups of friends or working committees go out to eat or order takeout, someone always suggests Asian food. Samuel, who had a lot to say about food, explained the problems that arise: "Let's say you go to a Chinese banquet. The first thing they serve on the platter is jellyfish and all that stuff. And you know, how many other races would say, 'Oh yeah, let me try that stuff!'" Resistance to trying "foreign" foods is an experience most of us can relate to. For those who choose to join Evergreen, eating Asian food is clearly part of the package, as it was for Steve, a young White member:

> I didn't like most Asian food at all before I came to Evergreen. I think
> I realized if I want to socialize and get to know people I've obviously
> got to give that a chance, and now there are a lot of things that I really
> like. But there are still some things I—it's not that I can't handle
> them, but I don't prefer them. Like whenever my friends go out for
> Korean barbeque, I try to persuade them away from that.

Like Steve, those who want to eat something other than Asian cuisine have to convince the Asian-food-loving majority to try something new. They are often outvoted, but they can use the tenets of racial reconciliation theology to challenge those in the majority group to get out of their comfort zones. Steve has learned from his time at Evergreen that even as a White American he has a culture to be proud of and share. The one time he convinced his group of friends to try his kind of food, he took them to Señor Fish for fish burritos, which he assured me everyone loved.

Potlucks present even more of a challenge for food inclusion. It is easy for groups to find a variety of restaurants, but the food brought to potlucks is dependent on individuals, and people generally bring what they like to eat and what they think others will like to eat. There were neither Jell-O molds nor jellyfish at the three potlucks I attended. According to Samuel, people tend to bring things that are "in the middle," meaning they leave the chicken's feet at home. They bring dishes that will not be seen as too "way out," as one woman put it. For his part, Samuel brings burritos, because he says everyone likes them, and he openly declares how tired he is of Asian food. As with many areas of tension at Evergreen, frustration with the Asian dominance is rarely expressed this directly, but there was at least one occasion when food inclusion became a public issue.

In January 2002, the *Pasadena Star-News* published a story on the efforts of Asian churches to become more diverse. The article described a young mixed-ethnic couple who had joined Evergreen because of the church's commitment to racial reconciliation and related an incident that happened at a church gathering:

> Last June, [Karen] organized a church luncheon. A pastor suggested picnic food, and she contributed her black-bean salad. On the day of the lunch, [Karen] noticed her salad had barely been touched. A Chinese-American acquaintance, seeing her dismay, asked what she had made, and she explained. He had seen something like this before, in an "American" restaurant, he said. He tentatively tasted it and called others over. Soon everyone had politely tried a few bites. Mortified, [Karen] brought home three-quarters of the salad.[5]

Even those who insist there is no food tension at Evergreen have to answer to this potluck incident. In response to my questions about it, I learned that many Asian members were very surprised and hurt to read the story in the newspaper. They had no idea Karen did not feel completely accepted. The incident was even addressed in a Sunday sermon by one of the assistant pastors. As one woman recalls, the point of this sermon was "bringing out the hurt for the whole congregation and calling people to think beyond the whole Asian thing." Many in the majority group began to see that the dominance of Asian-American cultures might make it hard for non-Asians to feel at home at Evergreen.

Recognizing that food can be a source of exclusion and doing something about it are two different matters. As one longtime Japanese American member put it, "I could see how she would feel like that because her food wasn't accepted. But I guess to us it's just different. How do you solve something like that, and try to be more sensitive?" It had bothered this woman for some time that the Prime Timers group for seniors is made up almost entirely of Japanese American members. Since the potluck incident she has become more sensitive to how it might feel to be one of the few non-Japanese Prime Timers: "I'm just wondering how they feel because, for example, for our monthly breakfast we always have rice. I wonder how [they feel]. It's just so slanted toward Japanese things." While the food tensions at Evergreen have not erupted into anything equivalent to "worship wars," they do contribute to a sense that non-Asians are outsiders or visitors rather than full participants.

Some multiethnic churches avoid the potential divisiveness of fellowship events by avoiding all things ethnic. Helen Ebaugh and Janet Chafetz observed this strategy at two multilingual/multiethnic churches in Houston: "At none of these events is ethnic food served or ethnic music or dance performed."[6] Instead, the churches rely on what is described as "American" food and music, which supposedly serve as a neutral basis for ethnic inclusion. Churches may justify this practice on the grounds that "ethnic" food and music are divisive, but they are in fact imposing a White American ethnic culture on the congregation. In practice, Ebaugh and Chafetz found that this ethnic avoidance strategy (a logical extension of the color-blind strategy) is not successful. Events are poorly attended, and those who do attend still self-segregate along ethnic and linguistic lines. More important, the insistence that "American" culture serve as the common church culture has not been accepted by the minority members of these churches: "At the multi-ethnic Catholic church, where the Parish Board is dominated by Anglos, Filipino and other immigrant groups strongly resent the fact that they have been kept from providing ethnic foods for parishwide events, where hot dogs and other 'American' foods constitute the staples."[7] At Evergreen, there has never been an effort to discourage members from bringing the kind of foods they like to eat to church functions. Nor has there been an institutional effort to insist on "American" food. Given that Evergreeners have strong ties to their ethnic cultures, it is hard to imagine such a strategy working.

In keeping with its insistence that ethnicity matters, Evergreen encourages a cosmopolitan appreciation of cultural difference. This was stated explicitly in the Sunday sermon after the potluck incident was published in the newspaper. Members are encouraged to bring the kind of food they eat at home *and* to taste what others bring. Without this exchange, a potluck can become an isolating affair rather than a shared eating experience. Since the potluck incident there has been greater sensitivity to making eating a more inclusive experience, and perhaps a greater willingness to try unfamiliar dishes such as Karen's blackbean salad. But I heard from many non-Asian members that there is still not enough give-and-take when it comes to food choices. Until those in the majority take the initiative in broadening their food spectrum, fellowship will continue to be a point of disconnection for some Evergreeners.

Family: Drawing Lines in the Sand

Mixed marriages are a common sight at Evergreen and have been for many years.[8] Jack, a single, forty-year-old White member, believes that they are an exciting sign of God's grace:

> When you see a multiethnic family, when you're getting ties down to that level of closeness where your family members are coming from other races, that's representing a breakthrough not only in our own hearts, but at the bottom that reflects to the world around us that there's something different, that there's something going on that's transforming.

From a theological standpoint, mixed marriages and the families they create are a powerful sign of racial reconciliation, and resistance to particular ethnic matches has clear racist, not to mention un-Christian, overtones. Jack's positive interpretation is shared by the young adults at Evergreen, but it is not shared by many of their parents.

Mixed marriages may be an accepted fact of life in Southern California, but they are more dreaded than celebrated by parents at Evergreen. Sociologists look at mixed marriage rates as an indication of social acceptance and integration, but they are also interpreted as a sign of assimilation and loss of ethnic distinctiveness. Many parents fear that if their children marry someone outside their ethnic group (however that is defined) it will erode their cultural and family ties. At the same time, how can these parents insist on in-group marriage without appearing racist? For young people, the decision to marry someone outside of their ethnic group, or outside the boundaries of those their parents regard as acceptable mates, can feel like a choice between their parents' values and their own, between honoring ancestral culture and assimilating. Given the intensity of the issue, it is somewhat of an understatement to call it a "disconnective point." Of all the areas of ethnic tension at Evergreen, marriage is the one arena in which, as one White member put it, lines are still drawn in the sand.

Trying to gauge the level of resistance to mixed marriage at Evergreen is difficult for two reasons. First, it is not socially acceptable to be opposed to mixed marriage. While people were quick to tell me about others in the congregation who had strongly opposed their children's marrying outside their ethnic group, few owned up to such attitudes themselves. It may also be the case that those who agreed to be interviewed for this study were more favorably inclined toward mixed marriage than the majority of Evergreen members. A second reason mixed marriage is a difficult issue to examine at Evergreen is that it is very much a live issue in this community. People are actively struggling with it and in the process are unsure of their true feelings. While everyone at Evergreen seems to accept the idea of mixed marriage in the abstract, it is quite another matter for them to say it is okay for *my* child to marry *that* kind of person. This ambiguity is not just a challenge for researchers. Singles at Evergreen have a difficult time figuring out the dating scene, according to Jack: "Is this even an open thing or am I swimming in the wrong pond?" In light of the church's commitment to racial reconciliation, however, it has become increasingly difficult for members to justify their objections to mixed marriage.

Everyone at Evergreen knows someone or has heard of someone who was disowned by his of her parents over a marriage partner, and this kind of parental response to mixed marriage is considered extreme and unacceptable. Everyone also knows parents who would be very upset, even horrified, if their child entered into a mixed marriage. This attitude is considered understandable, but not something to be proud of because it does not reflect Christian values. Everyone knows too that most of the Asian parents at Evergreen have "preferences" when it comes to marriage partners for their children; these preferences are generally seen as reasonable and not the same as racial prejudice. For example, when I asked a young Asian American member what she thinks about parents who impose limitations on their children's choice of spouses, she replied: "That is up to everyone's preferences, but I think in general if we are thinking along those lines of diversifying, then those lines about marriage and interracial marriage should be pretty open as well. I won't say they are right or wrong. It is really preference."

Framing opposition to mixed marriage in terms of "preferences" is quite common at Evergreen. Many people attributed this distinction between prejudice and preference to Pastor Ken, who, I was told, had said that there is nothing wrong with having preferences. It is significant that this is what people took away from his message because, according to Ken, what he actually teaches on the subject is quite different:

> When I talk to parents and they are struggling with their preferences and feeling guilty about that, I say, "I don't think having a preference is automatically sinning because you start somewhere, and it's typically what you're comfortable with. However, what we're trying to do at this church is to teach you what's lurking behind some of those preferences, because when a real person walks in the door and you reject them flat out of hand, even though they're a Christian, simply by how they look, then you have to deal with the fact that actually it's a prejudice.

As a parent, Ken understands the desire to have one's children marry someone who will easily fit into the family. One member who was really struggling with this issue told Pastor Ken honestly: "When I stand over my babies at night and I imagine one of them walking in the door someday with that person, it's either Chinese or Japanese, and Christian." With a four-year-old daughter himself, Pastor Ken can relate to the inclination to imagine a future in-law as "our kind of people."

Ken challenges parents to "get real" about the possibility of mixed marriage, telling them that because they live in Southern California there is a good chance the person their child marries is not going to look the way they had imagined. He warns them that if they do not accept that person who walks through the door, their children will see their prejudice for what it is. This has been a hard teaching for many to accept; Ken knows at least one person who has not joined the church because of it, and others who have chosen to ignore the church's racial reconciliation stance when it comes to their own family. For example, one longtime member told me about a man who came to Evergreen to ensure that his daughter would marry a Chinese man, because the thought of her marrying outside the culture was so horrific to him.

Parents at Evergreen sometimes ignore the application of racial reconciliation to family life, but more often they reframe their concerns as preferences. Whether marriage preferences are explicitly stated or only hinted at, parents let their children know that some types of people are more acceptable than others. The boundaries of acceptability are variable and form a hierarchy of ethnic groups perceived as most compatible.[9] Parents prefer that their children marry within their ethnic group, (e.g., Japanese American), but will accept an in-law who is perceived as similar enough (e.g., Americanized Asian American). Darren, a longtime White member of Evergreen who is married to a Chinese American, has given a lot of thought to how marriage preferences work at Evergreen. He told me about a conversation with a young Asian American member who claimed that she would marry anyone: "I said, 'Does that include African Americans?' and she said, 'Well, I meant someone like us.' So they say 'anyone,' but they really mean other Asians, Caucasians, or similar groups, and of a certain socioeconomic background." Darren sees these preferences organized as concentric circles, with Americanized Japanese and Chinese Americans in the middle, then Japanese and Chinese immigrants, followed by Anglos. Much further from the center are Filipinos, Pacific Islanders, and South East Asians, and furthest from the center are Blacks and Latinos.[10] While the specific order of preferences may vary, the placement of Blacks and Latinos as the least desirable marriage partners does not.

What bothers Darren most about the way people at Evergreen talk about preferences is that "they're kind of clueless about the extent that their culture dominates their attitudes and motivates their thinking." I would add to his insight that there is little recognition at Evergreen that such preferences are not natural, but have been formed by the racialization patterns of White Americans. The racial preference hierarchy of many Evergreeners mirrors that of White Americans, with one important exception: Whites are not at the top. Single, White men are often surprised to find that they are not warmly embraced at Evergreen but rather looked at with suspicion under the assumption that they are only there to find an Asian wife.[11] If Evergreen is successful at attracting more Latino and Black members in the future, I would expect that these lines in the sand will be pushed more into public view, and it will be harder to justify them as merely benign preferences. At the same time, church members will have to wrestle with the fact that while resistance to a particular match reflects prejudice against an entire ethnic group, the desire for in-group marriage privileges one ethnic group over others. Yet the argument can be made that an in-group marriage is a way to honor parents, pass on culture, and resist assimilation—all laudable activities in a church that places a high value on ethnicity.

Reproducing Ethnicity

If mixed marriages are a sign of weak ethnic ties, it makes sense that people who strongly value their ethnic heritage would be most resistant to them. Sociologists note that resistance to mixed marriage is strongest among immigrants. Immigrant parents worry that an out-group marriage will mean the disappearance of their way of life. How will the grandchildren learn the language if it is not spoken at home? How will the family continue its cultural traditions if the grandchildren are not properly trained? Many Americans, including social scientists, believe these concerns will fade away for the American-born generations as they become increasingly assimilated to the new culture. But the Americanized Asian Americans at Evergreen continue to have a strong preference that their children marry someone perceived as culturally similar. While their ethnic ties are not nearly as strong as those of immigrants, they too want to pass their ethnic heritages to the next generation.

It can be perplexing for children who have been pushed to be American to also be told that they should marry "someone like us." One young woman named Shin told me that while she was growing up her parents told her not to eat Korean food or speak Korean in public, so it came as a surprise to learn that her father expects her to marry a Korean: "But he knows that I am not *that* Korean where I can only marry a Korean guy." She thinks it would be nice to find a Korean American like herself, "not too Korean, not too anything, just a little Korean, but I don't see that happening." Many of the young adults at Evergreen were raised with this double message: Be American in all areas of your

life except family. At least some parents recognize that this expectation is difficult to meet. One father told me that by sending his daughter to private schools
with few other Asians, she became so comfortable in White culture that she
thought she was one of them: "I don't know if I want to say it was my fault, but it
was. . . . She sees herself as some Californian blonde, blue-eyed girl. I mean she
looks in the mirror and she doesn't see this Chinese girl." Not surprisingly, his
daughter married a White man.

Some parents think joining an Asian American church can narrow the
field of potential mates for their children and make up for the years of intermin-
gling with non-Asians. A church staff member told me that people occasionally
call Evergreen to ask if non-Asians attend because they really want their children to marry Asians. Obviously, the church's efforts to become multiethnic
undermine this possibility. It follows that those especially concerned about
mixed marriage would not be supportive of the church's reconciliation mission, but I found little evidence for this kind of thinking at Evergreen, at least
not expressed publicly. It is one thing to have preferences and quite another to
suggest that institutions need to be segregated in order to assure a good match.
Parents at Evergreen may hold on to their "preferences" about whom their children will marry, but by bringing their children to a church that is no longer exclusively Asian they are knowingly taking their chances.

Mixed marriage is widely accepted by the young people at Evergreen, many
of whom date and marry cross-ethnically. This should not be taken as an indication that they do not care about their family's ethnic heritage. All of the young
people I spoke with firmly intend to pass their ethnicity on to the next generation, regardless of whom they marry. Ben is an interesting example to consider
because he, like many of the young people at Evergreen, sees himself as bicultural. At twenty-six, he speaks Cantonese adequately but identifies as Asian
rather than Chinese because he says he has assimilated into the Asian American melting pot. Even though his parents really want him to marry someone
Chinese, Ben thinks they have given up on his retaining "their type of Asian
culture" and accepted that their grandchildren will be "American," meaning
they will have little connection to Chinese culture. However, when I asked him
if there was anything from his ethnic heritage he would like to pass on to his
children, he replied:

> I am sure they will eat all sorts of crazy things for breakfast. I think
> they will be Asian American in terms of learning how to be very con-
> siderate and polite, that is real important to me, and a high value for
> education. I would like them to be able to take off their shoes when

they come inside the house. They will definitely learn chopsticks at an early age.

While Ben is not going to pass on his parents' "type of Asian culture," he has very concrete ideas about his own type of Asian culture.

I met many young adults at Evergreen who, like Ben, described themselves as assimilated, Americanized, or "diluted," but when they spoke about raising children, it became clear how important their ethnic heritage is to them. What ethnicity means to them is described in terms of values, such as respecting elders, rituals, such as celebrating Chinese New Year, and cultural practices, such as eating rice for breakfast. Eating rice for breakfast was mentioned repeatedly as an important indication of still being Asian. Since Anglo Americans do not generally eat rice for breakfast, it is a clear sign of not having assimilated completely. More important than any particular ethnic marker is the sense of being different, the sense that one has not been completely Americanized.

While parents may fear that a mixed marriage means their grandchildren will have no connection to their heritage, young adults at Evergreen are much more optimistic that their ethnicity, however they understand it, will survive a mixed marriage. This may be a reflection of their youthful naiveté, but it also reflects their upbringing in an age of multiculturalism in which ethnic pride is encouraged. Rebecca Kim writes in her study of Korean Americans at UCLA, "The pressure to conform to a presumably unified white majority has declined and students have more liberty to explore and express their ethnic identities."[12] For these young people, reproducing ethnicity is a matter of intention, like choosing to send the children to Chinese school or taking them to Japan with their grandparents. Ben's Latina girlfriend has a clear plan of how to raise their future children. They will be tricultural: Latin, Chinese, and then American. She explained, "The kids will get time with Grandma speaking Cantonese and Grandma speaking Spanish. I think we're definitely still connected to our roots and want to pass that on." Ben added that ideally they would spend part of their lives doing mission work in both China and a Spanish-speaking country.

Reproducing ethnicity for this generation of Evergreeners is made easier by the cultural richness of the area. In Los Angeles there are ample opportunities, such as museum exhibits and ethnic festivals, to learn about one's ethnic heritage. Parents can also turn to private organizations, such as the weekend Chinese school, that teach children language and culture—tasks that were traditional carried out by ethnic congregations. In addition to learning about their own ethnic heritage, young people expect that their children will be multiculturally literate. As one young Chinese father explained, "I'd like them to know they are Chinese, and it would be terrific if they could speak Chinese, but it would be terrific if they could speak Spanish too." Another Chinese American father told me that, in addition to knowing the richness of their own history, "I want them to have a very diverse group of friends. I want them to be comfortable in any setting." For this generation, the survival of ethnicity as they understand and value it is not threatened by surrounding diversity or even diversity within the nuclear family. Instead, ethnic pride and cosmopolitanism are presumed to be natural companions.

Being Ethnic in a Multiethnic Church

There is little doubt that ethnic churches are effective spaces for reproducing ethnicity. Immigrants to the United States have always formed ethnic churches to meet both religious and social needs. Ebaugh and Chafetz argue that "immigrant religious institutions provide the physical and social spaces in which those who share the same traditions, customs, and languages can reproduce many aspects of their native cultures for themselves and attempt to pass them on to their children."[13] Even as a pan-Asian church, Evergreen continued to serve this function to some extent by validating and strengthening a shared Asian American identity, as well as Japanese and Chinese American identities. Can Evergreen now, as a multiethnic church, also strengthen ethnic ties? In other words, is it possible to be ethnic in a multiethnic church, or does diversity necessarily undermine ethnicity?

It is widely assumed that ethnic ties are weakened in diverse contexts. As we saw in chapter 3, InterVarsity Christian Fellowship has struggled with this concern as it pursues the dual goals of ethnic identity development and multiethnic community. Many people point to the history of European immigration to the United States as evidence that assimilation is inevitable. What they often fail to realize is that European immigrants were pressured to assimilate to Anglo American culture by a wide array of institutions, including churches, that purposely denigrated their ethnic cultures.[14] Even in the current climate of multiculturalism, which supposedly celebrates diversity, strong cultural forces like the market economy and popular culture continue to undermine ethnic ties. The question remains, though, whether assimilation to the dominant group is inevitable in a multiethnic institution.

Peter Wagner, the Fuller Seminary theologian who popularized the homogeneous unit principle, maintains that those in the majority inevitably force their cultural ways upon those in the minority.[15] Cultural chauvinism and forced assimilation are often not intentional, but because the consequences for minority groups are disastrous, Wagner promotes ethnic-specific churches. In the case of Mosaic, which was described in chapter 4, White members are not in a position of numerical dominance, but the church has chosen to use the "American acculturated center" as the cultural norm for the congregation and is intentionally promoting assimilation through its ethnic transcendence strategy.[16] Few contemporary multiethnic churches have developed as explicit a program of Anglicization as Mosaic; however, churches that rely on a color-blind strategy are intentionally or unintentionally forcing members to conform to White American norms. To avoid the complex negotiations required in ethnically diverse settings, these churches reject things that are seen as ethnic-specific in favor of "American" things, like hot dogs, which are promoted as "non-ethnic." Discourse that acknowledges ethnic differences is actively discouraged in this context. As a result these multiethnic churches are intensifying the pressures to assimilate to Anglo American cultural norms that people of color experience in the larger social context. Gerardo Marti, who studied Mosaic in depth, insists that ethnicity is not buried or erased at Mosaic because its young, urban members already value ethnicity and diversity.[17] What would happen in a multiethnic church that publicly values ethnicity and institutionalizes this value? Would ethnic differences be inevitably eroded in a color-conscious, multicultural multiethnic church?

As we have seen in the case of Evergreen, not all multiethnic churches encourage members to discard their ethnic ties and conform to White America or the cultural ways of the congregation's majority group. Churches that use an ethnic inclusion strategy affirm and encourage ethnic ties. Through the incorporation of ethnic-specific references, traditions, food, music, and language, multiethnic churches can reproduce ethnicity, though much less intensely than in the ethnic church because the necessary time, energy, and resources must be divided among the many different ethnicities present in the community.

There is some evidence from ethnographic research on multiethnic churches that interaction with people of different ethnicities can serve to strengthen ethnic identity. Patricia Dorsey observed this in her study of a large multilingual/multiethnic Assembly of God church in Houston: "Ironically, the context of a multi-ethnic church functions to reinforce ethnic identity because members simultaneously experience their ethnically rooted differences and find others of the same ethnicity."[18] On a typical Sunday, the church Dorsey studied has twenty-five hundred worshippers from almost fifty different countries. Dorsey found that this tremendous diversity heightened individuals' awareness of their own ethnicity, as they came to understand themselves better in relation to others. Pastor Ken, likewise, contends that increasing diversity at Evergreen will reinforce ethnic identity by bringing to light taken-for-granted cultural practices.

This has happened in his own life, especially in his marriage to a Japanese American woman. Several White members told me that this has been their experience, too. It was not until they came to Evergreen that they realized they had a distinctive ethnic culture. But not everyone at Evergreen is convinced. One Asian member was quite skeptical: "That is true in certain circumstances, and certainly as you compare them the differences become evident, but generally speaking, the flip side of that is you tend to assimilate or dilute." This member does not share the optimism of Ken and many of the young adults at Evergreen that diversity actually strengthens individual ethnic identity.

Awareness of difference does not necessarily translate into strong ethnic ties. At the Houston church Dorsey studied, members were exposed to differences while simultaneously able to interact with co-ethnics. In such a large and diverse setting, members could form ethnic subgroups after services and talk in their native tongues over coffee. Such co-ethnic interaction certainly serves to strengthen ethnic ties in the multiethnic church, just as it does in the ethnic church, but it also has the potential to undermine cross-cultural interaction. Because Evergreen is not nearly as large or diverse as the church Dorsey studied, it lacks the critical mass of minority members necessary to form substantial ethnic subgroups. While this can certainly be seen in a positive light as evidence of integration, the end result is that Evergreen cannot serve to reproduce ethnicity as well as institutions that allow greater opportunity for co-ethnic community formation.

When Pastor Ken first articulated his vision of a multiethnic Evergreen, Asian American members feared the church would have to give up its Asian American culture. As we have seen in this chapter, such drastic changes have not happened. Evergreen still feels very much like an Asian church. It has neither incorporated new ethnic practices nor discouraged Asian American ones. But one can sense that change is on its way, as more non-Asians are challenging the Asian cultural dominance. One thing that everyone seems to agree on is that no matter how diverse the church gets, it will always honor in some way its Asian American roots. Ken hopes that at some point there will be no dominant culture at Evergreen, but this is far different from suggesting that Evergreen will come to resemble the acculturated American middle. Because Evergreen values ethnic identity, it will encourage individuals to bring their ethnicity into the church culture, ostensibly creating a multicultural church. This process of sharing ethnicity is not the same as ethnic reproduction, which occurs naturally in ethnically homogeneous communities, but it does serve as a counterforce to societal pressures to conform to the habitus of the White American culture.

As we saw in chapter 4, Evergreen does not put much emphasis on incorporating different ethnic cultures into church services or social events. Diversity is not celebrated here as much as it is valued and respected. The response to the potluck incident is a clear example of how Ken and other church leaders push Evergreeners to think more seriously about what it means to live out their shared value for diversity. How members choose to live out their own ethnicity is up to them. No one is required to perform ethnicity in specific ways. There is a great deal of flexibility in how ethnicity is expressed at Evergreen. Samuel is free to bring chili dogs whenever he gets tired of Asian food and still be fiercely proud of his Japanese American heritage. Shin likes the fact that at Evergreen she is not pressured to conform to cultural expectations of Korean femininity. She can be loud and assertive at Evergreen, at least among the young people. By validating a fluid, flexible, adhesive, situational ethnicity, Evergreen functions as a haven from ethnic entrapment, just as Mosaic does. The difference is that at Evergreen members are not trying to escape from their ethnic identity, just from pressures to perform ethnicity according to a given social script.

Evergreen appeals to people who value ethnicity. They do not necessarily have strong ethnic ties, but they consider such ties valuable and want to be in an environment that affirms them. People turned off by the color-blind discourse of other multiethnic churches come to Evergreen, where they can have it all: being ethnic in a multiethnic world. Among the cosmopolitan members there is a great deal of optimism that this is possible, and their schooling in a climate of multiculturalism encourages them to challenge the assimilation paradigm. Like reproducing ethnicity within a mixed-ethnic family, holding on to who you are is seen as a matter of intentionality. As one White member explained, "I think it's harder. You'd have to find other contexts in which to connect to people of your same cultural background." A multiethnic church is simply not able to reinforce any particular ethnicity as strongly as an ethnic church does, but young Evergreeners do not see their church as the sole or even primary institution for ethnic reproduction.

If Evergreen continues to insist that ethnicity matters, rather than trying to avoid ethnic tensions by imposing a supposedly neutral American culture, it will continue to face points of disconnection and division. The prevalence of disconnecting points would certainly tear a church apart if it were not for countervailing forces that bind it together. Even though I purposely looked for areas of tension at Evergreen, it was clear that there is a great deal that Evergreeners love about their church, from the challenging worship services to the warm fellowship. These have certainly helped Evergreen flourish as a multiethnic church, but more important than these attributes are the underlying appreciation and tolerance of difference that helps Evergreeners weather the challenges that arise in the multiethnic setting. To some extent, those who are attracted to Evergreen already have this cosmopolitan outlook, but Pastor Ken has also worked to create a congregational culture that nurtures this outlook and applauds the ability to cross ethnic divides.

As a multiethnic church, Evergreen is still in its "toddler stage," as one member put it. If and how this church completes the transition to an intentionally inclusive, ethnically diverse community will depend very much on who joins in the coming years. An increase in immigrants will undoubtedly intensify the already existing fault lines in matters of language, food, and family life. An increase in cosmopolitans, with their fluid sense of ethnic identity and enjoyment of cross-cultural experiences, will reduce these tensions. But how many are attracted to Evergreen will depend very much on how the Asian American majority receives them. The church cannot become multiethnic without both institutional and individual effort. Those who are in the culturally-comfortable majority do not have to wait until a critical mass of Latino, White, or Black members stage a dim sum revolt before trying a new kind of restaurant. I do not mean to minimize the symbolic importance of such a choice. For the Asian American majority, to give up their cultural comfort is to sacrifice the very thing that brought them to Evergreen in the first place. It is Pastor Ken's hope that all Evergreeners will take up this challenge and learn to live with some discomfort rather than run from it.

6

The Culture of Discomfort

It is a painful process, this laying down stuff, making cultural mistakes, being uncomfortable. This is really investing in someone.
—Evergreen member

There are multiethnic churches in which ethnic tensions erupt into
full-blown conflicts on a regular basis, but Evergreen is not one of
them. At times, ethnic differences make people feel disconnected
from each other and uncomfortable, and Evergreeners see the challenge of belonging to an ethnically-diverse church in terms of discomfort rather than conflict. Discomfort is a subtler problem than
tension or conflict, but it is a greater burden on church communities
than it first sounds. In the sociological literature, it is widely thought
that the primary reason people join a church is to satisfy basic needs
of meaning and belonging. The discomfort of the multiethnic church
makes it more difficult for these needs to be met. As sociologists
Brad Christerson and Michael Emerson have put it so simply, there
are real costs to diversity.[1] Multiethnic churches must work harder to
form a sense of community and to help those who feel disconnected
find a way to belong. With so many homogeneous churches to
choose from, the multiethnic church can only thrive if members are
willing to put up with these additional costs.

Given the costs of belonging to a multiethnic church—especially
one that openly addresses ethnic tensions—the obvious question is
why anyone would want to join such a church. What motivates people

to stay in a multiethnic church once they find how difficult it can be to work around disconnective points? In this chapter I examine the ways in which Evergreeners experience discomfort and weigh this against the benefits they receive from this church. Both the Asian majority members and those in the non-Asian minority give up some comfort and familiarity in a multiethnic church, but the brunt of this sacrifice falls on the non-Asian members who are displacing themselves ethnically, so I spend time in this chapter getting to know these boundary crossers and what motivates them. In the last section I examine how Pastor Ken's teaching on the hard things required of Christians helps individual members find purpose in this struggle. Ken often challenges Evergreeners to live with discomfort because there is no way to create redemptive communities without giving up the familiar ease that is found in a church made up of "our kind of people." By creating a "culture of discomfort," Pastor Ken turns on its head the very notion of church as a place of comfort and belonging.

The Costs of Diversity

Even though Evergreen still "feels Asian," as so many people put it, the new Evergreen is a much more culturally complex place than the pan-Asian Evergreen. The Asian majority may be the primary shapers of the corporate culture, but they are not untouched by the changing demographics. One of these changes has been the loss of comfort that comes from being among co-ethnics. As a pan-Asian church, Evergreen offered an opportunity to form social bonds with people who share similar life experiences as a racialized minority group and served as a safe haven from the negative stereotypes that marginalize Asian Americans as "perpetual foreigners."

One woman who had recently moved to Los Angeles from a Midwestern state told me she had been looking for an Asian church: "I just wanted to be in a place where I didn't have to explain what it meant to be Asian American. Where there is at least a category for it." The need to explain oneself to non-Asians can be, as another member put it, emotionally exhausting. Growing up, she hated having to explain to her White friends why she always had to ask her parents' permission for everything and why she was never allowed to attend sleepovers at friends' homes. Now, as an adult, she simply wants to be surrounded by people who understand and accept her: "It is just nice when you don't have to say anything and people understand you. People understand I had to go to Chinese school every Saturday in the morning, and when you know someone who has been through that pain it is just an unspoken connection that draws people together." This unspoken connection among co-ethnics is often expressed at Evergreen through humor. Jokes referring to Jet Li or karaoke are common in sermons and conversation, but in a multiethnic community they require explanations that diminish the enjoyment of sharing a taken-for-granted reality.

With more non-Asians around, those in the majority are increasingly required to step out of a comfortable Asian American haven. There are some multiethnic churches where people naturally form ethnic subgroups that buffer some of the awkwardness of cross-cultural exchange. At Evergreen, everyone is expected to be warm and friendly to newcomers and to be culturally sensitive, even to the point of putting oneself in uncomfortable situations. These expectations raise an anxiety-producing dilemma for those in the Asian American majority: too much attention to the non-Asian visitor can be perceived as tokenism, and the wrong kind of attention can have the unintended effect of making the minority member feel uncomfortable. On the other hand, treating non-Asians as "the same as us" can be perceived as a lack of cultural sensitivity and even as racial prejudice. In the end, there is no surefire way to make others feel at home, for the multiethnic setting is fraught with the potential to offend the very person one wants to welcome.

The expectation that those in the majority be continually sensitive to the experiences of those in the minority requires a good deal of effort. When these efforts to be inclusive are not recognized and appreciated, or, worse, if those who are trying hard to be inclusive are accused of prejudice, it is easy for resentment to build. In 2002, a brief burst of conflict brought these feelings to the surface. A young Black member announced through a church e-mail list that she was bringing her mother to the church for the first time and warned, according to the person who told me the story, that "nobody better talk bad to her or otherwise I'm going to be on your case." The implicit accusation that anyone at Evergreen would treat her mother badly was deeply offensive to church members, especially those Asian American leaders who had been trying so hard to create a church welcoming of all people. After a few more such e-mails, the pastors intervened and told her not to write any more. The man who told this story is a longtime Asian American member who takes the ministry of hospitality very seriously. He commented, "I really had a hard time with that because I just thought, here we are trying our best . . ."

Listening to this story, I caught a glimpse of how much is at stake for those in the majority. By opening their doors, they make themselves vulnerable to scrutiny and harsh criticism that strikes at a very personal level. Theologians

Charles Foster and Theodore Brelsford found in their study of three multiethnic churches in Atlanta that even with many successes a sense of fear and weariness is never far away.[2] The multiethnic experiment is a fragile one whose success is entirely dependent on the willingness of those involved to bear the costs of diversity.

Costs to the Minority

It should come as no surprise to the non-Asians who come to Evergreen that it is harder to fit in here than at a church of their co-ethnics. From the moment they drive into the parking lot, they have stepped into an Asian American world in terms of numbers and the corporate culture of the church. For White members, Evergreen may be one of the few places where they experience life as a minority. One White woman told me how hard it was for her to feel at home here in the beginning: "I just felt that everything I did was really loud and big. It was hard. I feel like I'm sticking out." The non-Asians who choose to make Evergreen their faith community find some way to fit in, as this woman eventually did, but that does not mean they ever feel entirely at home.

Those in the minority group face the problem of being treated like perpetual visitors. A White man who had been at Evergreen for more than twenty years spoke about how much it bothers him to be treated like a guest in his own church. A much newer Asian member has repeatedly said to him how glad he was to have him at their church: "He would just make it sound like it's his culture's church and I'm a guest here." After so many years of contributing to this church, he wonders when he will stop being treated like an outsider. Other members shared similar experiences. Jill has experienced many years of feeling like an outsider. As a White woman, she originally came to Evergreen with an Asian friend so "it wouldn't be so weird," but after coming for several years people would still ask her if she was new. Her Asian friend, who had no trouble fitting in, joked that "it was cool because people would always think I am bringing a visitor." When people seem to have trouble getting to know them as individuals, it is even more difficult for the newcomers to feel a sense of belonging. According to Jill, Asian members often confuse her with other White women who attend. "They always think I am Karen, even though I'm like five inches taller than she is." It was not until she began taking on leadership roles that Jill stopped being an unknown entity and began to feel like an insider.

The 25 percent of the church who are not Asian American find themselves, in Samuel's words, "being drawn into the Asian world rather than meeting in the middle." Minority members are expected to learn about Chinese and Japanese

cultures but are rarely asked about their own. My interview with an older Hispanic woman is one example out of many:

GARCES-FOLEY   Do people at Evergreen ever ask you about your ethnic
heritage as a Hispanic?

EVERGREENER   I've never been asked.

GARCES-FOLEY   Do you wish they would ask you?

EVERGREENER   No. It doesn't bother me one way or the other.

GARCES-FOLEY   Do you think in terms of making the church more diverse, say in attracting more Hispanics, that it would be important for
people to try and learn about Hispanic cultures?

EVERGREENER   I think it would help, certainly . . . I think it would really
help if more people learned about the other races.

Given the rhetoric of "valuing ethnicity" at Evergreen, I found it surprising to
hear from several non-Asian members that no one had ever asked them about
their ethnic heritage. Even more remarkable to me is how accepting minority
members are of this lack of interest. John, a young bicultural member, told me,
"I would like them to ask more, but in a multiethnic Asian church they pretty
much know each other's culture. Folks aren't insensitive. It just doesn't cross
their minds to ask." This is quite different from his experience in InterVarsity as
a UCLA student; there, "folks were constantly interested in learning about someone else's culture in a very real way." Being in the minority at Evergreen means
being an unknown entity. While many minority members accept this reality, they
also acknowledge that more genuine cultural exchange would help non-Asians
feel more welcome and would lead to greater numbers of non-Asians joining.

From time to time, the church leadership does try to foster greater cultural
awareness. through events such as Cultural Day described in chapter 4 as an
example of church programming tied to the inclusive vision. The idea of Cultural Day is to celebrate cultures all over the world, and many of the Asian members mentioned this event as an example of what Evergreen is doing to become
more culturally informed. In contrast, several non-Asians mentioned Cultural
Day as an example of how little cultural awareness there is at Evergreen. Karen,
a White woman mentioned earlier, was so upset when she saw the plans for the
the event that she took her concerns to the organizers. The problem, she said,
was that the booths on various Asian cultures were terrific, but little thought
had gone into representing non-Asian cultures. Karen was especially offended
by the Africa booth, which centered on making animal masks. She explained,
"We are summing up a whole continent by the animals who live there. Great,

this is really teaching our children a lot." After she had voiced these concerns, some changes were made to "even things out," but the animal masks remained. Since memories of Cultural Day continue to evoke disappointment among non-Asian members, it is not surprising that this event has yet to be repeated. Though the intentions were good, rather than creating a welcoming climate, the event made several minority members feel even more marginalized and brought into the open how little genuine cultural exchange is happening at Evergreen.

Because of the small numbers of Black and Latino members at Evergreen, there is a tendency to put them in the spotlight in a way that can feel like tokenism. An Asian man concerned with this problem noted, "I am friends with two African Americans at this church and I know that they are always getting their pictures taken for every single church bulletin. There will always be a photographer coming around them because I guess they want to show that we have one." Being among the very few Black or Latino members at Evergreen means carrying the burden of dispelling negative stereotypes. Mark, a Black man in his fifties, sees this as part of his mission at Evergreen: "One Black individual could give them a bad taste in their mouth or a bad flavor for other Blacks, and I am happy that I can show them we are all not like that so they won't stereotype." Marisol, a Latina woman in her sixties, told me that people at Evergreen assume that she was raised Catholic and that she only eats Mexican food. They are always asking her to make tamales, but they don't ask what she likes to eat. She says such stereotypes are harmless and brushes them off, but the fact that she mentioned them to me says a great deal. The lack of cultural awareness about Blacks and Latinos contributes to their sense of being invisible and not belonging.

It would be easier to be a minority at Evergreen if the majority members were more attuned to how hard it is to feel included as a non-Asian. As one woman put it, "Churches often don't realize the height of the hurdle that other cultures have to go through to fit in." The Asian members of Evergreen are largely unaware of the discomfort the non-Asians experience. This explains in part why the "potluck incident" came as such a surprise. Ken gave me his explanation for this lack of insight:

> For the people in the majority or used to being in the majority, who are the primary owners of the corporate identity and culture, I really don't think they spend a lot of time thinking about it because they don't have to. If you're the one in the minority that feels marginalized and undervalued and invisible, you spend a lot more time thinking about it because you're trying to find a place.

Indeed, the non-Asian members I interviewed had lots of suggestions for what could be done to make themselves and other non-Asians feel more at home at Evergreen, which we will look at in a moment. To some degree, however, the discomfort of being in the minority can never be entirely eliminated.

Brad Christerson and Michael Emerson argue that those in the minority group bear a disproportionate share of the costs of diversity because, with fewer co-ethnics in the church, forming social bonds requires more effort and more risk.[3] In other words, it takes much more work for those in the minority to reap the benefit of belonging, and the smaller the size of the minority group, the greater the work. While cross-ethnic relationships are plentiful at Evergreen, as we have seen, these relationships often lack the ease of co-ethnic relationships and are subject to frequent misunderstandings. Christerson and Emerson note that given this greater burden, minority members are more likely to leave, making multiethnic churches inherently more unstable than ethnic churches. Those in the minority leave not only because they have weaker ties to the church but also because there are alternative ethnic churches where their need for belonging would be more easily met.[4] Given these high costs, why do those in the minority group put themselves in this position? Why join a church where they never quite fit in, where people never completely understand them and are sometimes downright offensive?

To answer this question, Christerson and Emerson conducted an in-depth case study of a small, Filipino-majority, multiethnic church in Los Angeles County. They found that both majority and minority members named "the joy of diversity" as the greatest benefit of belonging to their church. Here is how a Hispanic member describes her experience: "It's a taste of heaven on earth to have people from all these different backgrounds worshipping together. I feel like my worship of God is so much more pure and authentic when I look up there and see all of the nations represented."[5] Christerson and Emerson were surprised to find that even members who experience high levels of frustration remain strongly committed to the church: "It seems that for many of the congregants of this church, the value they have placed on worshipping in a diverse congregation is so high that they have simply ruled out the option of returning to a homogeneous congregation, even when they recognize the greater benefits they would receive by doing so."[6]

As we have already seen, Evergreeners likewise have a high value for diversity, and some members do, in the words of Christerson and Emerson, venture across ethnic boundaries for enjoyment and novelty. However, there is strong sense at Evergreen that crossing ethnic boundaries is not a joy but a necessary part of accepting Jesus' call to discipleship. The ministry of racial reconciliation is recognized as hard work requiring sacrifices on the part of everyone. The motivations that bring people to Evergreen and keep them there reveal a more complex picture of how the costs and benefits of the multiethnic church are weighed.

The Boundary Crossers

Evergreen could not change from a pan-Asian church to a multiethnic one without the willingness of non-Asian to cross traditional ethnic boundaries and join their church. These boundary crossers have put their commitment to racial reconciliation, together with their cosmopolitan recognition, acceptance, and eager exploration of diversity, into action by choosing to be in the ethnic minority of their congregation. As we saw in chapter 3, many of these boundary crossers are young cosmopolitans who grew up in diverse settings and have been schooled in the ideology of multiculturalism. For these young people, homogeneous settings are uncomfortable. After having been in a diverse college environment, one young White man said he could not imagine saying, "Okay, well I'm just going to be in this church now that's all White. It just didn't feel right."

At Evergreen I met boundary crossers in every age group and ethnic group. I talked with several Asian American members committed to boundary crossing who are at Evergreen *despite* the fact that it is primarily Asian American and who are anxious for the church to become more diverse. One member described those I am calling boundary crossers in this way: "They're very cross-cultural in their perspective. They're either missionary sorts of people or just people that have a mindset of seeing themselves as part of a global community, a global church in particular, and commit to that." Having a "cross-cultural perspective" is a point of pride for many boundary crossers who not only enjoy diverse settings but also operate effectively in them. It is not an exaggeration to say that they delight in their ability to move easily between worlds. They like trying new things, learning about cultures, and eating all kinds of foods. Listening to boundary crossers talk about how they prefer diverse settings, I began to question whether homogeneous churches really do offer greater benefits, as Christerson and Emerson assume.

One of the benefits of attending Evergreen, which I heard from all the boundary crossers, is that it reflects the "real world" instead of offering an alternative to it. My conversation with Mark, the new African American member mentioned earlier, was very helpful in this regard. Mark first came to Evergreen after reading about it in the *Los Angeles Times*. He was already attending a multiethnic church in Los Angeles but wanted to see how Evergreen was doing things. He is most comfortable in diverse settings and wants his children, who are of Asian and African American parentage, to be as well: "I look for places to put them in a mixed environment and not isolate them in either Black, White, or Spanish or Asian. I like them to be exposed to what the world is. The world is a mixture. It is like a tree and the leaves are many colors. They are not just green, especially in autumn." Like many of the boundary crossers at Evergreen, Mark has a special connection to Asian culture. He studied martial arts for twelve years and has previously been married to an Asian woman. Though he grew up in a Black church, he joined the Marines to see the world and ever since cannot imagine being in anything but integrated churches. For Mark, living in a diverse world is often not a joy. He is all too aware of the racism his children will face, but rather than shelter them, he wants to teach them how to live in the real world.

For many boundary crossers, being cross-cultural people makes it difficult for them to be entirely at home in ethnically homogeneous settings. In Mark's case, he found the Black community too confining. As a conservative Republican, Mark is not comfortable in all-Black settings and especially does not like Black churches: "They will start dancing in the aisle and hands will start flailing or they will either smack you or you will pass out on the floor, and I am not into all that show. I am into quietness . . . I don't care for all the nonsense." Mark's estrangement from the Black church is more extreme than that of anyone else I spoke to. Ben, a young Asian man who had previously been attending a Black church, has this to say about himself and other boundary crossers: "We don't totally fit in with our own group because we really like being around people that are different than us, and that is just not common for people." Ben also thinks being a minority in a church makes it easier to do cross-cultural ministry, something he is very committed to: "I feel like there is something about being a minority at a church that frees you to invite people of all ethnicities to come, because you are kind of in the same boat of 'Well, there are certain cultural things that seem crazy to both of us.' "

In Christerson and Emerson's analysis of the costs of diversity, it is assumed that those who join a multiethnic church are giving up the meaning and belonging they could more easily experience in a church of their co-ethnics, but for many of the boundary crossers at Evergreen, no such alternative exists. Shin, a twenty-four-year-old member of Evergreen, is not sure where she belongs. While she was visiting Evergreen, she was also checking out Korean churches because she is a second generation Korean: "I don't necessarily want to be a part of one, but I can't ignore my sense of comfort level when I go to the church." In the end Shin chose Evergreen in the hope it will become more diverse, because "I don't feel one hundred percent comfortable either being surrounded by all Asians." For this woman it is not clear who her kind of people are. In a Korean church Shin feels her "unKoreanness," and in a White church she feels her "Koreanness." Christerson and Emerson assume a social context in which everyone belongs to a single ethnic group with a corresponding ethnic church, but for many Americans this is not the case. Ethnic churches have many benefits, especially for people of color, but they can also be stifling and restrictive, compelling some individuals to look for settings in which there is more freedom to be ethnic in their own way. For many at Evergreen, the option is not between a comfortable church and an uncomfortable one but choosing among churches that are all uncomfortable.

The prevalence of homogeneous churches has long been explained by the fact that people are most comfortable with their co-ethnics. Sociologists call this the homophily principle, but it can be most simply stated as "birds of a feather flock together." Not only ethnicity, but class, age, education, and profession are also strong factors in the formation of social bonds. Of course, individuals do form relationships across these boundaries, as in the case of mixed-ethnic marriages, but when we look at society at large these patterns of homophily are still quite strong. Given this social fact, I began to wonder if the boundary crossers at Evergreen are some strange group of misfits, since they actually prefer diverse settings and seek out cross-ethnic friendships. In fact, far from being misfits, they are part of a much larger shift in attitude toward ethnic diversity, which I have described as the emergence of a cosmopolitan ethos. Given their experiences in diverse settings and their exposure to multiculturalism, it makes sense that the basis on which they identify "their kind of people" has shifted. While ethnicity is not their primary basis for forming social bonds, other factors, such as class, age, professional status, and educational background, take precedence and still function as strong forces toward homogeneity. This explains why Evergreen has had much more success creating (in the words of the vision statement) montages of culture, than montages of classes or circumstances.

Because they do not feel entirely at ease in ethnically homogeneous settings or they prefer cross-cultural exchanges, boundary crossers look for alternative bases on which to form social connections, such as a shared value for diversity. That does not mean that they have abandoned their ethnic identities or turned their backs on their co-ethnics. At Mosaic, Gerardo Marti found that members were happy to participate in White American culture. Marisol, the Latina woman mentioned earlier, would much prefer a multicultural experience. Even though she does not cook Mexican food at home, she likes to bring tamales to potlucks at Evergreen because there is always someone who will try Mexican food for the first time. She also hopes that many more Latinos will come to the church. For her, and many others at Evergreen, the opportunity to build both co-ethnic and cross-ethnic friendships is the best of all possible worlds.

If homogeneous churches are not always comfortable, is it possible that heterogeneous churches are not always uncomfortable? I was told many times that everyone gets along so well at Evergreen because they are used to being in diverse settings. Evergreeners do appear to get along well for the most part, and even though disconnective points persist, members have avoided the kinds of conflicts that have seriously fragmented other multiethnic churches. I am skeptical of the claim that any multiethnic church is free of tension, given the inevitable existence of prejudice, ethnocentrism, and conflicting lifestyles. If such churches do exist, Evergreen is not one of them.

One thing that is apparent from this study is that the costs as well as the benefits of diversity are experienced differently by members depending on their values, interests, and skills for functioning in diverse contexts. It is clear that the boundary crossers at Evergreen greatly enjoy the cross-cultural aspect of the church. They are more skilled at crossing ethnic boundaries and can make friends more easily with all kinds of people. In fact, they will enjoy Evergreen much more when it becomes more diverse and no longer has a dominant Asian American culture. While Christerson and Emerson are correct that those in the minority group bare the brunt of the costs of diversity, it is also true that those who willingly put themselves in this situation usually possess cosmopolitan traits that go a long way in lessening their discomfort. It follows that multiethnic churches will grow most easily among cosmopolitan, boundary-crossing churchgoers, because they experience greater benefits and fewer costs in this setting. The challenge for the church trying to become multiethnic is how to attract those who want to be in diverse settings to a church that is not yet diverse.

Building a Critical Mass

Whenever Elena sees someone at Evergreen who looks Latino, she makes a special point of welcoming her or him: "I'm more friendly, more open, inclusive. I make a special effort. It's kind of like, you know, saying I'm here and it's okay, so you can be here too and be okay." With so few Latinos at Evergreen, she thinks this kind of outreach is the only way to build a critical mass. Everyone I spoke with had ideas about how the church could be more welcoming of non-Asians: more education, less talk, more talk, more Cultural Days, no more Cultural Days, more action, more confrontation, and more biblical teaching. Like Elena, many people believe it all comes down to hospitality. What is needed, I was told, is "some serious befriending." Every week, Elena notices a couple of Latino families who sit together at the front of the church, and she wishes someone in leadership would be more proactive in helping them make friendships in the larger community. Mark, the Black man in his fifties I described earlier, told me he has been the target of some serious befriending; he is invited out to brunch almost every time he comes to Evergreen, but he has yet to accept an offer.

White visitors do not need this special treatment, I was told by a few White members, because there is already a critical mass of White members. In fact, Jill predicts that White people are going to start flooding in because Evergreen is already very White-friendly. If the church is really going to become multiethnic, she says, facetiously of course, it should not let any more White people in and definitely not hire any more White staff. As it happened, when Pastor Ken did hire a new staff person in January 2004, he selected a White woman. This is a big step for Evergreen, but it may not be a step in the right direction, according to Jill, who fears that if the church becomes too comfortable as an Asian/White congregation, it will be unable to attract Latinos and Blacks. To become truly multiethnic, Evergreeners will have to make more serious efforts to reach these groups.

Out of the Church Comfort Zone

What if church is not supposed to be a place of comfort? What if church is the place where you "get out of your comfort zone" so you can better fulfill the Great Commission? This is Pastor Ken's challenge to the congregation. In the April 2004 church newsletter, he wrote that Evergreen was becoming a model twenty-first-century church, "from being a haven for comfortable, suburban, self-sustaining people to becoming those willingly drawn out of our comfort requirements in order to meet, love and serve Jesus in others."[7] "Get out of your comfort zone" is a popular phrase in evangelical circles today, just as it is in American popular culture in general. The concept derives originally from the work of Russian developmental psychologist Lev Vygotsky in the late nineteenth century, but the popular usage of the comfort zone discourse in recent decades is far removed from its origins in developmental psychology. Since the 1980s, "get out of your comfort zone" has become a stock phrase of evangelical discourse, though long before the 1980s Christians were exhorting one another to place Christian discipleship above cultural comfort. Among its wide range of applications, comfort zone discourse is used by evangelicals with regard to cross-cultural evangelism.

Applied to cross-cultural ministry, getting out of one's comfort zone means interacting with and, ideally, evangelizing persons with whom one would not normally relate. Pastors use the image of the comfort zone to encourage people to engage in missions and urban projects. When Ken talks about getting out of the comfort zone, it carries this same meaning; however, he also applies it to life at Evergreen by drawing attention to the ways that ambiguity and cultural dis-ease have shifted from outside the walls of the church to inside.[8] The kind of thinking that motivates missionaries to go to foreign lands and college students to spend summers in the inner city is now used to motivate church members to try new foods at potlucks. Other multiethnic pastors apply the comfort zone dis-course to their own churches; Pastor Dave Gibbons of the multiethnic New Song church in Orange County has actually coined the phrase "a theology of discomfort."[9] A step up in sophistication from talking about comfort zones, this theology provides a biblical basis for intentionally putting oneself in uncomfort-able situations in order to follow the Gospel. When this theology is applied to the multiethnic church, it turns on its head the idea that church is supposed to be a place of familiarity and comfort.

The theology of discomfort reframes the costs of the multiethnic church in light of the Gospel, imbuing even minor inconveniences with theological sig-nificance. The multiethnic church member is expected to embrace difference and to find religious growth in cross-cultural encounters, which are fraught with ambiguity and discomfort. In other words, the experience of discomfort becomes a primary source of faith development. At Evergreen, this reframing of discomfort has been very effective. In fact, there is so much talk about "get-ting out of comfort zones" at Evergreen that I began to think of the church as having a culture of discomfort. Many people explained they came to Evergreen because they were too comfortable at other churches, not just ethnically but also in terms of their commitments to social transformation. Others come seeking a comfortable Asian American church and find instead that being "pushed out of their comfort zones" is a good thing, a sign of Christian matu-rity. The theme of discomfort frames much of what happens at Evergreen, from volunteer work in Rosemead to a 2003 advent sermon series, "The Uncom-fortable Christmas." Evangelical churches are known for their smart packaging of religious themes, and Ken admits that there is some of that going on, but the basic message is one he firmly believes in: following God's call is going to bring some discomfort. He reminds members frequently of this, especially as a preface to sermons on controversial topics like racism at Evergreen: "We need to start having these uncomfortable situations because people are suffer-ing if we don't."

With so much talk about discomfort at Evergreen, I began to wonder if the expectation is really that everyone at this church is going to feel uncomfortable all the time. Ken gave me a helpful clarification:

> We are not going to have no culture here. We are not going to have
> any predominant culture here. We want to be a redemptive culture

here. And so that means that maybe right now I don't like your food, but over time we've all learned to eat foods that at first we didn't like . . . I don't think the goal should be to make you 100 percent uncomfortable 100 percent of the time, because nobody can live like that, but it is trying to find comfort in what we're trying to do and then encouraging people to grow so that they make uncomfortable choices willfully.

The goal of the theology of discomfort is not to make everyone uncomfortable all of the time but to broaden the boundaries of what is perceived as comfortable. The hope is that everyone can learn to appreciate cross-cultural experiences and develop the skills that allow those experiences to flow more smoothly. Even difficult conversations about racism and ethnocentrism can become easier if people are committed to racial reconciliation. Since those in the minority group are already making uncomfortable choices willfully, this encouragement is really directed at the Asian American members. As the owners of the corporate culture at Evergreen, they are the ones who need to make some uncomfortable choices if the church is to become more inclusive of non-Asians. As for the boundary crossers, they have already wholeheartedly embraced the theology of discomfort.

On a Mission for the Lord

Most of the non-Asians who come to Evergreen have had prior cross-cultural experiences through InterVarsity, overseas or domestic missions, friendships and family, or attending churches in which they were in the minority. They had already committed themselves to bearing the costs of diversity for, in their words, the sake of the Gospel. This explains why they are willing to join a church in which, as one Asian member put it, "they do have to cross a couple of barriers or kind of jump through a couple of hoops in order to say, well, we're going to be part of this." When they do experience exclusion at Evergreen or are offended by something, it is not the joy of diversity that keeps them there but their sense of being called by God for this mission of reconciliation.

Jacob, whom we met in chapter 3, is a good example of a boundary crosser who is on a mission. He is passionate about racial reconciliation and believes racism can only be defeated by the cross. A recent college graduate, Jacob moved to Rosemead because of Evergreen. He is one of seven InterVarsity graduates who have formed an intentional Christian community, the Rosemead Neighbors, in partnership with Evergreen. Besides their paying jobs, the Rosemead Neighbors are involved in a number of service-related activities for at-risk youth, particularly immigrants.[10] As a person of mixed-ethnic heritage—Mexican, Spanish, Apache, Navajo, and Honduran—Jacob hopes his presence at Evergreen will help other people of color feel comfortable. As a multiracial person, he believes that racial reconciliation is God's mission for him. This strong sense of calling keeps him motivated when progress at Evergreen is slow. Knowing that racism is alive and well in Los Angeles, Jacob is not surprised that there are tensions at Evergreen. The issue of interracial dating affects him personally, since he would like to date a Chinese girl from the church but knows her parents would not approve. Jacob accepts her parents' rejection of him as understandable, given that they have not yet been convicted with the truth of racial reconciliation. Their rejection is simply part of the difficult mission God has given him.

The challenge of pursuing racial reconciliation and the challenge of living in a multiethnic church are themselves strong incentives for bearing the costs. As Christian Smith has argued persuasively in *American Evangelicalism*, evangelicals thrive under the perception that they are an embattled people with a strong sense of mission.[11] In the case of racial reconciliation, embattlement often comes from other evangelicals. These "scoffers," as Ken calls them in a 2004 newsletter article, claim that the multiethnic church will never work, or that it will only work through a color-blind approach. Strong convictions do not provide a protection against discouragement. Many Evergreeners told me that they reflect frequently on the progress or lack of progress at the church: am I having an impact here? Without signs of progress, or "bearing fruit," it is tempting to look for an easier place to do God's work. It can be tempting to leave Evergreen, not for a homogenous church, but for a church that is more receptive to the message of racial reconciliation, where their gifts would be put to better use. The temptation to give up is also present because, as one man explained, "Whenever you try to do something like that, spiritually speaking, the enemy is going to try to attack." The enemy in this case is Satan, whether in the form of "scoffers" or the allure of a church that appears to be having more success with racial reconciliation. By framing the costs of diversity in theological terms and stressing the worthiness of the struggle, boundary crossers imbue their burdens with theological significance and gain satisfaction from fulfilling their mission.

Having Fun with Diversity

Not everyone at Evergreen takes the theology of discomfort so seriously. Evergreen is a surprisingly light-hearted place. Before going into ministry, Ken wanted to be a stand-up comedian. He writes in the October 2003 newsletter,

"God has used my sense of humor as a preacher to disarm people for what He wants to say instead." Humor does have a disarming effect, and it can diffuse tensions that would otherwise build. Ken has used humor effectively to help the congregation deal with the discomfort of diversity. In his sermons he often shares stories of cultural miscues; at one sermon I heard, he recalled how awkward it had been as a boy to visit the homes of his White friends where the cultural norms were very different from what he was used to. When offered a drink, for example, he would refuse, expecting to be asked several times, as is the Chinese custom, and end up without a drink. Ken also shares funny stories from his own multiethnic family, which many in the congregation can personally relate to. Becker found humor to be an important aspect of the two multiracial churches she studied in Oak Park, Illinois. She writes, "Through sermons, as well as other forums, the pastor provides both an interpretive rationale for multicultural ministry and an opportunity for members to laugh good-naturedly at their own discomfort and find ways of moving beyond it before it becomes the basis for prolonged and painful conflict."[12] In his preaching, Ken models for the congregation a way of living with diversity that is both respectful and light-hearted. Humor in this context serves as a tool for making the uncomfortable more comfortable, as long as everyone is willing to laugh.

There is a good deal of "ribbing" that goes on at Evergreen. Judy, a young Asian American woman, shared the following story with me. One Sunday as people were finding seats in the church, she heard a Black and a White woman make a joke about how all the Asian girls are so skinny. One of them said, "Come sit near me because you have an ass and they all don't." Judy thought this was funny rather than offensive. She added that this comment was probably their way of dealing with the awkwardness of being among the few non-Asians in the crowd. Judy is not afraid to make cultural mistakes because she finds them amusing and hopes other people take them that way, too. Food is often a topic of jokes at Evergreen as well. I have heard non-Asian members make jokes about having rice again or being served things they would not think of eating, like chicken's feet. Beneath such ribbing lie real tensions, real discomfort, real potential for conflict, and it would be a mistake to think that humor somehow removes this discomfort. Humor often diffuses these tensions, allowing people to move on, but it can also mask tensions, allowing them to fester until they build into more serious conflict.[13]

At Evergreen, members are encouraged to put up with small offenses in good humor, but this may mask how deeply offended they are—feelings that are too strong to be voiced in this atmosphere of light-heartedness. There are of course times when humor is inadequate, as in the service following the September 11 attacks, when there was no humor in the connection drawn between the forced internment of Japanese Americans and racial attacks against Arab-looking Americans. There was no humor when an e-mail accused members of treating Blacks poorly. For the church leaders who are trying to model a way of living with diversity, it takes skillful reading of the congregation to know when humor will be an effective response to conflict and when other tools, like theological reflection, are needed.

It is not easy to cultivate a church culture in which members willingly choose to do things that make them uncomfortable. It takes persuasive theological teaching to convince members to bear the costs. It takes people with strong convictions and cross-cultural skills to be the first boundary crossers who carry the lion's share of the burden of making the multiethnic church a reality. It takes skillful management of the discomfort and tensions that inevitably arise to keep these disconnective points from building into serious conflict. As Christerson and Emerson suggest, the multiethnic church is an unstable entity, but diversity is not only a source of instability and burden. For many Evergreeners, the multiethnic church offers a spiritual challenge that brings them a sense of purpose and self-esteem while also providing opportunities for enjoyment.

7

The Multiethnic Church in Society

As an emerging institutional form, the multiethnic church involves a good deal of trial and error. It makes sense to think of it as an experiment rather than a finished product. Through culture work, multiethnic churches experiment with strategies for convincing members to pursue the goals of diversity and to accept the costs involved. To create a sense of inclusivity, they experiment with ways to institutionalize diversity in leadership, programs, and corporate worship. They also experiment with discourses for framing the salience of ethnic identity in relation to Christian identity. What makes the multiethnic church most like an experiment, though, is its uncertain outcome. Will Evergreen succeed in making the transition from an Asian American church to a multicultural, multiethnic church? The authors of *United by Faith* urge Christians to make the twenty-first century the century of multiracial congregations, but given how difficult such congregations are to create and sustain, will we see a significant number of churches moving in this direction?[1] And, perhaps most important, what difference, if any, will multiethnic churches make in our highly racialized society? Though I cannot predict the future, in this concluding chapter it seems fitting to speculate on what the future holds for Evergreen and the significance of the multiethnic church experiment more generally. We may get some glimpse of what the future holds for American congregational life by looking more closely at the relationship between institutional change and social context.

Adapting to a Multiethnic Society

Social institutions are not known for their adaptability, and churches seem particularly inclined toward maintaining the status quo. For an eighty-year-old Japanese American church to become a multi-Asian/multi-ethnic church is quite extraordinary. For this reason, some scholars predict that churches that begin with a multiethnic vision have a much greater chance of success. What about the more than three hundred thousand religious congregations that already exist? What are the factors that propel a church toward radical institutional change? Many Christians would like to know how to get their churches to move in this direction, but there is no simple map to follow, and there may be as many different routes as there are churches.

Institutional adaptation is always a response to something, whether it is the arrival of a new group of people, a burning bush, or a financial downturn. In the case of American congregations, churches have often made radical changes in response to changing demographics in the surrounding neighborhood that threaten the institution's survival. In fact, some would argue that most churches in the United States will open their doors to "others" only when forced to, but there are always other options. In her comprehensive study of congregational change, sociologist of religion Nancy Ammerman identifies four patterns of response to changing environmental context.[2] The most common response is to proceed with business as usual, a strategy that will eventually lead to the death of the congregation. Peter Wagner writes, "It is a social fact, however, that some groups of people prefer the death or dissolution of their group to the alternative of accepting people into their group they perceive, for whatever reasons, as being incompatible."[3] Another common response is to relocate along with church members—typically to the suburbs. Relocation, commonly called "White flight," is often the preferred response of people with the economic means to do so, as the Evergreen move from the Latino-dominated Boyle Heights area to the San Gabriel Valley demonstrates. A congregation that chooses to stay in its neighborhood as the ethnic demographics change has two choices: become a "niche" congregation, drawing commuters from a wide region, or open their doors to the newcomers in the neighborhood and take on a multiethnic identity.

The decision whether to leave in the hope of not changing or to stay and change is very difficult to make. Either choice results in a significant upheaval in the life of the congregation. Racism, classism, and a host of other "isms" can lead a church to flee its new neighbors, as can the desire to maintain its traditional identity and corporate culture. But what leads a church to stay in the face of changing demographics and make ethnic inclusion a goal?

The decision to become, or try to become, multiethnic may be entirely pragmatic. It may cost less money or require less effort to stay and diversify than to move. This is the conclusion Penny Edgell Becker drew from her study of two churches in the Oak Park area, outside of Chicago, that took on a goal of racial inclusion in the 1990s after losing many members to White flight.[4] Assessing the social processes that led to this decision, Becker concludes it was ultimately pragmatic and reactive, as opposed to ideological and proactive. For these churches, theological reflection was not a motivating factor but a tool used to legitimate the racial inclusion goal and to inspire the necessary institutional changes to make this goal a reality. Like Becker, Michael Emerson and Karen Chai Kim found through the nationwide Multiracial Congregations Project that "resource calculation" is a primary impetus for developing multiracial congregations, but they also found that mission and a mandate for diversity from an external authority structure, such as a denominational body, could stimulated such radical change.[5] Becker's juxtaposition of pragmatic and ideological, and Emerson and Kim's three-part framework of resource calculation, mission, and external authority structure are useful conceptual tools for analyzing the factors that propel churches toward greater diversity, but like all conceptual schemas they bring clarity by abstracting from the complexity of real life.

In real life, motives are always mixed, and particularly when it comes to religious congregations—organizations purportedly created to pursue spiritual ideals—separating the ideological from the pragmatic may be impossible. In the case of evangelical churches, such a distinction is all the more blurred because spreading the Gospel and gaining new converts is intrinsically part of evangelical theology. Thus the church growth movement urged Christians to use the most pragmatic means possible to achieve this goal, but churches have also been known to take up very unpragmatic strategies, sociologically speaking, on the sheer faith that their ideological motivations will be rewarded. Just as practical demands are intertwined with religious ideals, the internal social processes of churches are embedded within social and theological contexts. Changing attitudes in society at large may prompt churches to reconsider their practices, and church leaders may draw new insights from reflecting on Christian tradition, scripture, and congregational history, or from listening to and watching what other church leaders are doing. Few churches are given mandates from an external authority to integrate, but many are prompted to do so as they learn of new ideas and church development strategies, particularly those that have gained legitimacy within a church's institutional field. Normative pressure to follow the practices of other churches perceived as highly successful is particularly strong within evangelical institutional fields. Rather than isolate any one of these factors from the others, it is fruitful to examine the way demography, social attitudes to diversity, new theological ideas and strategies, and pragmatic considerations all weigh on the development of multiethnic churches.

The Case of Evergreen

Throughout its history Evergreen has been adapting to demographic shifts. Its orientation from the start was a niche congregation, first serving the needs of Japanese immigrants and their English-speaking children. Because it was also a locally-oriented congregation, Evergreen was strongly affected by changes in neighborhood demographics. When Boyle Heights was literally emptied of Japanese Americans during World War II, Evergreen closed its doors, and quickly reopened them when the members returned from their imprisonment. The church's relocation to the San Gabriel Valley in the 1980s was prompted by the influx of Latino residents to Boyle Heights and the growth of the Asian American population in the Valley. At its new location in Rosemead, Evergreen continued to draw commuters from all over Los Angeles and had little connection to the city. In the 1980s, Evergreen's niche orientation evolved from an English-speaking Japanese congregation to a pan-Asian church. This development in the life of the church is explained, in part, by Mark Mullins's theory of the life-cycle of the ethnic church.[6]

Based on his study of Japanese Christian and Buddhist congregations in Canada, Mullins predicted that immigrant churches will "de-ethnicize" over time as their members shed their ethnic identity and become assimilated to the dominant culture of the host society. In Mullins's theory, immigrant churches go through stages of assimilation as they develop bilingual, bicultural ministry for the children of immigrants and a "de-ethnicized," multiethnic ministry in order to attract subsequent generations and remain solvent.

We can clearly see these life cycles in the history of Evergreen as it moved from serving immigrants to serving the American-born generations and from serving Japanese Americans to serving Asian Americans. However, rather than "de-ethnicize," in the sense of intentionally discarding their Asian American ethnic identity, Evergreen continued to encourage ethnic identity after it became a pan-Asian church. Certainly Mullins is correct that some American-born offspring of Asian immigrants do leave ethnic churches for White-majority churches, just as some people intentionally reject their ethnic heritages, but as the existence of pan-Asian churches makes clear, this is not always the case. Many studies of Asian American churches have found Mullins's model flawed because it assumes that social assimilation inevitably leads to Anglo-conformity instead of allowing for the possibility that Asian Americans can be both highly assimilated and have a strong ethnic identity.[7] It was this recognition of dual identity that led Pastor Ken to develop his model of pan-Asian ministry in the 1980s. The question still remains, however, whether Evergreen was forced to broaden its niche orientation because it could no longer attract a sustaining membership of Asian Americans.

As it happens, the San Gabriel Valley is predicted to become home to an even larger number of Asian Americans.[8] Given these demographics, a pan-Asian Evergreen would have had a sufficient target population to maintain itself. In fact, with Ken's established reputation and the growing Asian population in the San Gabriel Valley, it would have been much easier to rebuild the congregation after the hive as an Asian American church than to take a new direction. Given the accepted status of the homogeneous unit principle at the time, there was every reason to think a multiethnic church would fail. Every reason, that is, except Ken's own experience in his diverse family and friendships. Changing demographics did not force Evergreen to become multiethnic, but they played a significant role in the decision nonetheless.

Adapting to Diversity

From its informal worship style to the Hawaiian shirts men wear in the summer, Evergreen is an L.A. church, and it thinks of itself as situated in this larger context. To understand what Evergreen was responding to, it is helpful to consider the rapid changes occurring in the greater Los Angeles area. Two related demographic changes directly affected Evergreeners: increasing rates of mixed marriages and multiethnic offspring and increasing diversity within their social networks. As was noted in chapter 1, the number of Angelenos who identified as multiracial in the 2000 census was more than twice the national average, and among U.S.-born Asian Americans rates of exogamous marriages are reaching 30 to 50 percent.[9] Given these statistics, it comes as no surprise that an increasing number of Evergreeners were experiencing greater diversity within their own families. In addition, they could not help but be affected by the tremendous growth in diversity in the Los Angeles area since 1960. In workplaces and schools across the region they had occasion to make social contacts with people from all over the world and a vast array of ethnic backgrounds.

While the census data makes it undeniably clear that there is more diversity in Los Angeles than ever before, such diversity does not necessarily translate into a mixing of people across ethnic divides, and the deadly riots of 1992 demonstrated how volatile race relations are in this region. As one Evergreener put it, "This city blows up every ten years and only on the issue of race and nothing else." Such violence has little direct impact on the professional, middle-class members of Evergreen who experience Los Angeles as an oasis from the racial tensions that plague other parts of the country. For them, Los Angeles is a place of tolerance and mixing, and surprisingly few had experienced any racism living there. I heard several "war stories" from Evergreeners who ventured outside California's urban, coastal centers and suffered stares, coldness, and occasionally racial slurs from less tolerant Americans. Such trips make them appreciate the cosmopolitan atmosphere of Southern California all the more. The *perception* that Los Angeles cultivates a unique "ethic of mixing" played an important role in Evergreen's decision to become multiethnic.[10] As a multiethnic church, the new Evergreen hopes to mirror the "real world," or at least the world as Evergreeners would make it.

Evergreen's decision to reflect the demographic diversity of the larger Los Angeles region served a very important pragmatic function. If the church became multiethnic, Asian American members would be comfortable bringing their non-Asian family members and friends there, but the tradeoff for this benefit was the loss of Asian Americans seeking a pan-Asian church. From the perspective of the church growth movement, the new Evergreen would not flourish, because most people do not want to cross ethnic boundaries to go to church. When Pastor Ken announced the new vision after the hive, many Evergreeners feared that the experiment would fail, but Ken's relationship to Inter-Varsity also gave him reason to be hopeful that young adults would be attracted to a church that was pursuing racial reconciliation. Ken told his staff that Evergreen would be "good news" to a hidden group of people coming out of college, people who were "discipled" in the new apostolic paradigm of the postmodern church. He believed they would be willing to commute to Evergreen to be part of this exciting vision, and this has proven to be true, though it is undeniable that Evergreen would have grown faster as a pan-Asian church. Seeking to be a "montage of cultures, classes, and circumstances," Evergreen has no target population, and yet its reconciliation vision does serve as a kind of niche orientation that attracts evangelicals committed to this value from all over Los Angeles. While not all Evergreeners care deeply about this vision, the fact that so many have joined precisely because of it presents a serious challenge to the homogeneous unit principle, which is still taught in many seminaries. It appears from the Evergreen case that, at least in Southern California, not all Christians prefer to be in churches with their own kind of people.

There has been a cultural shift in values in Southern California, which has opened up even greater opportunities for crossing ethnic divides, and Evergreen has strategically tapped into the emerging cosmopolitan ethos of the region. Rather than being pushed by changing demography to become multiethnic, Evergreen was pulled in this direction by the opportunity such change presented. Taking this opportunity to appeal to evangelicals of diverse backgrounds would not have been the most pragmatic choice if the goal of the church were growth of members and resources. We cannot understand Evergreen's development without noting how social changes are interpreted through and examined in light of an array of resources church leaders have at their disposal.

New Ideas, New Goals

The social factors that push churches to change do not occur in isolation from theological reflection but are interpreted through a religious lens that is not static, but evolving in relation to the new ideas and strategies shared within institutional fields. Evergreen's institutional field is American evangelicalism, and within that context Pastor Ken was drawn toward racial reconciliation theology.

Pastor Ken's exposure to racial reconciliation theology through InterVarsity set him on a radically new ministerial path, and he chose to take the church with him. Evergreeners would have rejected his new vision if he had not skillfully presented reconciliation as a theological value worthy of pursuit. In contrast to the churches Becker studied in Chicago, Pastor Ken did not use theological reflection as a legitimating tool to pursue a pragmatic goal. To the contrary, it was an impetus to pursue an extremely unlikely goal: creating a church that draws people across the boundaries of class, culture, and circumstance. Emerson and Kim have suggested that churches that become multiethnic out of a sense of mission will be more likely to sustain diversity than those that do so as a means of economic survival or because they have received an external mandate for change.[11] If their hypothesis proves true, then Evergreen's future looks promising, and to the extent that other church leaders are moved by a sense of mission to take advantage of the diversity surrounding them, we will see many more mission-driven multiethnic churches in the future.

The story of Evergreen is a unique one, but the factors that propelled it toward greater diversity are not. Increasing ethnic diversity and ethnic mixing, rising intermarriage rates, and changing attitudes toward diversity are factors pressing on churches all over Southern California and more and more on urban churches all over the country. The story of Evergreen's transformation demonstrates the complex relationship between pragmatic concerns and ideological commitments in the decision-making processes of religious institutions. Evergreen was not reacting to changing neighborhood demographics, a diminishing target population, or pressure to conform to expectations of White evangelicals, but it was responding to changes in the larger cultural milieu of Southern California and American evangelicalism more generally, which opened up the possibility of the multiethnic church as both desirable and attainable.

The Future of the Multiethnic Church

What lies ahead for Evergreen and its racial reconciliation efforts is hard to predict. A change in leadership, especially the loss of Pastor Ken, would seriously test the community's resolve. Evergreen could easily become a predominantly Asian/White congregation, making it difficult to attract Latinos and Blacks. An influx of new immigrants would strain the church's shared American identity and might push the church to become multilingual. The loss of young people would deflate the church's energy for outward social engagement, leading to a more inward, family-focused congregational culture. Evergreen's appeal to young people as a dynamic, postmodern, multiethnic church is a precarious one, depending largely on Ken's ability to inspire the established members to buy into his vision. Charles Foster and Theodore Brelsford conclude from their study of culturally diverse churches in Atlanta that "the possibility of dramatic, perhaps tragic change is always within sight."[12] Indeed, the multiethnic church is a fragile, unstable experiment continually facing new challenges, but it is also a vibrant, exciting experiment impelled forward by even the smallest signs of success.

Young adults, raised with a cosmopolitan ethos and passionate about reconciliation, will play a key role in the growth of these congregations. Those who strongly value diversity will look for churches that espouse this value. In turn, churches hoping to attract this target population will adapt to meet their desires. Pressure to adapt will be strongest in urban areas, where young people are more likely to move in diverse social networks and to look for churches that reflect this reality. Like the seeker churches of the 1990s, multiethnic churches will become their own niche. With changing demographics and shifting attitudes toward diversity, ignoring diversity issues may not be an option for urban churches much longer, and even churches in less diverse areas will feel pressure to make at least symbolic gestures toward ethnic inclusion. In a spiritual marketplace with a large number of churches to choose from, the demands of the consumer may go a long way in changing the conscience of a church.

A Praxis of Multiplicity

What difference, if any, will multiethnic churches make in a society so marked by racialization? Across confessional traditions, Christian leaders assert that churches have divinely-inspired resources distinct from secular institutions, which they bring to bear on racial divisions. The authors of *United by Faith* predict that "multiracial congregations will be called on in the years ahead to use their experience to provide a healing salve for the wounds of racial division, cultural misunderstandings, and even the lingering pain of traumatic events."[13] Though many Christian leaders believe multiethnic churches will be able to make a positive impact on race relations in the United States and around the world, this is a bold claim given the Christian churches' long history of segregation and collusion in maintaining White privilege.[14]

Will the development of multiethnic churches signal a radical departure from this dismal history? It depends greatly on how they engage the thorny issues of ethnic, racial, and cultural diversity. Not all multiethnic churches foster the kind of wide-ranging discourse about race that is necessary for churches to engage in the struggle for racial equality.[15] Color-blind churches certainly do not, and even color-conscious churches may prefer to celebrate diversity rather than examine it. I am inclined to agree with Penny Becker that if churches refuse to deal with the reality of social structural inequality or to acknowledge the legitimacy of group-based interests, and if they fail to mobilize their members for social change, there is little hope of their building anything more than isolated communities of social integration. Is this what Evergreen has done, created an island of social integration?

One of the difficulties of gauging the impact churches have on society is that few churches engage in the kind of headline-grabbing political activity that is easy to spot. Mainline Protestant and Catholic churches may mobilize to support a living wage or keep a Wal-Mart superstore from opening, but evangelical churches have generally limited their political activism to family issues such as abortion, pornography, and gay marriage.[16] While I am aware of Roman Catholic and mainline Protestant multiethnic churches that are actively involved in progressive social issues in Los Angeles, evangelical multiethnic churches rarely speak out on social issues in the larger society.[17] The fact that Evergreen's pastors occasionally make "political" statements, as in their response to the mistreatment of Arab Americans after the September 11 attacks, has given the church a negative "liberal" reputation among some evangelicals. Social activism has not been part of the mainstream evangelical tool kit in recent decades, but churches like Evergreen are pushing the boundaries of what is considered appropriate social engagement for evangelicals. Even when racial reconciliation is pursued as a call for healing rather than political reform, it can have an impact on social relations beyond church walls and beyond the level of personal relationships.

The racial healing ministry of Curtis May has yielded notable results. May is director of the Office of Reconciliation Ministries (ORM) for the Worldwide Church of God, headquartered in Pasadena, California.[18] He has been a key figure in bringing together religious and civic leaders across the country to talk about racial healing. In 1999, ORM was instrumental in organizing a large Pasadena-wide conference that featured the city's mayor, Chris Holden. May serves on the race relations task force for Los Angeles mayor Jim Hahn and was asked to conduct a racial sensitivity workshop for the Pasadena Police Department in 2003. He writes in the ORM newsletter of one of his latest victories, "Won my own 'public relations battle' with a prominent restaurant chain in the Los Angeles area concerning the elimination of lawn jockey depictions of stereotypical African Americans as lazy, thick-lipped, naïve buffoons."[19] ORM has also participated in city-led responses to racial violence, such as the Diversity Day held in the city of Duarte after incidents between Latino and Black youths. When I met with May in the fall of 2003, he was pleased to show me an array of plaques and "keys to the city" he has received from mayors all over the country in appreciation for his racial healing workshops. If evangelical multiethnic churches do become players in the struggle for racial equality, I suspect it will be through the kind of racial healing work that ORM is already being called upon by public leaders to provide.

In addition to providing social and religious services, churches also have an impact on society in more subtle ways. They are public spaces, arenas for interaction and discourse. Churches foster collective norms and encourage specific values and practices that reflect moral choices. In his study of public religion in Chicago, Lowell Livezey found that while few congregations engaged in political action on race issues, they frequently addressed questions of race or ethnicity nonetheless:

> Whether or not to conduct a worship service in an additional language, whether to add or change a picture or icon, how hard to try to evangelize a neighborhood or to recruit new members from a wider

region—choices such as these entail racial values and choices. And
the decision of whether to articulate the racial dimension or to leave it
latent beneath the surface is itself a moral choice.[20]

All multiethnic churches are arenas for interaction across ethnic boundaries,
and all promote the values of diversity and tolerance, but how these values are
carried beyond church walls depends on the ways in which diversity issues are
framed and addressed within the organization. The ethnic transcendence strategy used by color-blind, multiethnic churches is carried by members into civic
life—into schools, workplaces, neighborhoods, and voting booths.[21] Churches
that use an ethnic inclusion strategy promote a strong value for diversity that is
likewise carried into the public sphere.

Reflecting on the kind of civic habits Evergreen is fostering, I am encouraged by the wide-ranging discourse about race I heard there. Many of the members connect their concern for racial reconciliation with a commitment to economic justice, a link not often drawn in middle-class churches and certainly not
in middle-class evangelical churches. Evergreeners are not political activists, but
they are much more likely to support social changes that redress structural inequality than members of churches that refuse to acknowledge that ethnicity
matters.

What I found potentially most socially subversive about multiethnic
churches was the willingness of Evergreen's members to put up with a fair
amount of discomfort and tension and to operate in ambiguity on a regular
basis. It would be much easier to use an ethnic transcendence approach that ignores ethnic differences, or to go to the opposite extreme and insist on rigid
racial constructs, but Evergreeners have taken a much more challenging path.
Charles Foster and Theodore Brelsford concluded from their Atlanta study that
diverse congregations can foster a new kind of consciousness: "They engage in
a public hermeneutic, a hermeneutic of multiplicity, negotiation, and change,
both within and beyond their walls."[22] I believe that a similar consciousness—
what I have called a cosmopolitan ethos—is fostered at Evergreen. More than
just a consciousness of multiplicity, Evergreen encourages what Foster and
Brelsford call a "praxis of multiplicity."[23] Church leaders model skills, such as
humor, cultural sensitivity, humility, and fearlessness in the face of difference,
and they promote a commitment to the discomfort of diversity as essential to
Christian life. These skills and values enable church members to flourish in a
complex world of cross-cutting identities and permeable boundaries and motivate them to face the challenges of this new world.

Multiethnic churches are training grounds for boundary crossers, but they
can only teach those willing to learn. To the extent that such churches are able,

in the words of Evergreen's mission statement, "to equip God's people to be ministers of reconciliation, healing, and transformation," they are also forming citizens who will create a cosmopolitan society. Cosmopolitanism does not necessarily lead to a racially just society, and it benefits most those with the economic and educational resources to exercise their ethnic options and explore the diversity around them. A society that fosters the recognition, acceptance, and eager exploration of diversity is not the Promised Land that Martin Luther King, Jr., described, but it is a big step in the right direction.

Appendix A: Methods

This research project began in December 2001 as a case study of a multiethnic church, Evergreen Baptist Church of Los Angeles. Over a two-and-a-half-year period, I studied the church's literature, Web site, historical documents, and sermons, and made fourteen site visits during which I observed worship services, meetings of the single-adult group, and a quarterly congregational meeting. These observations and my examination of the church materials provided a context from which to develop interview questions for staff and members.

Interviews with Evergreen's staff and members, both formal members and regular visitors, began in April 2002, after I was introduced to the congregation at Sunday morning services, and continued until January 2004. Pastor Ken encouraged the congregation members to speak with me. As a result, some members did seek me out on their own. For the most part, I initiated the interviews in person, by phone, or by e-mail, using names that church members and staff provided in response to my request for names of those who had a strong interest in or opinions about racial reconciliation. Almost everyone I asked was willing to meet with me. I interviewed male and female members ranging in age from 23 to 79. Each subject was asked to fill out a questionnaire about his or her educational background, occupation, and ethnic identity. These interviews were semi-structured, meaning that they followed a standardized set of questions that were open-ended, with new questions added as needed to explore pertinent themes. Most interviews were an hour in length. In all I conducted thirty-three formal interviews with members and six with ministry staff, as well as a final two-hour interview with Pastor Ken in January 2004. In June 2003 I was able to hold a focus group with the Prime Timers senior group. Since nearly a hundred people attended this meeting, we broke up into several small groups, and I listened in as members discussed the ways in which ethnicity matters to them personally and in the life of the church.

It quickly became apparent during the research that the members most interested in the subject matter were young adults who had been exposed to racial reconciliation in college Christian fellowships. To understand the role of young evangelicals in the racial reconciliation movement, I expanded my study to include the Greater Los Angeles division of InterVarsity Christian Fellowship as a secondary research focus. Through their Web site and contacts at Evergreen I was able to contact staff members for interviews. Between July 2002 and February 2003, I interviewed ten staff workers, four of whom are also Evergreen members, and attended one Race Matters meeting at UC–Santa Barbara. Though I hoped to attend a Race Matters meeting at UCLA, where this format was first constructed, I was unable to get scheduling information from the InterVarsity staff there. With the help of staff members, the InterVarsity Web site, and InterVarsity press materials, I did considerable background research on the racial reconciliation movement in InterVarsity nationwide, including two phone interviews with staff at the national office in Wisconsin.

The last important piece of this project came from research on the racial reconciliation movement at the national and Southern California regional level. My goal was to understand Evergreen's immediate and wider institutional field. In addition to examining articles on racial reconciliation in evangelical magazines and on denominational and para-church Web sites, I conducted ten interviews with evangelical pastors and para-church leaders involved in racial reconciliation the Los Angeles area. These interviews provided valuable data on how other local churches and organizations conceptualize and pursue racial reconciliation. Most of these evangelical leaders were familiar with Evergreen and provided insightful evaluation of its efforts, which helped me understand what impact Evergreen is having on others within its institutional field.

All of the interviews were audiotaped with permission and then transcribed. They were later analyzed in conjunction with field notes from participation observation and the racial reconciliation literature. I organized the data around common themes that emerged from the interviews, which later came to serve as the outline for the book. All names have been changed except those individuals who spoke to me as the public representative of an organization.

My status as a White, middle-class researcher from a secular university did not appear to be an obstacle to finding interview subjects. Evergreen has been the subject of several academic studies in recent years, though to my knowledge all these prior studies were undertaken by church members. Most of the people I talked with asked what my religious affiliation was, and few knew what to make of my being a Unitarian Universalist. To my surprise, no one showed an interest in converting me. Because of my outsider status, many people felt the need to explain "evangelical-ese" or to avoid using it altogether. I encouraged them to use the discourse they are most comfortable with during the interviews.

In their study of multiracial churches, Charles Foster and Theodore Brelsford express the concern that their questions contributed to the sense members had of the fragility of their multiracial church and brought into the open latent issues and conflicts.

My research may have forced some Evergreen members to become aware of tensions they had previously not been attuned to; however, because I solicited interviews from persons interested in the subject matter, those willing to be interviewed had already given much thought to issues of diversity. Similarly, the InterVarsity staff members I spoke with were not expressing their concerns for the first time, since they are encouraged in their organization to be self-reflective and critical of their processes. I provided Evergreen Baptist Church with a copy of my dissertation, which was discussed in the January–February 2005 church newsletter. I suspect that some members were troubled to learn how marginalized the non-Asian members felt, but I also suspect that the church leadership did not find any surprises there. As I was making final revisions on the book manuscript in early 2006, I revisited Evergreen's archival sources, namely the newsletters and Web site, and contacted the church office to learn more about recent developments such as the creation of a Racial Reconciliation Resource Team and the hiring of Brenda Salter McNeil as a consultant.

Appendix B: Comparing Models of Ethnically Diverse Congregations

While "church" is a common enough word, the evolving institutional arrangements of churches are not as well known. Some churches are forced to manage the diverse population that floods through their doors, and others seek ways to maximize their diversity by inviting new groups to share their space. In urban areas it is common for a single church building to house several congregations, which can be very confusing, since we often use "church" and "congregation" synonymously. It is not always clear, even to those involved, what the boundaries are between these groups. Several institutional models for diversity have been developed in addition to the multiethnic church, which I have defined as an inclusive, ethnically diverse community. The most common forms are the space-sharing church, the multilingual church, and the pan-ethnic church. Comparing each of these with the multiethnic church will provide a clearer sense of what is distinctive about the multiethnic church experiment.

THE SPACE-SHARING CHURCH

In urban areas, space-sharing is a frequent arrangement; new religious communities rent space from established churches until they can buy their own building. This relationship provides declining churches with needed revenue and small start-ups with furnished facilities. Often these newly formed churches are serving small immigrant populations, and many churches and denominations take pride in this gesture of hospitality to the newcomer. They may even provide the space without charge as part of their social-justice or mission outreach. Space-sharing arrangements may also come about when an established church starts a new mission church to serve an ethnic group with a different language. If successful, the mission church will eventually become autonomous, even though it continues to share space with the parent organization. Looking at church signs in downtown Los Angeles, it is difficult to know how the two or three, or even more, groups holding services at a single facility are connected.

Space-sharing churches have separate by-laws of incorporation, separate membership books, and separate finances. In some cases the groups will have virtually no contact apart from procedural issues of space use negotiated by the leadership. Such arrangements are fertile ground for conflict given the imbalance in power between the "hosting" church and the "guest" church. However, due in part to the growing attention to diversity in churches, space-sharing groups are increasingly trying to improve ethnic relations. They look for ways to foster interaction through workshops, social events, service activities, communication-sensitivity workshops, and shared worship. The more they do together, the more they begin to look like a multiethnic church. In some cases, space-sharers are connected through shared resources. The member congregations consider themselves separate, autonomous wings of a single organization. Peter Wagner believes that this arrangement, which he calls the multicongregational church model, holds outstanding promise for applying the sociological, theological, biblical, and ethnic principles of pluralism in inner-city America.[1]

THE MULTILINGUAL CHURCH

A second model, that of the multilingual church, was developed to serve immigrants who wanted to worship in their native tongue. Unlike the space-sharing church, the multilingual church is a single entity that manages its diversity by holding separate services for the main language groups. This arrangement is common in Catholic parishes, which often have a large immigrant membership, but it is also used by Protestant churches in urban areas and immigrant churches serving several generations. A typical parish in the Catholic Archdiocese of Los Angeles, where masses are said in more than fifty languages, will hold several Spanish- and English-language masses on Sunday. If it has additional language groups, such as Tagalog or Vietnamese, it may hold occasional services in those languages, but the ability to secure a regular language mass is dependent on the size and influence of the group and the availability of priests who speak the language. To better address the needs of all the constituent language groups, some multilingual parishes have created separate lay parish councils for each major group. Each council serves its own people, and interaction occurs between parish leaders as they negotiate the limited resources of space, funds, and attention of the shared clergy.

Because of linguistic and cultural barriers and institutional separation, members of multilingual churches may not think of themselves as part of a single church community. The multilingual model has been criticized for encouraging "ethnic balkanization" and forming de facto "parallel congregations." In practice, the multilingual church can come to look much like a space-sharing arrangement. Based on their study of immigrant congregations in Houston, Helen Rose Ebaugh and Janet Saltzman Chafetz suggest that such internal subdivisions can actually be beneficial for members: "While cause for some concern because of its potential to disrupt congregational unity, self-segregation allows immigrants the opportunity to communicate comfortably, exchange news and gossip from the old country and about the local ethnic community, and in general, to celebrate and reinforce their ethnic identities."[2] They also point out that the bonds members form among their co-ethnics enhance their commitment to the whole church.

Without substantial efforts to forge interaction among the various subgroups, the multilingual church will be strongly fragmented. In the Archdiocese of Los Angeles and other Catholic dioceses around the country, efforts are being made to counteract the subdivisions within the multilingual church. Ethnic-specific parish councils are being phased out in favor of a single parish council with proportional representation of each sizable ethnic group. Multilingual/multicultural services are another way churches try to bridge ethnic divisions and form a sense of community. Despite much creative experimentation, such services have not been widely adopted. Members like the idea of a common service but find the end result less than satisfying.[3]

As a compromise, many multilingual churches hold joint services only periodically. For example, the Catholic Archdiocese of Los Angeles encourages "multicultural masses" on special holy days, such as Pentecost Sunday and Holy Thursday. The multicultural mass draws on the language and culture of the main parish groups, utilizing both translation and multilingual songs, as well as a combination of musical styles. Such services are difficult to do well, but parishioners are more inclined to appreciate their symbolic unifying value when they are held only occasionally. Other strategies used to foster cross-cultural interaction are multicultural social events, such as an annual fiesta at which members can taste each other's food and hear each other's music. Through the efforts of bilingual/bicultural members, multilingual churches try to forge a common sense of identity and bonds of caring, but without a common language such churches remain strongly fragmented.[4]

THE PAN-ETHNIC CHURCH

Unlike the multilingual church, the pan-ethnic church has no institutionalized divisions along ethnic lines. The designation of "pan-ethnic church" has come into scholarly usage recently to describe the creation of pan-Asian churches designed to serve those Ken calls "Americanized Asian Americans." As we saw in the case of Evergreen, the pan-Asian church emerged as an alternative to the ethnic-immigrant church and the White-dominated church. Russell Jeung, who was the first to study pan-Asian churches in depth, argues that they developed out of a shared sense of Asian American identity fostered through the multicultural ethos of the San Francisco Bay area.[5]

The distinguishing features of the pan-ethnic church, as I see the term being used today, are a common language and a shared racialized status among people who identify with distinct ethnic groups. For example, a church made up of members from various cultures in Latin America may think of itself as pan-Latino. The Native American Church, or Peyote Church, developed in the early twentieth century as a consciously pan-Indian religious community. In the mid-twentieth century, European Christians moved away from immigrant churches to pan-Euro churches. It could be argued that even today some White and Black churches are better thought of as pan-ethnic rather than ethnic because of the distinct ethnic identities of members within these ascribed racial categories. The appropriateness of the pan-ethnic label depends on the degree to which members identify with a distinctive ethnic group within the racial category.

Like the multiethnic church, the pan-ethnic church strives for inclusivity across diversity, but the ethnic boundaries within pan-Asian churches are less formidable than racial boundaries. In other words, because they share an ascribed racial category, people mix more easily within these categories than between them. Jeung writes that in the context of multiculturalism, acculturated Asian Americans do not make group distinctions based on cultural affinities.[6] Pastor Ken based his pan-Asian ministry on the perception that there are many commonalities between Americanized Japanese and Chinese Americans in particular. Jeung also found that while pan-Asian churches attract these two groups, as well as Korean Americans, they rarely include Vietnamese, Filipino, Thai, or other Southeast Asians. For this reason, Pyong Gap Min argues that they should be called "East Asian" congregations rather than "pan-Asian," a term he sees as misleading.[7] Pan-Asian churches have managed to bridge the differences among college-educated, professional, Americanized East Asians without the degree of ethnic strife that multiethnic churches have encountered.

In crossing not only ethnic but also racial boundaries, multiethnic churches face a much greater challenge than pan-ethnic churches do. Interestingly, by the time Jeung published his research on pan-Asian churches in the Bay Area, several of these churches followed Evergreen in broadening their boundaries to include non-Asians. In addition to developing mission statements declaring their ethnic inclusivity, some of these pan-Asian congregations have made intentional efforts to attract a multiethnic membership. In 2004, I collaborated with Jeung on a national study of Asian American–led multiethnic churches, which included interviews with the twenty-seven pastors of these churches. We found that, like Pastor Ken, most were impelled in this direction by a desire to bring healing to the society and drew upon racial reconciliation theology as they pushed their congregations to become color-conscious, multicultural, multiethnic churches.[8]

Notes

INTRODUCTION

1. I spoke with Bishop Fred Caldwell by telephone on June 1, 2004. See Diane Haag, "Church to Pay White Visitors," *Shreveport Times*, July 30, 2003.

2. DeYoung et al., *United by Faith*, 2. The authors define a multiracial church as one in which no single racial group accounts for more than 80 percent of the membership. For more findings of the Multiracial Congregations Project, see http://www.congregations.info/facts.html.

3. For a concise overview of the history of racial divisions in American Christian churches, see DeYoung et al., *United by Faith*, chapter 3.

4. A large and growing number of books on multiethnic churches are written from a theological standpoint; for an extensive bibliography, see the Web site of the Multiracial Congregations Project. Two books that combine theological and sociological concerns were of great use to me: Paul DeYoung, Michael O. Emerson, George Yancey, and Karen Chai Kim, *United by Faith: The Multiracial Congregation as an Answer to the Problem of Race*, and Charles R. Foster and Theodore Brelsford, *We Are the Church Together: Cultural Diversity in Congregational Life*. From a strictly sociological standpoint, three ethnographic studies strongly shaped my approach to the subject matter: Penny Edgell Becker, "Making Inclusive Communities: Congregations and the 'Problem' of Race"; Patricia Dorsey, "Southwest Assembly of God: Whomsoever Will"; and Gerardo Marti, *A Mosaic of Believers: Diversity and Religious Innovation in a Multiethnic Church*. From the Multiracial Congregations Project, Michael O. Emerson and Karen Chai Kim, "Multiracial Congregations: A Typology and Analysis of Their Development," and Brad Christerson, Korie L. Edwards, and Michael O. Emerson, *Against All*

Odds: The Struggle for Racial Integration in Religious Organizations, were immensely useful.

5. K. Connie Kang, "Building on the Gospel of Inclusion," *Los Angeles Times*, December 8, 2001.

6. According to DeYoung et al., 15 percent of Roman Catholic churches in the United States are multiracial, but the percentage in the Los Angeles region is much higher than this. I have examined the Archdiocese's promotion of the multicultural parish in an unpublished paper titled "The Project of Multiculturalism in the Los Angeles Catholic Church," which was delivered at the 2002 meeting of the American Academy of Religion.

7. For example, in Christerson et al., *Against All Odds*, all of the case studies involve this dynamic of a White church allowing people of color in. *Congregation and Community*, Nancy Ammerman's extensive study of congregational change, highlights several multiethnic churches, all of which began as White-majority churches.

8. Statistics on evangelicalism vary widely, as do the definitions of "evangelical" used in survey research. Christian Smith cites the number of Protestant, church-going evangelicals as 7 percent of all U.S. citizens (*American Evangelicalism*, 1). In his survey of baby boomers, Wade Clark Roof found that 33 percent have the religious identity of "Born-again Christian" (*Spiritual Marketplace*, 321). An older book by James Davison Hunter cites the proportion of evangelical North Americans, understood broadly as theologically conservative Protestants, as 31.7 percent (*Evangelicalism: The Coming Generation*, 5). The Gallop organization has been asking participants if they would describe themselves as "born again" or "evangelical" since 1976. Positive responses have ranged from a low of 33 percent in 1987 to a high of 47 percent in 1998 (Eskridge, "Defining Evangelicalism").

9. Emerson and Smith, *Divided by Faith*, 63.

10. In their national survey, Emerson and Smith found that 40 percent of all White evangelicals and 51 percent of "strong" evangelicals had heard of racial reconciliation (*Divided by Faith*, 127–28).

11. Becker, "Making Inclusive Communities."

12. The term "racialization" has come into common usage in race and ethnic theory. It refers to the social processes through which racial categories are created and sustained. For an overview of the term, see Pierce, "The Continuing Significance of Race." The most well-known study of the concept of racialization is Omi and Winant, *Racial Formation in the United States*.

13. For more on adhesive identity, see Yang, *Chinese Christians in America*.

14. Becker, "Making Inclusive Communities," 453.

15. While it is customary in scholarly writing to refer to persons by their last names, in this study I follow the practice in evangelical communities of referring to the pastor by first name, with or without the preceding title of Pastor.

16. On the greater ethnic flexibility afforded White Americans, see Waters, *Ethnic Options*.

17. For a cogent argument for the continued use of "race" instead of "ethnicity" in diversity studies, see Pierce, "Continuing Significance of Race."

CHAPTER 1

1. My first meeting with Pastor Ken in January 2002 was a brief one. I interviewed him formally on January 29, 2004, and, unless otherwise cited, this information comes from the latter interview, which was taped and transcribed.

2. Revelation 22:2b. All biblical quotations are taken from the New Revised Standard Version.

3. This brief history derives from two sources: Ken Fong, "Taking the Baton and Running Our Leg of the Race," and an older history of the church available in the church archives, author unknown.

4. McGavran, *Understanding Church Growth*, 198.

5. Jacket copy, Wagner, *Our Kind of People*.

6. Ken Uyeda Fong, *Pursuing the Pearl*, 4.

7. The only comprehensive study of pan-Asian churches is Jeung, *Faithful Generations*.

8. Sociologist Pyong Gap Min argues that such churches should be identified as East Asian since they are not really pan-Asian. He attributes this pattern of Japanese American–Chinese American churches to "perceptions of similarities in physical characteristics, culture, and premigrant historical experiences" ("A Literature Review," 24).

9. Fong, *Pursuing the Pearl*, 25. Though I did attempt to contact Pastor Cory Ishida to learn his version of events, I was unable to do so.

10. Ken reiterated this in the church newsletter of March 2002, after an article about the church had been published in the *Pasadena Star-News* on January 20. He writes, "In trying to sum up my thoughts the reporter made it sound like the reason folks went with Evergreen-SGV in 1997 was because they weren't in favor of pursuing diversity. I made sure to call Pastor Cory Ishida [the senior pastor at San Gabriel Valley] that afternoon, to make sure that he knew that I had never made that statement in that context."

11. As given on the Web site for Evergreen Baptist Church San Gabriel Valley, the mission statement is: "To make and grow disciples of those who closely identify with the English speaking Asian American culture so that people everywhere can come to know Jesus Christ" (http://www.evergreensgv.org).

12. Ken Fong, "A Church Empowered to Reconcile," church sermon given on November 10, 2002, transcribed from audio recording produced by church staff. Audio recordings of all sermons are sold at the church or made available for downloading on the church Web site: http://www.ebcla.org.

13. This phrase comes from the church mission statement, which is also printed on all church materials along with the church values: hope, humility, and hospitality.

14. "Branding: An Evergrowing, Everloving, Everchanging Process," church newsletter, May 2002, 1–2.

15. Swidler, "Culture in Action."

16. These are the processes Penny Becker identifies in her study of two churches that became multicultural/multiracial, "Making Inclusive Communities: Congregations and the 'Problem' of Race."

17. Sedaqah communities are home-based Bible study groups formed throughout the Los Angeles region. At the time of the 2004 survey, 55 percent of respondents reported that they participated in a sedaqah group. The wording of the vision statement was slightly altered in 2006 to "Evergreen Baptist Church of Los Angeles will demonstrate Jesus' passion for reconciliation by building Sedaqah Communities—redemptive fusions of cultures, classes and circumstances—brought together by the Spirit to bring God's coming future into every life."

18. Sermon, see note 12.

19. When Ken teaches on reconciliation he always addresses all three areas, so this may be a misperception on my part, but the question has been raised in the sociological literature whether crossing ethnic or cultural boundaries is easier than crossing class boundaries. For a brief discussion of this issue, see Dougherty, "How Monochromatic Is Church Membership?"

20. Church newsletter, May–June 2005, p. 3. It is a testament to how far Wagner's ideas have now gone out of fashion that Ken introduces the concept to a new generation of Christians as one that was "all the rage" fifteen years ago.

21. Sermon, see note 12.

22. Smith, *American Evangelicalism.*

23. Ken adds that it is all the more amazing that God is bringing about reconciliation through a church that belongs to a declining and historically ethnocentric denomination (church newsletter, January 2004).

24. All names have been changed except those individuals who spoke to me as the public representative of an organization and gave me permission to use the quoted material.

25. Shinagawa and Pang, "Asian American Panethnicity and Intermarriage." C. N. Le has compiled and analyzed data from the 2000 census ("Interracial Dating & Marriage").

26. The term *hapa* (or *happa*) derives from the Hawai'ian pidgin term *hapa-haole,* literally "half-white." Today it has multiple meanings. Some people use it to refer to children of mixed Japanese-White parentage, but it is increasingly used to identify any person who is part Asian. Because of the Spanish influence, Filipinos more commonly use the term *mestizo* for Filipino-White offspring.

27. Park, Myers, and Wei, "Multiracial Patterns in California by County,"; C. N. Le, "Multiracial/Hapa Asian Americans." According to Le, "Demographers predict that by the year 2020, almost 20% of all Asian Americans will be multiracial and that figure will climb to 36% by the year 2050."

28. Church newsletter, December 2003.

29. During this same period, four new members described Evergreen as an Asian American church in their biographies.

30. While attendance at Evergreen is approximately 700 on a given Sunday, the number of official members is much smaller, approximately 350 in January 2004. The surveys that are used to compile demographic data are given out at church services to adults and, thus, are representative of those who attend rather than those who are formal members. Throughout this book I have used the term "member" in the broad

sense of all those who think of themselves as belonging to Evergreen regardless of their status as formal, tithing members.

31. New themes and metaphors may also be introduced out of necessity—even after several years of practice, members still find it arduous to explain what "sedaqah" means.

CHAPTER 2

1. Yancey, *Beyond Black and White*, 53.

2. Matthew 28:19; see also Mark 16:15, Acts 1:8.

3. Wagner, *Our Kind of People*, 109.

4. Ibid., 136.

5. Ibid.

6. DeYoung et al., *United by Faith*, 20.

7. Conn, foreword to *One New People*, 9.

8. Perkins and Rice, *More Than Equals*, 154–55.

9. Harper et al., *Creating an Acts 6 Racially Reconciling Community*, 16.

10. DeYoung et al., *United by Faith*, 28.

11. For an overview of various positions on this issue, see Bruce W. Fong, *Racial Equality in the Church*.

12. Emerson and Smith, *Divided by Faith*, 47.

13. Martin, *A Prophet with Honor*, 296; quoted in Emerson and Smith, *Divided by Faith*, 47.

14. Emerson and Smith, *Divided by Faith*, 47.

15. Graham, "Racism and the Evangelical Church," 27.

16. For a superb discussion of this tension in another evangelical multiethnic church, see Marti, *A Mosaic of Believers*, 79–85.

17. For a concise overview of this historical tension over social action within evangelicalism, see DeYoung, "Tensions in North American Protestantism."

18. Alumkal, "American Evangelicalism in the Post–Civil Rights Era."

19. Emerson and Smith, *Divided by Faith*, 54.

20. Alumkal, "American Evangelicalism," 200.

21. Emerson and Smith, *Divided by Faith*, 46.

22. Ibid., 56.

23. Tapia, "The Myth of Racial Progress"; Graham, "Racism," 27.

24. Underwood, "The Memphis Miracle."

25. Morgan, "First Stride in a Long Walk," 48.

26. "Seven Promises," Promise Keepers Web site, http://www.promisekeepers.org.

27. Emerson and Smith, *Divided by Faith*, 52.

28. Ortiz, "Commitment to Reconciliation," an address presented as the Ritter Lecture at the Evangelical School of Theology in November 1997.

29. Emerson and Smith, *Divided by Faith*, chapter 4.

30. Bartkowski, *Promise Keepers*, chapter 6.

31. Alumkal, "American Evangelicalism," 203–4.

32. Ibid., 205.

33. Taped interview by author, November 12, 2002. The Harambee Christian Family Center was founded in 1982 by Dr. John Perkins to build community among Latino and African American residents.

34. Alumkal, "American Evangelicalism," 201.

35. For a list of these contemporary leaders, see Emerson and Smith, *Divided by Faith*, 59. Michael Emerson advocates alternative models to mainstream racial reconciliation, such as "the more holistic approach of the Christian Community Development Association (stressing three Rs—relocation, redistribution, and reconciliation—rather than just one)" ("Why Racial Reconciliation Alone Cannot End Racial Strife," 70).

36. For a thoughtful appraisal of the changing demographics within American Christianity, see Warner, "Coming to America."

37. For more on the relationship between African American churches and evangelicalism, see Albert G. Miller, "The Rise of African-American Evangelicalism."

38. This data comes from the Hispanic Churches in American Public Life (HCAPL) research project directed by Gaston Espinosa, Virgilio Elizondo, and Jesse Miranda. A summary of findings released in January 2003 can be downloaded from http://www.pewtrusts.com/pdf/religion_hispanic_churches.pdf. Many Latinos prefer the label *evangelico,* which can be translated as "Protestant" but most often refers to an evangelical Protestant.

39. Michael Luo, "Seeking to Integrate the Pews: Asian Churches Struggle with MLK's Call for Inclusion," *Pasadena Star-News,* January 20, 2000.

40. Busto, "The Gospel According to the Model Minority?" See also Kim, "Emergent Ethnicity."

41. For the viewpoint that the Asian American "silent minority" is becoming increasingly active within mainstream evangelicalism, see Yamamoto, "Silent No More."

42. The Institute for the Study of American Evangelicals, located at Wheaton College, has completed a project titled "The Changing Face of American Evangelicalism," which includes a study I co-authored with Russell Jeung, "Asian American Evangelicals in a Multiethnic Society." See http://www.wheaton.edu/isae/NewLuceGrant.html for more details on this project, which was funded by a grant from the Henry Luce Foundation. For a description of meetings among evangelicals of color on the topic of racial reconciliation, see Carrasco, "Pivotal Minority Movements."

43. Articles addressing these themes can be found in the October–November 2001 and May 2003 issues of the church newsletter.

44. On voting, see the church newsletter of November–December 2004. For Pastor Ken's views on abortion, see the May 2002 issue.

45. Brenda Salter McNeil is a national speaker and consultant to churches on racial reconciliation. She preached at Evergreen on the subject of racial reconciliation on May 18, 2003, Dec 5, 2004, and December 11, 2005. Rudy Carrasco and Derek Perkins, directors of the Harambee Christian Family Center, led the annual Family Camp in 2002 on the theme of "biblical reconciliation with an emphasis on racial reconciliation."

46. That Asian American evangelicals have borrowed much more heavily from White evangelicals than from Black evangelicals is apparent in worship and polity styles. Russell Jeung notes that particularly in their worship style, pan-Asian churches identify with the broader American evangelical subculture rather than with the more traditional forms of worship found in ethnic churches; see Jeung, "Asian American Pan-Ethnic Formation."

47. Alumkal, *Asian American Evangelical Churches*, 143, 182.

CHAPTER 3

1. After directing Overflow Ministries from 1995 to 2004, Salter McNeil founded a new organization called Salter McNeil & Associates, LLC, which is also a racial and ethnic reconciliation training, consulting, and leadership development company based in Chicago. She recently co-authored the book *The Heart of Racial Justice: How Soul Change Leads to Social Change.*

2. Overflow Ministries newsletter, Spring 2003.

3. Hollinger, *Postethnic America*, 84.

4. At the time of the 2004 survey, 12 percent of respondents were married with children under age 18. This question was not asked in the 2002 survey.

5. Carroll and Roof, *Bridging Divided Worlds*, 7.

6. Ibid., 21.

7. Beaudoin, *Virtual Faith*, 27.

8. Donald E. Miller, *Reinventing American Protestantism*, 24.

9. Giddens, *Modernity and Self-Identity*, 20–21.

10. Both of these positions have been widely held among conservative Christians since the early twentieth century. Premillennialism, the belief that the world has become increasingly corrupt before Jesus' imminent return to usher in a thousand-year period of peace, is discussed in chapter 2. Dispensationalism is the belief that world history has been divided into distinctive eras in which God has related to humanity in different ways. Many conservative Christians believe that we are living in a special dispensation, which began at Pentecost and will end with the rapture of the saved before God releases his wrath on a sinful world.

11. Carroll and Roof, *Bridging Divided Worlds*, 19.

12. U.S. Census Bureau, "Census 2000 Data for the State of California."

13. Myers and Park, "Racially Balanced Cities in Southern California." At the same time, in some areas of Los Angeles the neighborhoods are becoming increasingly segregated, and some school districts bus students to create more racially balanced schools. See Ethington, Frey, and Myers, "The Racial Resegregation of Los Angeles County, 1940–2000."

14. Los Angeles Almanac, "Language Spoken at Home," http://www.laalmanac .com/population/po47.htm.

15. Tatum, *"Why Are All the Black Kids Sitting Together in the Cafeteria?"* 52.

16. This trend should not be applauded uncritically, however, because as diversity gains currency it also becomes a new form of exploitation of people of color and may

reflect a long-standing Western practice of exoticizing people of color rather than making a sincere effort to create an ethnically inclusive society.

17. Wuthnow, "Culture of Discontent," 32.

18. Glazer, *We Are All Multiculturalists Now*, chapter 2.

19. For a review of these debates surrounding the adoption of new social studies textbooks, see Olsen, *Made in America*, 262 n. 33.

20. Robert Bellah offers a cogent analysis of why American culture has been so receptive to multiculturalism as an ideology in his essay "Is There a Common American Culture?"

21. Kennedy, *Interracial Intimacies*, 126.

22. Ibid., 36. Kennedy cites several small polls on racial attitudes on 544 n. 40.

23. Root, "Rethinking Racial Identity Development," 206.

24. Park, Myers, and Wei, "Multiracial Patterns in California by County." The multiracial children statistic comes from the U.S. Census Bureau, *The Two or More Races Population: 2000*.

25. Beaudoin, *Virtual Faith*, 137.

26. Mary Waters explores this phenomenon in her book, *Ethnic Options*, chapter 2.

27. Cornell and Hartmann, *Ethnicity and Race*, 73–90.

28. Waters, *Ethnic Options*, chapter 3.

29. For an intelligent appraisal of the incident, see Kamiya, "Cablinasian Like Me."

30. For an excellent study of how these pressures affect first-generation Americans in a California high school, see Olsen, *Made in America*.

31. Sociologist Herbert Gans uses the term "symbolic ethnicity" to describe the expressive feeling of ethnic identification that lacks actual cultural connection. See Gans, "Symbolic Ethnicity" and "Symbolic Ethnicity and Symbolic Religiosity."

32. For a complete list of clients, see http://www.saltermcneil.com/about/company.asp.

33. Salter McNeil originally thought that the reconciliation generation would develop out of today's college students, but she now believes that those in junior high and high school will be the ones to accept this mission. Phone interview by author, June 2, 2003.

34. John M. Perkins Foundation, "Biography of Dr. John M. Perkins," http://www.jmpf.org/jp_bio.html.

35. Schools like George Fox University, Seattle Pacific University, and Houghton College have offices for multiculturalism that bring racial reconciliation experts to campus.

36. More accurately, evangelical fellowships can be found at non-evangelical schools, including Catholic and mainline Protestant colleges.

37. Busto, "The Gospel According to the Model Minority," 171.

38. InterVarsity president Alec Hill, "Church," InterVarsity Christian Fellowship/USA, June 30, 2003, http://www.intervarsity.org/news/news.php?item_id=674.

39. Alumkal, "American Evangelicalism in the Post–Civil Rights Era," 206.

40. Alec Hill, "Core Commitment #10," The President's Page, InterVarsity Christian Fellowship/USA, June 24, 2003, http://www.intervarsity.org/news/news.php?item_id=648.

41. Rudy Carrasco and Derek Perkins, taped interview by author, November 12, 2002.

42. This tension came to a head at an Urbana meeting in 1970, when the Black delegates, after hearing a moving talk on racial prejudice by Tom Skinner, asked that the focus be changed from missions to racism and poverty, and their request was denied. See Hunt and Hunt, *For Christ and the University*, 274–76.

43. Urbana 2003, http://www.urbana.org/u2003.facts.cfm.

44. Urbana 2000 Fact Sheet, http://www.urbana.org/u2000.factsheet.cfm.

45. Busto, "The Gospel," 180–81.

46. Keith Hirata, phone interview by author, July 11, 2002.

47. According to Paul Tokunaga, who has been on InterVarsity's staff for thirty years and currently serves as the National Asian American Coordinator, there has been an increasing recognition that both multiethnic and ethnic-specific fellowships have strengths and weaknesses. Phone interview by author, February 26, 2002.

48. Washington and Kehrein, *Breaking Down Walls*.

49. Doug Schaupp, taped interview by author, November 14, 2002.

50. Carl Ellis is a nationally-known speaker and writer on multiethnic ministry, among other topics. He has led training workshops for InterVarsity staff across the country.

51. Carrasco and Perkins, taped interview by author, November 12, 2002.

52. Evergreen's 2004 survey of adult members, provided by the Evergreen staff.

53. Samuel Chetti, taped interview by author, July 1, 2002.

CHAPTER 4

1. DeYoung et al., *United by Faith*, 1–5. For more information on this survey, see http://www.congregations.info/facts.html.

2. This famous statement is usually attributed to Martin Luther King, Jr., who used it in the sermon "Remaining Awake Through a Great Revolution," which he delivered many times but most famously at the National Cathedral in Washington, D.C., on March 31, 1968, four days before he died. Peter Wagner attributes the statement to Liston Pope, but in this text (*The Kingdom Beyond Caste*, 105) Pope puts the phrase in quotation marks, suggesting he heard it elsewhere.

3. A third option was expressed in the September–October 2005 newsletter by a young man who described EBCLA as "a 2nd generation Chinese church that he feels very comfortable going to."

4. Becker, *Congregations in Conflict*, 4–5.

5. Michael Mata, quoted in Ortiz, *One New People*, 149.

6. Two instances where I noted this change in terminology from "racial reconciliation" to "ethnic reconciliation" are on the InterVarsity Web site and in the Overflow Ministries brochure. Brenda Salter McNeil explained that this shift in terminology mirrors the shift from the original focus on Black-White reconciliation to concern for reconciliation among all groups of people; phone interview by author, June 2, 2003.

7. Bellah, "Is There a Common American Culture?" 617.

8. Spickard and Burroughs, "We Are a People," 10.

9. DeYoung et al. contrast this model with the Pluralist Multiracial Congregation and the Integrated Multiracial Congregation; *United by Faith*, 166–71.

10. Roger Greenway, quoted in Ortiz, *One New People*, 150.

11. Wuthnow, *Producing the Sacred*, 44.

12. Becker identifies four congregational models: House of Worship, Family, Community, and Leader. Close, family-like attachments are stressed in the Family and Community models. See *Congregations in Conflict*, 15.

13. Jeung, "Asian American Pan-Ethnic," 236.

14. Ken Fong, "Notes from the Journey," church newsletter, October 2002.

15. These three categories are similar to those Penny Becker uses in her study of multiracial churches: formal and ritual inclusion. See "Making Inclusive Communities," 452.

16. The multiethnic church movement has spawned a number of books on the subject of power-sharing and how to negotiate different cultural styles of communication and leadership. Eric Law, an Episcopal priest, has written several books on the topic that are used within liberal and mainline churches; see Law, *The Bush Was Blazing But Not Consumed* and *The Wolf Shall Dwell With the Lamb*.

17. The May–June 2004 newsletter also includes reports from the study groups on unwed mothers and HIV/AIDS.

18. Two years prior to the creation of the Rec'ing Crew, a civil rights movie and discussion night, based on the film *My Big Fat Greek Wedding*, was held at the church, but this discussion centered on generational and cultural clashes rather than racism.

19. Church newsletter, May–June 2005.

20. Marti, *A Mosaic Of Believers*.

21. McManus has also published *Seizing Your Divine Moment: Dare to Live a Life of Adventure* and *Uprising: A Revolution of the Soul*.

22. McManus, *An Unstoppable Force*, 30.

23. This material on Mosaic comes from two sources: *A Mosaic of Believers* and a taped interview with Marti conducted on October 24, 2002.

24. Mosaic is one of four churches highlighted in DeYoung et al., *United By Faith*, 84–87.

25. This phrase is not found very often in the current missiological literature when the topic is the relative "cultural distance" between the evangelizer and the potential convert. For an overview of one system of classifying cultural distance, see Winter, "The New Macedonia." Terms in quotation marks in this paragraph are from Marti's *A Mosaic Of Believers*, chapter 7.

26. Marti explains this term in an earlier version of *A Mosaic of Believers*, his dissertation "A Mosaic of Believers: Diversity and Religious Innovation in a Multiethnic Church," 330.

27. Marti, *A Mosaic of Believers*, 164.

28. I am indebted to Rudy Busto for pointing out to me that ethnic identity can be given enhanced meaning and legitimacy by containing it within a Christian framework.

29. Jeung, "Asian American Pan-Ethnic Formation," 239.

30. Becker, "Making Inclusive Communities," 468.

31. This quote comes from a news article describing a new, multiethnic, "post-black" church in Minneapolis that has looked to McManus for guidance (Martha Sawyer Allen, "Where We Worship: New Church Isn't Waiting to Become Multicultural," *Minneapolis Star Tribune*, March 6, 2004).

32. Marti discusses these other congregations in the unpublished paper "Can Lightning Strike Twice? A Comparative Analysis of Two Large Multi-Ethnic Congregations in Los Angeles" (presented at the annual meeting of the American Academy of Religion, Atlanta, 2003).

33. Marti, *A Mosaic of Believers*, 187–190.

34. Ibid., 161.

CHAPTER 5

1. When Evergreen re-formed after World War II it was primarily English speaking, and in the 1950s the smaller Japanese-speaking group formed a separate church, the Japanese Baptist Church of Los Angeles.

2. At the time of the 2004 survey, 31 percent of Evergreeners were immigrants and 34 percent were born in the United States to immigrants, compared to 9 and 21 percent, respectively, in 2002.

3. For a concise overview of this role, see Ebaugh and Chafetz, *Religion and the New Immigrants*, chapter 6.

4. Asian food is of course a very broad category. Some of those I interviewed differentiated between "real" Chinese or Japanese food and Asian food that has been Americanized to appeal to the Southern California consumer.

5. Michael Luo, "Seeking to Integrate the Pews," *Pasadena Star-News,* Jan 20, 2002.

6. Ebaugh and Chafetz, *Religion and the New Immigrants*, 88. The authors do not explain what they mean by "ethnic" food, but it is clear from the context that it is anything other than the stereotypical White American fare.

7. Ibid., 91.

8. Since the church became a Japanese-Chinese congregation, there have been many marriages between members of these groups. Now that the church includes more non-Asians, there are also many marriages between Asians and non-Asians. Since either is a significant boundary crossing to the members of this congregation, I use the term "mixed marriage" to encompass both.

9. For more on how this hierarchy has historically functioned in the United States, see Spickard, *Mixed Blood.*

10. It was not clear to me where Koreans fit in this marriage hierarchy, since no one I spoke with at Evergreen mentioned them in this context.

11. For more on this issue, see Espiritu, *Asian American Women and Men.*

12. Kim, "Second-Generation Korean American Evangelicals," 26.

13. Ebaugh and Chafetz, *Religion and the New Immigrants,* 80.

14. For a classic study of this phenomenon, see Gordon, *Assimilation in American Life*. For an examination of the contemporary pressures to assimilate, see Alba and Nee, *Remaking the American Mainstream*.

15. Wagner, *The Healthy Church*, 60–62. Wagner develops the idea of "people blindness": "the malady that prevents us from seeing the important cultural differences that exist between groups of people living in geographical proximity to one another," 60.

16. Marti, "A Mosaic of Believers," 161.

17. Ibid., 156. I had the opportunity to hear Marti explain this point at a consultation meeting on Multiracial Congregations held at the Louisville Institute in April 2004.

18. Dorsey, "Southwest Assembly of God," 245.

CHAPTER 6

1. Christerson and Emerson, "The Costs of Diversity in Religious Organizations."

2. Foster and Brelsford, *We Are the Church Together*, 165.

3. Emerson and Christerson, "The Costs of Diversity."

4. The sociological terms for these processes are the *niche edge effect* and the *niche overlap effect*. See Popielarz and McPherson, "On the Edge or In Between."

5. Emerson and Christerson, "The Costs of Diversity," 176.

6. Ibid., 177.

7. Church newsletter, April 2004.

8. Foster and Brelsford talk about this shift from negotiating ambiguity outside the church to inside the multiethnic church in *We Are the Church*, 123.

9. New Song began in 1994 with a handful of Korean American members but with a vision to become multiethnic from the start. When I interviewed Pastor Dave by telephone in October 2002, the church, which by then had more than fifteen hundred members, had diversified to 20 percent non-Asian members. Since then New Song has planted several churches in the Los Angeles area that draw members from their Latino and/or African American neighborhoods. For more on this large, young, multiethnic church in Southern California, see http://www.newsong.net/about/press.php.

10. Church newsletter, May 2003.

11. Smith, *American Evangelicalism*.

12. Becker, "Making Inclusive Communities," 459.

13. I am indebted to Edwin Apointe for pointing this out to me in his response to my paper "The Culture of Discomfort," given at the annual meeting of the American Academy of Religion in Atlanta, November 2003.

CHAPTER 7

1. DeYoung et al., *United by Faith*, 2.

2. Ammerman, *Congregation and Community*.

3. Wagner, *The Healthy Church*, 65.

4. Becker, "Making Inclusive Communities," 467.

5. Emerson and Kim, "Multiracial Congregations."

6. Mullins, "The Life-Cycle of Ethnic Churches."

7. See Alumkal, *Asian American Evangelical Churches*, and Yang, *Chinese Christians in America*.

8. Myers, Pitkin, and Park, "2005 Full Report: California Demographic Futures."

9. Park, Myers, and Wei, "Multiracial Patterns in California by County."

10. I learned this phrase from Professor Paul Spickard, who does not remember where he first heard it.

11. Emerson and Kim, "Multiracial Congregations," 225.

12. Foster and Brelsford, *We Are the Church Together*, 172.

13. DeYoung et al., *United By Faith*, 76.

14. On the role homogeneous churches play in supporting racialization in the larger society, see Emerson and Smith, *Divided by Faith*, 153–168.

15. Becker, "Making Inclusive Communities," 468–70.

16. An effort by the Wal-Mart Corporation to build a mega-store in Inglewood, California, was stopped by a coalition of religious and civic organizations, including the Southern California Leadership Conference and Nation of Islam. In Los Angeles, many liberal churches and synagogues support activist groups such as Clergy and Laity United for Economic Justice and L.A. Metro, an Industrial Areas Foundation organization. Interestingly, a Wal-Mart store was subsequently proposed in Rosemead, and as of September 2004, Evergreen members were discussing whether to have a voice in this proposal.

17. Two examples of activist, multiethnic churches in Los Angeles are All Saints Episcopal Church and Immanuel Presbyterian Church. New Song in Orange County is not as diverse as Evergreen, but it does focus more on issues of social justice.

18. See *http://atimetoreconcile.org* for more information on ORM's mission and activities.

19. *Reconcile,* ORM Newsletter, Fall–Winter 2003.

20. Livezey, introduction to *Public Religion and Urban Transformation*, 23.

21. An example of a civic version of color-blind churches appeared on the California ballot in October 2003, as the Racial Privacy Initiative (Proposition 54), which stated, "The state shall not classify any individual by race, ethnicity, color or national origin in the operation of public education, public contracting or public employment." It failed to pass.

22. Foster and Brelsford, *We Are the Church*, 157.

23. Ibid., 115.

APPENDIX B

1. Wagner, *Our Kind of People*, 159.

2. Ebaugh and Chafetz, *Religion and the New Immigrants*, 88.

3. Among the newest trends is the use of headsets providing simultaneous translation. These are very costly, but several Los Angeles pastors told me they hope to purchase

them in the future. First Baptist Church of Los Angeles has used them for several years with positive results, according to Interim Minister Dennis Plourde; taped interview by author, December 4, 2003.

4. What is often overlooked in multilingual churches is the diverse ethnic makeup of those attending the English-speaking service.

5. Jeung studied dozens of pan-Asian churches in the Bay area and published the results in *Faithful Generations: Race and New Asian American Churches.*

6. Jeung, "Asian American Pan-Ethnic Formation and Congregational Culture," 240 n. 4.

7. Min, "A Literature Review," 23–24.

8. Garces-Foley and Jeung, "Asian American Evangelicals in a Multiethnic Society."

Bibliography

Alba, Richard, and Victor Nee. *Remaking the American Mainstream: Assimilation and Contemporary Immigration.* Cambridge, MA: Harvard University Press, 2003.

Alumkal, Antony. "American Evangelicalism in the Post–Civil Rights Era: A Racial Formation Theory Analysis." *Sociology of Religion* 65:3 (Fall 2004): 195–213.

———. *Asian American Evangelical Churches: Race, Ethnicity, and Assimilation in the Second Generation.* New York: LFB Scholarly Publishing, 2003.

Ammerman, Nancy. *Congregation and Community.* New Brunswick, NJ: Rutgers University Press, 1999.

Bartkowski, John P. *The Promise Keepers: Servants, Soldiers, and Godly Men.* New Brunswick, NJ: Rutgers University Press, 2004.

Beaudoin, Tom. *Virtual Faith: The Irreverent Spiritual Quest of Generation X.* San Francisco: Jossey-Bass, 1998.

Becker, Penny Edgell. *Congregations in Conflict: Cultural Models of Local Religious Life.* Cambridge: Cambridge University Press, 1999.

———. "Making Inclusive Communities: Congregations and the 'Problem' of Race." *Social Problems* 45:4 (November 1998): 451–72.

Bellah, Robert. "Is There a Common American Culture?" *Journal of the American Academy of Religion* 66:3 (Fall 1998): 613–25.

Busto, Rudy V. "The Gospel According to the Model Minority? Hazarding an Interpretation of Asian American Evangelical College Students." In *New Spiritual Homes: Religion and Asian Americans,* edited by David K. Yoo, 169–87. Honolulu: University of Hawai'i Press, 1999.

Carrasco, Rodolpho. "Pivotal Minority Movements Strive for Racial Unity." *Christianity Today,* January 8, 1996, 70.

Carroll, Jackson W., and Wade Clark Roof. *Bridging Divided Worlds: Generational Cultures in Congregations.* San Francisco: Jossey-Bass, 2002.

Christerson, Brad, Korie L. Edwards, and Michael O. Emerson. *Against All Odds: The Struggle for Racial Integration in Religious Organizations.* New York: New York University Press, 2005.

Christerson, Brad, and Michael Emerson, "The Costs of Diversity in Religious Organizations: An In-Depth Case Study." *Sociology of Religion* 62:2 (Summer 2003): 163–81.

Conn, Harvie M. Foreword to *One New People: Models for Developing a Multiethnic Church,* by Manuel Ortiz. Downer's Grove, IL: InterVarsity Press, 1996.

Cornell, Stephen E., and Douglas Hartmann. *Ethnicity and Race: Making Identities in a Changing World.* Thousand Oaks, CA: Pine Forge Press, 1998.

DeYoung, Curtiss Paul. "Tensions in North American Protestantism: An Evangelical Perspective." *Journal of Ecumenical Studies* 35:3–4 (Summer 1998): 400–404.

DeYoung, Curtiss Paul, Michael O. Emerson, George Yancey, and Karen Chai Kim. *United by Faith: The Multiracial Congregation as an Answer to the Problem of Race.* New York: Oxford University Press, 2003.

Dorsey, Patricia. "Southwest Assembly of God: Whomsoever Will." In Ebaugh and Saltzman, *Religion and the New Immigrants,* 234–57.

Dougherty, Kevin D. "How Monochromatic Is Church Membership? Racial-Ethnic Diversity in Religious Community." *Sociology of Religion* 64:1 (Spring 2003): 65–86.

Ebaugh, Helen Rose, and Janet Saltzman Chafetz. *Religion and the New Immigrants: Continuities and Adaptations in Immigrant Congregations.* Walnut Creek, CA: AltaMira Press, 2000.

Emerson, Michael O. "Multiracial Congregations Project." Hartford Institute for Religion Research. http://hirr.hartsem.edu/org/faith_congregations_research_multiracl .html.

———. "Why Racial Reconciliation Alone Cannot End Racial Strife." *Christian Scholar's Review* 28:1 (Fall 1998): 58–70.

Emerson, Michael O., and Karen Chai Kim. "Multiracial Congregations: A Typology and Analysis of Their Development." *Journal of the Scientific Study of Religion* 42 (2003): 217–27.

Emerson, Michael O., and Christian Smith. *Divided by Faith: Evangelical Religion and the Problem of Race in America.* New York: Oxford University Press, 2000.

Eskridge, Larry. "Defining Evangelicalism." The Institute for the Study of American Evangelicals. http://www.wheaton.edu/isae/defining_evangelicalism.html.

Espiritu, Yen Le. *Asian American Women and Men: Labor, Laws, and Love.* Thousand Oaks, CA: Sage Publications, 1996.

Ethington, Philip J., William H. Frey, and Dowell Myers. "The Racial Resegregation of Los Angeles County, 1940–2000." *Race Contours 2000 Study, Public Research Report No. 2001–04.* May 12, 2001. http://www.usc.edu/schools/sppd/research/ census2000/race_census.

Fong, Bruce W. *Racial Equality in the Church.* Lanham, MD: University Press of America, 1996.

Fong, Ken Uyeda. "Taking the Baton and Running Our Leg of the Race." Evergreen
    Baptist Church of Los Angeles. http://www.ebcla.org/history.asp.
———. *Pursuing the Pearl: A Comprehensive Resource for Multi-Asian Ministry*. Valley
    Forge, PA: Judson Press, 1999.
Foster, Charles, and Theodore Brelsford. *We Are the Church Together: Cultural Diversity
    in Congregational Life*. Valley Forge, PA: Trinity Press International, 1996.
Gans, Herbert. "Symbolic Ethnicity: The Future of Ethnic Groups and Cultures in
    America." *Ethnic and Racial Studies* 2 (1979): 1–19.
———. "Symbolic Ethnicity and Symbolic Religiosity: Towards a Comparison of Eth-
    nic and Religious Acculturation." *Ethnic and Racial Studies* 17 (1994): 577–91.
Garces-Foley, Kathleen. "The Culture of Discomfort." Paper presented at the annual
    meeting of the American Academy of Religion, Atlanta, Georgia, November
    2003.
———. "The Project of Multiculturalism in the Los Angeles Catholic Church." Paper
    presented at the annual meeting of the American Academy of Religion, Toronto,
    Ontario, November 2002.
Garces-Foley, Kathleen, and Russell Jeung. "Asian American Evangelicals in a Multi-
    ethnic Society." Paper presented at a consultation meeting, Institute for the Study
    of American Evangelicals, Wheaton, Illinois, October 14, 2005.
Giddens, Anthony. *Modernity and Self-Identity: Self and Society in the Late Modern Age*.
    Stanford: Stanford University Press, 1991.
Glazer, Nathan. *We Are All Multiculturalists Now*. Cambridge, MA: Harvard University
    Press, 1997.
Gordon, Milton M. *Assimilation in American Life*. New York: Harper Collins, 1964.
Graham, Billy. "Racism and the Evangelical Church." *Christianity Today*, October 4,
    1993, 27.
Harper, Lisa, Doug Schaupp, Sandy Schaupp, and Tracey Shyr. *Creating an Acts 6
    Racially Reconciling Community: How "Race Matters" Works as a Campus Strategy*.
    Manual, InterVarsity Christian Fellowship, October 2000.
Hollinger, David A. *Postethnic America*. New York: Basic Books, 1995.
Hunt, Keith, and Gladys Hunt. *For Christ and the University: The Story of InterVarsity
    Christian Fellowship of the U.S.A., 1940–1990*. Downer's Grove, IL: InterVarsity
    Press, 1991.
Hunter, James Davison. *Evangelicalism: The Coming Generation*. Chicago: University of
    Chicago Press, 1987.
Jeung, Russell. "Asian American Pan-Ethnic Formation and Congregational Culture."
    In *Religions in Asian America: Building Faith Communities*, edited by Pyong Gap
    Min and Jung Ha Kim, 215–44. Walnut Creek, CA: AltaMira Press, 2002.
———. *Faithful Generations: Race and New Asian American Churches*. New Brunswick,
    NJ: Rutgers University Press, 2004.
Kamiya, Gary. "Cablinasian Like Me." *Salon Magazine*, April 30, 1997. http://www.salon
    .com/april97/tiger970430.html.
Kennedy, Randall. *Interracial Intimacies: Sex, Marriage, Identity, and Adoption*.
    New York: Pantheon, 2003.

Kim, Rebecca Y. "Emergent Ethnicity: Second-Generation Korean American Campus Evangelicals' Religious Participation and Ethnic Group Formation." Ph.D. diss., University of California–Los Angeles, 2003.

———. "Second-Generation Korean American Evangelicals." *Sociology of Religion* 65:1 (2004): 19–34.

Le, C. N. "Multiracial/Hapa Asian Americans." *Asian-Nation: The Landscape of Asian America.* http://www.asian-nation.org/multiracial.shtml.

———. "Interracial Dating & Marriage: U.S.-Raised Asian Americans." *Asian-Nation: The Landscape of Asian America.* http://www.asian-nation.org/interracial.shtml.

Law, Eric. *The Wolf Shall Dwell with the Lamb: A Spirituality for Leadership in a Multicultural Community.* St. Louis, MO: Chalice Press, 1993.

———. *The Bush Was Blazing But Not Consumed: Developing a Multicultural Community through Dialogue and Liturgy.* St. Louis, MO: Chalice Press, 1996.

Livezey, Lowell, ed. *Public Religion and Urban Transformation: Faith in the City.* New York: New York University Press 2000.

Marti, Gerardo. "Can Lightning Strike Twice? A Comparative Analysis of Two Large Multi-Ethnic Congregations in Los Angeles." Paper presented at the annual meeting of the American Academy of Religion, Atlanta, Georgia, 2003.

———. *A Mosaic of Believers: Diversity and Religious Innovation in a Multiethnic Church.* Bloomington: Indiana University Press, 2004.

———. "A Mosaic of Believers: Diversity and Religious Innovation in a Multiethnic Church." Ph.D. diss., University of Southern California, 2002.

Martin, William. *A Prophet with Honor: The Billy Graham Story.* New York: William Morrow, 1991.

McGavran, Donald A. *Understanding Church Growth.* Grand Rapids, MI: Eerdmans, 1970.

McManus, Erwin Raphael. *Seizing Your Divine Moment: Dare to Live a Life of Adventure.* Nashville, TN: Thomas Nelson, 2002.

———. *An Unstoppable Force: Daring to Become the Church God Had in Mind.* Loveland, CO: Group, 2001.

———. *Uprising: A Revolution of the Soul.* Nashville, TN: Thomas Nelson, 2003.

Min, Pyong Gap. "A Literature Review with a Focus on Major Themes." In *Religions in Asian America: Building Faith Communities,* edited by Pyong Gap Min and Jung Ha Kim, 15–36. Walnut Creek, CA: AltaMira Press, 2002.

Miller, Albert G. "The Rise of African-American Evangelicalism in American Culture." In *Perspectives on American Religion and Culture,* edited by Peter W. Williams, 259–69. Malden, MA: Blackwell Publishers, 1999.

Miller, Donald E. *Reinventing American Protestantism: Christianity in the New Millennium.* Berkeley: University of California Press, 1997.

Morgan, Timothy C. "First Stride in a Long Walk: Evangelicals Labor to Heal Old Hurts." *Christianity Today,* February 6, 1995, 48.

Mullins, Mark. "The Life-Cycle of Ethnic Churches in Sociological Perspective." *Japanese Journal of Religious Studies* 14:4 (1987): 321–34.

Myers, Dowell, and Julie Park. "Racially Balanced Cities in Southern California." *Race Contours 2000 Study, Public Research Report No. 2001–05*. Rev. May 17, 2001. http://www.usc.edu/schools/sppd/research/census2000/race_census/.

Myers, Dowell, John Pitkin, and Julie Park. "2005 Full Report: California Demographic Futures." *Demographic Futures for California*, Population Dynamics Group, University of Southern California School of Policy, Planning, and Development, 2001. Rev. Jan. 27, 2005. http://www.usc.edu/schools/sppd/futures.

Olsen, Laurie. *Made in America: Immigrant Students in Our Public Schools*. New York: New Press, 1997.

Omi, Michael, and Howard Winant. *Racial Formation in the United States: From the 1960s to the 1980s*. New York: Routledge, 1986.

Ortiz, Manuel. "Commitment to Reconciliation: In Cost and the Future." *Evangelical Journal* 16:2 (Fall 1998): 89–98.

———. *One New People: Models for Developing a Multiethnic Church*. Downer's Grove, IL: InterVarsity Press, 1996.

Park, Julie, Dowell Myers, and Liang Wei. "Multiracial Patterns in California by County." *Race Contours 2000 Study, Public Research Report 2001–03*. April 11, 2001. http://www.usc.edu/schools/sppd/research/census2000/race_census/.

Perkins, Spencer, and Chris Rice. *More Than Equals: Racial Healing for the Sake of the Gospel*, 2nd ed. Downer's Grove, IL: InterVarsity Press, 2000 [1993].

Pierce, Lori. "The Continuing Significance of Race." In *We Are a People: Narrative and Multiplicity in Constructing Ethnic Identity*, edited by Paul Spickard and W. Jeffrey Burroughs, 221–28. Philadelphia: Temple University Press, 2000.

Pope, Liston. *The Kingdom Beyond Caste*. New York: Friendship Press, 1957.

Popielarz, Pamela, and J. Miller McPherson. "On the Edge or In Between: Niche Position, Niche Overlap, and the Duration of Voluntary Association Memberships." *American Journal of Sociology* 101 (1995): 698–721.

Roof, Wade Clark. *Spiritual Marketplace: Baby Boomers and the Remaking of American Religion*. Princeton, NJ: Princeton University Press, 1999.

Root, Maria. "Rethinking Racial Identity Development." In *We Are a People*, edited by Paul Spickard and W. Jeffrey Burroughs, 205–20. Philadelphia: Temple University Press, 2000.

Salter McNeil, Brenda, and Rick Richardson. *The Heart of Racial Justice: How Soul Change Leads to Social Change*. Downer's Grove, IL: InterVarsity Press, 2005.

Shinagawa, Larry Hajime, and Gin Yong Pang. "Asian American Panethnicity and Intermarriage." *Amerasian Journal* 22 (1996): 127–52.

Smith, Christian. *American Evangelicalism: Embattled and Thriving*. Chicago: University of Chicago Press, 1998.

Spickard, Paul R. *Mixed Blood: Intermarriage and Ethnic Identity in Twentieth-Century America*. Madison: University of Wisconsin Press, 1989.

Spickard, Paul, and W. Jeffrey Burroughs. "We Are a People." In *We Are a People*, edited by Paul Spickard and W. Jeffrey Burroughs, 1–19. Philadelphia: Temple University Press, 2000.

Swidler, Ann. "Culture in Action: 'Symbols and Strategies.'" *American Sociological Review* 51 (1986): 273–86.

Tapia, Andrés. "The Myth of Racial Progress." *Christianity Today,* October 4, 1993, 16–27.

Tatum, Beverly Daniel. *"Why Are All the Black Kids Sitting Together in the Cafeteria?" And Other Conversations about Race.* New York: Basic Books, 2003.

Underwood, B. E. "The Memphis Miracle." International Pentecostal Holiness Churches Archives and Research Center. http://pctii.org/arc/underwoo.html.

U.S. Census Bureau. *The Two or More Races Population: 2000.* Brief prepared by the Racial Statistics Branch of the Population Division. http://www.census .gov/prod/2001pubs/c2kbr01-6.pdf#search=%22The%20Two%20or%20More %20Races%20Population%3A%202000%22.

———. "Census 2000 Data for the State of California." http://www.census.gov/ census2000/states/ca.html.

Wagner, C. Peter. *Our Kind of People: The Ethical Dimensions of Church Growth in America.* Atlanta: John Knox Press, 1979.

———. *The Healthy Church: Avoiding and Curing 9 Diseases That Can Afflict Any Church.* Ventura, CA: Regal Books, 1996.

Warner, R. Stephen. "Coming to America: Immigrants and the Faith They Bring." *Christian Century,* February 10, 2004, 20–24.

Washington, Raleigh, and Glen Kehrein. *Breaking Down Walls: A Model for Reconciliation in an Age of Racial Strife.* Chicago: Moody Press, 1993.

Waters, Mary C. *Ethnic Options: Choosing Identities in America.* Berkeley: University of California Press, 1990.

Winter, Ralph D. "The New Macedonia: A Revolutionary New Era in Mission Begins." In *Perspectives on the World Christian Movement,* edited by Ralph D. Winter and Steven C. Hawthorne, 157–75. Pasadena, CA: William Carey Library, 1992 [1981].

Wuthnow, Robert. "The Culture of Discontent." In *Diversity and Its Discontents,* edited by Neil J. Smelser and Jeffrey C. Alexander, 19–36. Princeton: Princeton University Press, 1999.

———. *Producing the Sacred: An Essay on Public Religion.* Urbana: University of Illinois Press, 1994.

Yamamoto, J. Isamu. "Silent No More." *New Man Magazine,* May 1997. http://www.newmanmag.com/may97/ny197108.htm.

Yancey, George. *Beyond Black and White: Reflections on Racial Reconciliation.* Grand Rapids, MI: Baker Books, 1996.

Yang, Fenggang. *Chinese Christians in America: Conversion, Assimilation, and Adhesive Identities.* University Park: Pennsylvania State University Press, 1999.

Index